PERSONALITY AND
SOCIAL CHANGE

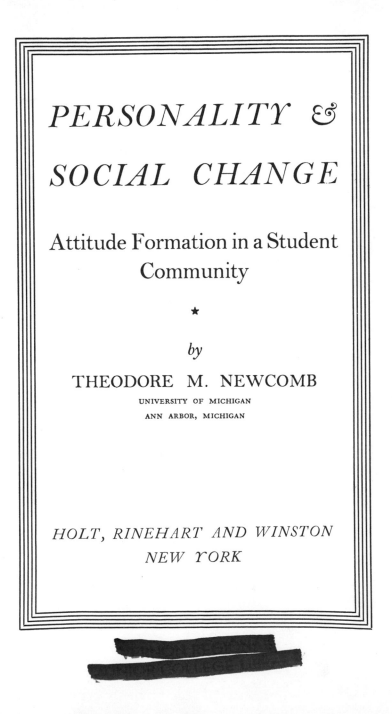

PERSONALITY &

SOCIAL CHANGE

Attitude Formation in a Student Community

★

by

THEODORE M. NEWCOMB

UNIVERSITY OF MICHIGAN

ANN ARBOR, MICHIGAN

HOLT, RINEHART AND WINSTON

NEW YORK

2064657

6 7 8 9

To the students of Bennington College
between the fall of 1935 and the spring of
1939, whose willing participation in this
study made it possible

Preface to the 1957 Edition

The excuse for reissuing this little monograph after fourteen years is simply that it has been out of print for a full decade, and that even at this late date I still receive inquiries as to where it may be obtained. I am grateful to The Dryden Press* for agreeing not only to reprint it, but also to issue it at minimum cost.

No one, I suppose, would feel that a work completed so long ago could not be improved, and I am aware of some of the shortcomings in the original report. But it, like all research documents, must stand on its own empirical legs, and I have therefore decided that, except for typographical errors, the present edition should be identical with the original.

Since 1943 I have published a set of supplementary findings, not included in the present report (*Journal of Abnormal & Social Psychology*, 1946, XLI, 291-302), and an alternative interpretation of many of the original findings (*Readings in Social Psychology*, Second Edition, edited jointly with G. E. Swanson and E. L. Hartley, Henry Holt & Co., 1952, pages 420-430). Since both of these are readily available, I have not included them in this reissue of *Personality and Social Change*.

T.M.N.

* Now part of Holt, Rinehart and Winston, Inc.

Preface

THERE IS SCARCELY a member of the Bennington College community who has not helped with this study. My colleagues of the Social Studies faculty have granted me Divisional funds for clerical purposes. President Robert D. Leigh and Professor Alvin C. Eurich, a part-time community member, have given me encouragement and criticism. The late Doctor Wilmoth Osborne spent many hours with me, amiably and acutely culling pertinent notes from student records, and more recently Doctor Joseph O. Chassell has given me equally valuable help. Gardner Murphy, Lois Barclay Murphy, and my colleague Dwight W. Chapman have read the entire manuscript and have made suggestions for want of which this report would have been much the poorer. Marie Louise Maguire was my ever-willing and indispensable assistant for two years while the study was in progress, her services being made possible by two successive grants-in-aid from the Social Science Research Council for the purpose of conducting the study. Jacquelin Griffiths and Marjorie Beebe gave valiant service in the final typing of the manuscript. Mary Shipherd Newcomb, my wife, has had a hand in almost every stage of the study.

1943   THEODORE M. NEWCOMB

Table of Contents

Part Three: Individual Studies

Part Four: Summary and Interpretation

Appendix

PART ONE:

The Setting

The Problem and Its Setting

THE DECADE OF THE 1930's brought profound social changes in America, changes which for present purposes may be symbolized by the phrase, "The New Deal." To say this is but to indicate that changes came to be accepted by large numbers of our citizens. They were accepted with every conceivable degree of willingness, of course, but this study proposes to contrast two general zones on the scale of willingness. It is reasonably clear that by and large they were accepted readily, if not enthusiastically, by a very great number. A considerable minority bitterly opposed them. An unknown number shifted, with the passage of years, part or all of the way between these positions.

What kinds of people gave ready allegiance to the new ways, and what is to be said of those who resolutely clung to the old? It is easy to reply, of course, that most business and financial leaders opposed the changes, while the majority of the unemployed favored them. But he who is curious about what happens to individual personalities in the face of immediate social change will want to know more. He will recall that by no means all business and financial leaders resisted the new ways, nor did every one at the other end of the economic scale embrace them. The question as to what kinds of people met the changes with what degrees of willingness involves far more than this.

Any social change, provided it has any relevance at all, is loaded with varying degrees of threat or opportunity for different individuals. Threats and opportunities will not, however, be assessed in the same terms by every one who views a given change. Each individual will see threats or opportunities in the light of what are to him dominant values. Indeed, many individuals will perceive both threats and opportunities following in the wake of the same change, because more than one value of importance to them is involved. Other persons may come to see threats where before they saw only opportunities, or vice versa, because they have come to see that previously unsuspected values are involved. One clue, then, to the question of what kinds of people showed what degrees of tolerance for these particular social changes is to be found in the pursuit of individual values.

This study lays no claim to answering such an ambitious question for the total population. But it does present data which have some relevance for contemporary college students. The reader is free to draw his own conclusions as to the applicability of the findings of the study to other than student groups. No inferences are intended by the writer, however, except for contemporary American college students, within certain limitations which are discussed in Chapter 17.

Ideally, of course, one would study a wide range of students in every sort of American college in searching out kinds of individuals who have accepted changes with varying willingness or unwillingness. But if one really intends to learn very much about individuals and the values in terms of which they look at social change, such a project becomes hopelessly ambitious. Methodologically, moreover, there is something to be said in favor of limiting such a study to a single community in which certain values, at least, are shared. The investigator is thus free to explore the varying ways in which a given sort of social change is seen by different individuals to impinge upon the more or less commonly shared values within the community.

The limitations of studying a single community are obvious. But it is patent that, for most individuals, whatever changes are in prospect must be mediated through the immediate social surroundings. Since values come to be values largely through the mediation of the groups with which an individual has direct contact, one cannot very sensibly study individuals' values apart from groups.

It should be noted that the phrase "commonly shared values"

does not imply that all individuals within a given community bear the same relationship to the common values. Their achievement is of more central importance to some than to others. For some their achievement is remote, and for others, almost or quite at hand. Every individual thinks of himself as accepting to a greater or less degree whatever he considers the dominant values of his own community, and as being at a certain point along the line of achieving them. His reaction to a proposed social change, then, will be in part determined by what he considers those values and his own relationship to them to be. All this is involved in the question, "What kinds of contemporary American college students accept certain social changes with what degrees of willingness?"

The Bennington College community was chosen for study not only because it happened to be available to the writer, but also because, as shown in the following pages, it was a closely knit community of manageable size in which the issues symbolized by the phrase "the New Deal" were taken seriously. More important still, many of the kinds of personality data essential to such a study were at hand, and the rest could be obtained from the entire student population without great difficulty.

The social changes which were occurring in the 1930's were, in a sense, remote to these young women. Most of them were aware of various ways in which their parents' incomes and their family status were apt to be affected. For most of them, however, the impact of these issues was felt rather through the college community than through home and family groups. (The evidence for this statement is contained in the remainder of the book.) In the sense and to the degree that these issues really came to matter to these students, as seen in later pages, they were not remote to them.

The values, in terms of which the issues took on meaning as something near rather than remote, were primarily just those which might be expected to be found among young women in such a college. The remaining chapters are devoted, in large measure, to the presentation of evidence concerning these values. By way of anticipating the findings, it may be said that they had largely to do with emancipation from parents and the establishment of independent, personal status within the community.

Such values, obviously, would not come to be associated with changes in attitude toward New Deal issues except under certain kinds of community conditions. These conditions we must now describe.

Bennington College owes its being to a group of sponsors who believed that a definite plan of education was both feasible and desirable.[1] The first class of some ninety freshmen was admitted in the fall of 1932. In the fall of 1935, when this study was begun, the fifty remaining students from this group constituted the first senior class. The 250 women students then enrolled represented the maximum number which could be provided for; this number has since remained constant. By 1935 the faculty had nearly reached its present membership of approximately fifty, including a few part-time instructors. This group of about 300 individuals is henceforth referred to as "the college community."

During the years covered by this study, the Admissions office received from three to five times as many applications for admission into freshmen classes as could be accepted. The college admissions policy is unusual only in that there are no fixed prerequisites in terms of subject matter, and in that very rarely the prerequisite of graduation from a secondary school is waived. The average "intelligence" level of entering freshmen is very high, relative to most other American colleges.[2]

The majority of students, in spite of a liberal scholarship policy, come from families that can afford to pay a tuition of $1000, in addition to room and board. Approximately thirty-five per cent of all students receive scholarship aid, ranging in amount from $100 to $1000. About one-quarter of all students earn a part of their expenses by various kinds of work. About one-third have their own automobiles at college.

The college grounds consist of several hundred acres situated on a hilltop a mile and a half from a tiny Vermont village, and four miles distant from the village of Bennington, whose population is slightly under 10,000. Community members make little use of the village facilities except the movies, the small shopping centers, and the churches. Since less than a majority of all students attend

[1] See the college bulletins for a description of this plan, beyond the meager details included here.

[2] The median score on the American Council on Education Psychological Test is consistently at about the 85th percentile for the several thousand college students who take it each year.

village churches with any regularity, and since most of their shopping needs are provided for at the college,[3] it may be said that the average student visits the village about once a week. The average student spends about one week-end a month away from the college.

Students live in houses accommodating about twenty each. Each house includes a few freshmen. Other students choose their own houses, though the formation of exclusive cliques is discouraged. Each house includes a faculty apartment, usually occupied by an instructor and his family. This instructor is charged with no supervisory responsibilities whatever; students are welcomed into his apartment to whatever degree he chooses; he is there as a community member, not as a don. A considerable majority of the faculty during the years of this study lived either on the campus or very near it. Their lives, except for the additional shopping necessitated by their families' needs, were nearly as completely contained within the college as those of the students.

All meals are served in the central Commons building, each student being free to eat with any group at any table in any of four dining rooms at any meal. Faculty members are frequently invited to eat with a group of students, although a separate faculty dining room is provided. Both students and faculty are served mainly by student waitresses. There are never as many such jobs available as are desired by students; no stigma whatever is attached to them.

The self-sustaining character of the community is further maintained by a recreation program and an evening meetings program. There is no gymnasium, but instruction in such sports as golf, tennis, hockey, and skiing is provided in season. A student-faculty Recreation Council plans a year-round program of dances and varied entertainments, all held at the college. There are no "extracurricular" clubs or organizations (except for a small Chapter of the American Student Union), the educational assumption being that if it is worth while for a student to carry on a given sort of activity, it should be fully legitimized within her program of college work.

[3] The college co-operative store, owned by community members, sells all types of student supplies, foodstuffs, ice cream, soft drinks, tobacco, etc. It arranges exhibits and sales of clothing from large metropolitan stores. It maintains a gasoline pump and a beauty parlor. There is also a post office and a Western Union office at the college.

During the years covered by this study, evening meetings were held, on the average, twice a week. These usually included a music or dance program, and a lecture by an outside speaker. A large majority of the entire community attended almost every one of these evening meetings. Lectures, particularly when a series of them was arranged about a single topic, often provided subjects for eager discussion for days or weeks afterwards. Reference was often made to them in classes. It was part of the community mores to take attendance at these meetings for granted.

Student-faculty relationships are, in general, friendly and informal. Most classroom groups include only six or eight students. Classes are conducted as workshops, studios, laboratories, or as discussion groups far more frequently than by the lecture method. Every student does part of her work, and often a considerable part, in individual conference with an instructor. Other community arrangements, mentioned later, tend to further an atmosphere of camaraderie. The total community numbers only about 300 individuals, and since most of them spend most of their time in very limited environs, formal sorts of arrangements would be difficult to maintain, even if they seemed desirable.

Community government is the responsibility of student-faculty committees. Faculty members, however, are greatly outnumbered; while their advice is apt to count heavily, they hold no veto powers, and decisions are made by majority vote. Several decisions of which faculty members disapproved are on record. General policies were laid down by these committees, early in the history of the college, according to which a maximum amount of responsibility was allotted to each student for her own conduct. It was not found necessary, for example, to limit the number of evenings in a week on which a student might leave the college grounds, or to state a fixed hour at which she must return, but it was found necessary to devise a rigorous system of signing out, so that the whereabouts of each student were known.

The student Educational Policies Committee is an important institutional device for assuring student-faculty collaboration on educational matters. One student member of this Committee is elected by the students of each Major Division of the college, from a list of names nominated by students and approved by the faculty of that Division. This committee is responsible both for initiating suggestions concerning desirable educational procedures and for criticizing and evaluating existing procedures. Once a year all students are interviewed by members of the Committee concerning their work with all their instructors, and individual reports are made to each instructor in which the information gathered during these interviews is frankly presented to him. Members of this Committee commonly attend meetings of the faculty members of their own Major Divisions, and their counsel concerning many sorts of educational problems is sought.

The college faculty during these years was, as such bodies go, a relatively youthful group. There were not more than two or three instructors whose ages exceeded forty, and none over fifty. Most of them were selected with an eye to capacity for smooth community relationships as well as to their professional qualifications.

Partly as an outgrowth of the college's total educational plan, and partly because of the limitations of near-by extra-college attractions, the community at this time was to a very unusual degree self-sufficient and self-contained. Partly because of the youth of the institution, and partly because of the relative novelty of its plan, it was also rather self-conscious. Many of its critics would probably have labeled it self-satisfied. At any rate it was not only a highly integrated community, but its members always referred to it by precisely that term. No phrase was more constantly on our lips than "the college community."

One further aspect of the community life must be mentioned. The faculty, which has been described as rather young and as having friendly, informal relationships with students, was almost universally described by those familiar with the college as "liberal." There were a few charges of "radicalism," but probably no more than were directed against many other college faculties.

It is probably an important datum for the evaluation of this study that its author was invariably included among the group of instructors most likely to be pointed out as "pretty liberal" or "radical." He is probably not aware of every point at which this reputation had significance for the study. It almost certainly had some bearing upon the degree of *rapport* established with different individuals during senior interviews.

It probably was one of the selective factors operating at such times as responses to attitude scales were less than 100 per cent complete, although the data cited later indicate that it could not have been a major factor. It is the writer's belief that it had little or no constant bearing upon the nature of actual replies to the attitude scales. Some of the students whom he knew best, and with whom his *rapport* seemed most satisfactory were those whose attitude scores, as hereinafter defined, were most conservative. A slightly larger number of those with whom his *rapport* seemed particularly good were among those whose scores were least conservative. It is possible, of course, that consistent errors were involved. Perhaps most students tended to reply in what they considered to be the direction approved by the investigator. Perhaps those who believed their attitudes to be like his tended to exaggerate the degree of their "liberal" replies, while those who believed their attitudes to be opposed to his tended to exaggerate the degree of their conservatism. These problems in themselves are worthy of research, but the data with which to answer them are not at present available. The significant fact, however, is that, regardless of the degree of "radicalism" attributed to the investigator, he was believed by nearly all students to represent the majority trend of the faculty.

Attitude change is here viewed as an adaptation in ways of coming to terms with certain sectors of contemporary public life. Like any other adaptation, it is made by a specific organism having, at any given moment, specified capacities and limitations. It is made by an organism with a specific history predisposing it toward certain sorts of activity and away from others. (Such predispositions, commonly referred to as motives, are as fully operative in the development of social attitudes as in the development, say, of vocational ambitions or of habits of social dominance.) It is an adaptation which is made not in a social vacuum, nor in all conceivable social environments, for each individual. The adaptation, particularly within these areas of public life, will therefore be made with reference to whatever social forces within that environment are perceived by the individual as impinging upon him.

Translated into terms of this particular investigation, this means that the writer has framed his problem specifically as follows: Each year some ninety young women, most of them seventeen or eighteen years old, leave homes [4] in which they have led a relatively sheltered

---

[4] A considerable proportion of Bennington students come directly from private boarding schools, but the adjectives "sheltered" and "conservative" are quite as applicable to these schools as to the students' homes.

existence. They leave families whose opinions about contemporary public issues are, as the term is currently used, definitely conservative. (There are, of course, individual exceptions to all of these generalizations.) Both home and school influences have been such that there was little or no necessity for them to come to any very definite terms with public issues. Such adaptations as they have made in these areas are apt to be of this nature: "Why, of course, practically every one of intelligence and good breeding agrees with my family and my family's friends about such matters."

They come from schools where they have had to face, with varying degrees of intensity and with varying degrees of success, the problem of achieving independent personal status. Many of them describe school situations in terms of acute and almost constant personal competition. All of them, by the time of arriving in college, have habits which predispose them to view the college situation in terms of certain degrees of competitiveness, and in terms of certain areas where certain forms of endeavor are significant for them, and others which are not.

They view their own problems of achieving independent personal status not only in terms of competition with their peers, but also in terms of loosing parental bonds. Some are only vaguely aware of this, while for some it dwarfs all other problems. Some of them phrase it in terms of freedom to go and come as they please and with whom they please; some feel bound chiefly by their parents' moral and religious standards and practices; for others it is cast in an intellectual framework. It is a problem for all, and it is not left behind on coming to college.

From such backgrounds and with such predispositions they come to a college where community life is intense; where they are granted unprecedented degrees of personal freedom and personal responsibility for their own conduct; where students are so selected that they offer much more competition than was met in school (so it is believed, at any rate); where there is much more pressure to come to terms with public issues, and where there are people of intelligence and good breeding (upper-class students and faculty, in the main) who do *not* agree with their families and their families' friends regarding contemporary public affairs.

And so some form of adaptation must be made. Previous modes may be more or less suitable, but some degree of modification is inevitable. It is not likely that the adaptations will exclude all areas of public affairs in this community, just as they could scarcely exclude football in some colleges, or dramatics in others.

Try as he will, it is not likely that any instructor can be completely successful in trying to present a student's-eye view of adaptation under a given set of circumstances. The writer therefore considers himself fortunate in being able to present a document, written by a sophomore in the throes of "emancipation," concerning the very process he has tried to describe. The document was not solicited, nor was it written with any notion of publication. He was told of its existence by another student. It is reproduced herewith by permission of the author, whose identity cannot be divulged, but to whom gratitude is hereby expressed.

MORE THAN THE TUITION

"It suddenly dawned on me that we'd never be able to go on like this, walking carefully around everything controversial, because everything controversial turned out to be all the vital things.". . . "After awhile all the laughter and gaiety rang false — it was like a steady diet of waltzes and swing with never a symphony for serious times.". . . "Two years ago we agreed about everything, and we would have gotten married but I thought I wanted a degree.". . . "I don't want to go home this vacation — there's no one I want to see for more than five minutes."

An increasing crescendo of scattered remarks of my friends mounts up in my mind and culminates in a dissonant, minor chord. What is the matter with these dissatisfied, bewildered, cynical girls? It's a simple answer, yet dishearteningly complex. Bennington is their trouble. I can't speak for all of us, but a hell of a lot of us are in this fix. We come from fine old Tory families who believe firmly in Higher Education — God knows why. So they sent us to a well-spoken-of college with an interesting-sounding scheme of education. Mary Jane could pursue her interests at Bennington and not get a nervous breakdown over Math the way Mummie did at Wellesley. So we went to Bennington, and our friends went to Vassar, Yale, Sarah Lawrence, Harvard, finishing school, St. Paul's-to-broker's-office. They came home, changed, a little. A slightly smarter jargon, unerring taste in clothes and Things To Do, and one and all, victrola records of the conventional ideas. We came home, some of us, talking a new language, some cobwebs swept out, a new direction opening up ahead we were dying to travel. Liberal, we thought we were. "What the hell's happened to you? Become a Parlor Pink?" "Well, hardly, Ha ha." It was a little bewildering. Oh, well, let's dance.

And then that fatal day came when we met The Man. God, but he's cute. And he likes us, and we have such a wonderful time together. House-parties, football, dances, skiing, and laughter, laughter. It's love,

all right. And Society approves, beamingly. Our backgrounds are the
same and we meet our respective parents' ideals.

He's got a job, now, and as soon as He's making enough we'll be married. We talk together about it a lot. We get a little more serious about
what's ahead, and we start to talk soberly together for practically the first
time. About all kinds of things. "We've known each other for such a
long time now, but we've never had time to talk about this, Johnny, —
or this. What do you think about —?" "Oh, come on, darling, let's have
another drink — you'll get over it."

And we did get over it — with a jolt — but not what He thought. Sud-
den desperation — if I can't get along with Him — what the hell? to hell
with Bennington? The more education, the broader-minded — and the
narrower the circle of kindred souls. It's closing in on us now. Soon we'll
graduate, and what then? Back to the old "set" which we've outgrown.
To people we can never be completely satisfied with again as friends, and
who distrust us now, if we've been brave enough to show our colors.
Most of us have played ball instead of that, and been hypocrites, with a
sick feeling. Let's dance. Have another drink.

This, in part, is what the Bennington community was like during
the years of this study. It must be repeated that it is not a "typical"
community; strictly speaking, of course, there is no such thing.
The particular ways in which public issues came to be related to
individual values in this community would not necessarily be
characteristic of other communities. In one respect, however, in the
writer's opinion, it is utterly characteristic of all communities. Whatever the manner in which public issues come to be related to individual values, the relationship will be established through the
medium of whatever group or groups of which the individual is a
member.

The question, then, "What kinds of individuals react in what
ways to proposed social changes?" must be rephrased somewhat
as follows: "What kinds of personal characteristics, in any student
community, determine those social relationships which in turn lead
to varying reactions to proposed social changes?" Such is the
problem of this study.

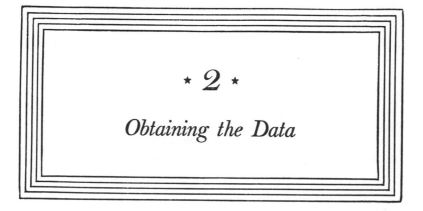

★ 2 ★

Obtaining the Data

THIS STUDY MAKES use of three major types of data: paper-and-pencil
questionnaire responses, written reports on individual students filed
in the college offices, and individual interviews. The purpose of
this chapter is to describe the conditions under which these data
were obtained.

In the fall of 1935 the writer placed in the post office box of every
student in college a mimeographed letter in which he stated his
purpose of conducting a four-year study of attitude change in the
college community. The letter went on to say that within a few
days every student would receive a questionnaire, and explained
why it was important to have responses from all students, and
ended by asking all those who had any misgivings as to their own
participation, or who had questions of any sort to ask to consult
the investigator.

It was also carefully explained in this letter that the investigator
was not interested in knowing the identity of individuals, but that
since it was to be a follow-up study, some method must be used
to identify each questionnaire. The use of code numbers was therefore proposed. It was explicitly promised that the investigator (who
would, of course, retain a list of names and code numbers) would
never associate names with responses without receiving personal
permission from each individual to do so, until the individuals in
question had permanently left the college. This was rigorously
adhered to throughout the study. The code numbers that appear

in these pages are not those which were used while the study was in progress.

Some twenty individuals consulted the investigator about his plans and purposes, mostly after receiving the first questionnaire. Most of their queries concerned the sociometric questions having to do with personal preferences among other students. All but two students seemed satisfied following such consultations, and only two of the 250 students refused to submit questionnaires.

Each questionnaire was labeled with a code number and inserted in an envelope bearing the name of the individual to whom the code number belonged. When filled out, questionnaires were dropped into a locked ballot box.

Only two minor variations were introduced into this procedure in succeeding years. During the early fall of the second, third, and fourth years of the study, brief mimeographed letters were sent to all students. These letters again described the general purposes of the study; it was stated that while at least once during each year it was important to have a response from every student in college, for most purposes this was not necessary. Each student was asked, finally, to sign and return to the investigator (if she felt so inclined) a brief appended statement indicating her intention (*not* her promise) to participate in the year's program to the extent of filling out three or four questionnaires to be submitted at irregular intervals. The promise was made that each student who cared so to participate would later receive a mimeographed summary of the complete results of the study. During each of these three years about 80 per cent of all students signed these statements, and of these 80 per cent about 75 to 90 per cent actually returned each questionnaire submitted.

In the spring of the third and fourth years of the study a different procedure was used to obtain replies from all students. At such times only the back-bone attitude scale of the study (later referred to as P.E.P.; see Chapter 3) and one or two sociometric questions were included. In order to do this, the aid of one student in each house was enlisted. Care was taken to choose a willing student, and one respected by her fellow students. She was simply asked to collect all the questionnaires, enclosed in sealed envelopes, from the students in her house, making such reminders as might be necessary, and using such pressures as she thought desirable.

The system worked almost perfectly. During each of these two years not more than two or three students proved either excessively dilatory or recalcitrant. The investigator then interviewed the latter students, in most instances obtaining what he considered a good-natured compliance with his request.

Several types of college records were used. Most important were instructors' reports. These consist not merely of letter grades, but ratings on several aspects of the student's work, followed by a brief essay concerning the student's particular strengths and weaknesses (including personality characteristics considered relevant to her work), and any kind of comments concerning the individual qualities of the student which the instructor cares to include. In addition to these, each student's counselor twice a year writes a more detailed and more systematic account of her development "in all its aspects." These were particularly valuable, since it is usually the student's counselor who knows her best.

The investigator did not consult directly the medical records, with all the personality data that they contain. But the present and the former college physician, both specialists in psychiatry, gave generously of their time in reading and commenting fully about every student concerning whom they were consulted, including all the members of three senior classes. The investigator did have access to the complete minutes of the meetings of the Student Personnel Committee which, in weekly or semi-weekly meetings throughout the year, discusses at considerable length the work and personalities of a large per cent of all students. He also made some use, as will be seen, of the records of objective tests.

The method by which the Guess Who ratings were obtained is fully described in Chapter 9, and the procedure by which interviews with seniors were obtained is presented in Part III. Concerning these, all that needs to be said here is that by the time these requests were made, students had developed such a feeling of having a vested interest in the study, because of their own regular participation in it, that acceptance was eager and unanimous. The study had by this time become an accepted community institution. It seems to the writer that for two years he has scarcely met a student who has not asked him how the study is coming along, when it will be finished, and when she will receive her promised copy of the summarized results.

PART TWO:

The Quantitative Data

★ 3 ★

The Attitude Scales:
Their Nature and Content

BY ATTITUDE IS meant simply a viewing with some degree (including zero degree) of favor or disfavor. Almost anything, obviously, may be so viewed. The term will be reserved in these pages, however, to viewings of public issues of controversial character.

Viewing is an essentially private, subjective process. The investigator of such a process can deal only with objective manifestations of it. Of several possible such manifestations, that of pencil responses to printed verbal statements was chosen.[1] That which is viewed is thus whatever is symbolized for each individual by the words included in the statements, and hence suffers from the variability which inevitably inheres in the use of words. The reader may judge for himself as to the degree of such variability by a perusal of one of the series of statements which is reproduced in the Appendix.

The to-be-described methods of handling the pencil responses are such that each individual's totality of viewing an entire scale of statements is symbolized by a number. The methods are such that the greater the number, the greater the degree to which the individual views the question with disfavor. There is a numerical point, for each scale, which represents zero degree of favor and zero degree of disfavor. The reader should bear in mind that values above this theoretical zero point do not necessarily represent a

[1] The advantages and disadvantages of such methods are discussed in Murphy, G., Murphy, L. B., and Newcomb, T. M., *Experimental Social Psychology*, 1937, pp. 907–912.

consistent viewing with disfavor of every statement in the scale, nor do values below it necessarily represent a viewing with favor of every statement. The numerical value, in short, represents a degree of preponderance of favorable over unfavorable viewing of the total issue, or vice versa.

One consideration was decisive in determining the nature and content of the attitude questionnaires: concerning what issues, within the realm of public affairs, does it appear likely that student attitudes are being modified as a result of experiences within the college community? The decision to limit the area to that of public affairs was an arbitrary one; some limitation was necessary, and the writer's interests happened to lie here. The fact that the issues included were almost exclusively contemporary ones was not the result of an arbitrary decision, but a consequence of the basic consideration stated above. To study current changes in attitudes to public affairs, it is necessary to study issues currently considered to be important.

Since the study was to extend over a four-year period, and since the measurement of change necessarily involves the repeated application of the same measure, a certain amount of risk was involved in the selection of the to-be-repeated measures. They had to deal with issues which were currently hot, and likely to remain so. It was also desirable, if possible, to use already existing attitude scales, rather than to create new ones, so that the results of this study might be compared with others. The history of American attitude research seems to show that nearly every investigator considers all existing measures inadequate for his special purposes, and so he constructs one for himself. But the same history also shows that the most carefully designed questionnaire, demonstrably valid and relevant for the population for which it was constructed, may have little value for other populations. For the purposes of this study the consideration of relevance for this particular population was primary. To use an already "standardized" measure was desirable, but of secondary importance.

The writer, at the time when this study was being planned, familiarized himself with nearly all the published attitude scales. One of them seemed almost perfectly to meet his demands for what might be considered the foundation scale, the one to be regularly repeated over the four-year period to be covered by the study. This

published scale[2] was of recent construction; it dealt with several
fairly specific but interrelated issues; and its several items had been
selected as coherent and valid for several populations. Best of all,
the issues dealt with were precisely those which were then alive in
the Bennington community, and bid fair to continue so. They
were, by and large, issues made prominent by the New Deal administration, then in its first term of office. They had been selected
by their author, after a careful perusal of the literature of the subject, as representing the essentials of "fascist" attitudes. This term,
however, has been discarded in the present study in favor of "Political and Economic Progressivism," the initials P.E.P. being used
throughout. The issues deal for the most part, as will be seen in
Appendix A, where the scale is reproduced, with attitudes toward
public relief, labor unions, and the public role of private and cor-
porate wealth.

While the content of this questionnaire seemed almost perfectly
suitable, the method by which subjects were directed to respond to
the attitude statements did not. For reasons elsewhere described,[3]
the writer believes that the Likert method[4] of scoring attitude questionnaires is superior, for most purposes, to other methods now in
use. This method provides for one of the following responses to
each statement in the scale by the subject: strongly agree, agree,
uncertain, disagree, strongly disagree. Some of the Stagner items
had to be reworded in order to be responded to by the Likert
method. A few of them could not be used at all, and the writer
added two or three new ones. But the P.E.P. scale remains sub-
stantially the Stagner scale in content.

The scoring method was as follows: responses indicating strong
agreement, agreement, uncertainty, disagreement, and strong disagreement were respectively scored either 5, 4, 3, 2, 1 or 1, 2, 3, 4, 5,
depending upon the wording of the statement in relation to which
of the two attitude extremes was to be scored high and which was to
be scored low: thus, strong agreement with a statement *favoring*
Loyalist Spain was scored 1, moderate agreement 2, moderate disagreement 4, and strong disagreement 5; strong agreement with a
statement *opposing* Loyalist Spain was scored 5, moderate agreement

    [2] Stagner, R., "Fascist Attitudes: an Exploratory Study," *J. Soc. Psychol.,* 1936,
Vol. 7, pp. 309–319.
    [3] Murphy, G., Murphy, L. B., and Newcomb, T. M., *op. cit.,* pp. 904–906.
    [4] Likert, R., "A Technique for the Measurement of Attitudes," *Archives of Psy-
chology,* 1932, No. 140.

4, moderate disagreement 2, and strong disagreement 1. Uncertain responses were always scored 3. Total score is simply the sum of the individual item scores. For all scales of the Likert type, *high* scores have been assigned to responses labeled *conservative*.[5] If the preliminary assignment of the conservative label to either agreement or disagreement with a given attitude statement proved to be in error, the fact was easily discoverable by the methods of validation described in Appendix B.

So much for the P.E.P. scale, which is the backbone of the measurements used in this study. Many other attitude scales were used, but only two others were repeated beyond the second time. One of these [6] was a scale of international attitudes, adapted from Likert.[7] Even in 1935 the writer felt that this scale was obsolete in part; by 1939 the dominant international issues had so changed that comparatively few of the items in this scale reflected problems of primary moment to the average observer. At any rate this scale did not correspond very closely to the major issues being discussed in this college community. In spite of a few revisions introduced into this scale to make it more relevant to the Bennington community, it never succeeded in measuring significant and controversial issues, and few significant changes in attitude score, even over a four-year period, were observed.

The other attitude scales were used, in the main, not for the purpose of tracing change from year to year, but for the sake of getting a more complete attitude-picture of individuals with reference to issues currently hot. As such, there was little reason to repeat the questionnaire after the issue had cooled off. Examples of such waxing and waning issues are the Spanish Civil War, President Roosevelt's Supreme Court proposals, and the Munich settlement.[8] Some of the questionnaires, such as those dealing with the CIO

[5] The writer attaches no significance whatever to this term beyond the actual content of the attitude statements. It happened that in this community (and in most other similar ones) during these years there was almost complete unanimity as to which of the two extremes of each attitude continuum should properly be labeled conservative. As used hereafter, the term is not to be thought of as a general personality characteristic, but as indicating a specific kind of response to specific attitude statements.

[6] The other was a scale of attitude toward Loyalist Spain.

[7] Likert, R., *op. cit.*

[8] Another example is the attitude toward President Roosevelt's selection of Senator Hugo Black as an Associate Justice of the Supreme Court, measured by a scale given in the fall of 1937. Its split-half reliability, however, proved so low that it was discarded.

and the New Deal, represented issues which remained decidedly warm. But these issues were included, though briefly, in the P.E.P. scale, and the limitations of time were such that not every scale could be repeated every year. Hence these scales were given only once or twice.

The attitude measures not making use of the Likert method were more or less standard. They were, respectively, measures of social distance and of degree of satisfaction with contemporary conditions and institutions. They were used as described by their original authors.[9]

[9] Bogardus, E. S., *Immigration and Race Attitudes,* 1928; and "A Social Distance Scale," *Sociol. and Soc. Res.,* 1933, Vol. 17, pp. 265–271.

Murphy, G., and Likert, R., *The Individual and Public Opinion,* 1938.

⋆ 4 ⋆

Attitude Norms

THIS IS A STUDY of attitude change. Its major purpose is that of discovering factors associated with different degrees and rates of change by individuals. But change in an individual's score has little or no meaning without a background against which it may be interpreted. The first essential in that background is a view of attitude changes by the various groups of which individuals are members. Hence this chapter will deal largely with mean scores.

THE P.E.P. SCALE

In Table I are presented the mean scores of all groups to which the P.E.P. scale was given. The number of subjects included in each group is given in parentheses, following the mean score.

TABLE I. MEAN SCORES, P.E.P. SCALE

Class Entered	Fall 1935	Fall 1936	Fall 1937	Spring 1938	Fall 1938	Spring 1939
1932	65.8 (45)					
1933	68.6 (47)	60.1 (27)				
1934	66.5 (74)	62.3 (37)	58.9 (27)	59.9 (37)		
1935	74.5 (88)	68.5 (55)	64.1 (45)	63.7 (50)	63.2 (40)	62.7 (45)
1936		75.8 (69)	72.3 (72)	69.1 (85)	68.4 (37)	68.5 (58)
1937			71.9 (64)	70.6 (86)	69.5 (40)	70.0 (62)
1938					75.9 (55)	72.8 (73)

The significant observation to be made from Table I is the slow but steady drop in scores from freshman to senior year. Reading from bottom to top, or from left to right, the mean scores diminish year by year. There are but two exceptions to this general rule.

The class entered in 1937 does not show the trend; and changes from fall to spring (within the same academic year) are slight for juniors and seniors. The first of these exceptions is due partly to the sample of the class from whom responses were obtained in 1937; the drop in score over this two-year period for subjects who responded at both times is somewhat greater than that indicated in Table I, though statistically unreliable. But the fact is that, regardless of sampling limitations, no class showed any very significant drop in score following the spring of 1938, and only one class (that entered in 1936) showed a perceptible decrease after the fall of 1937. Certain changes, elsewhere described in these pages, had taken place in the college community. It is likely that these cultural changes are responsible for the fact that score decrease between fall and spring of the same academic year is so slight, for the use of the P.E.P. scale in the spring was not begun until 1938.

These more or less characteristic mean scores for each of the four college classes, ignoring for the time being the above-mentioned changes in the community-at-large, are as follows (all freshmen, all sophomores, etc., are grouped together, regardless of the date of their entrance):[1]

276 freshmen, entering 1935–38 .... 74.2
241 sophomores, entering 1934–37 .... 69.4
166 juniors, entering 1933–36 .... 65.9
155 seniors, entering 1932–35 .... 62.4

Not all students in the college answered all questionnaires, and hence the question of selection arises. The per cent of responses to the P.E.P. scale, in its six administrations, ranged between 69 (fall 1938) and 99 (1935 and spring, 1938); the other percentages are 79, 85, and 96 for 1936, 1937, and 1939, respectively. As appears from the data in Appendix D, however, the selective factors involved had little or no influence on the group results.

Just how important are these freshman-to-senior changes? By either of two tests they are large enough to be statistically "safe," as shown in Appendix E. During each of the four years of the study, freshman scores are more conservative than those of juniors

---

[1] Fall responses rather than spring responses are used throughout this table, except for seniors entered in 1934 and in 1935, for which groups fall samples are small. . . . The critical ratios of these differences are 4.8, 3.2, and 2.7, respectively, for freshmen-sophomores, sophomores-juniors and juniors-seniors.

and seniors, by an amount greatly exceeding chance expectations. Even freshman-sophomore differences, during the first two years of the study, were highly significant in the same sense. Or, if we compare the freshman scores (of the only two classes which were studied for three or more consecutive years) with the same individuals' scores as juniors or as seniors, again the differences are far too great to be attributable to chance. It may be said with very great certainty that the measured differences are true differences. As the term is used in these pages, juniors and seniors are clearly less conservative than freshmen.

Mean scores of each class according to other attitude scales were also computed. For attitude toward Internationalism and toward Loyalist Spain, which scales were given more than once, mean scores of each class in any year were much like those of other years, except that all mean scores of attitude toward Internationalism were higher in 1939.[2] Summarized scores only are therefore given

TABLE II. MEAN SCORES, ACCORDING TO YEAR IN COLLEGE, ON ATTITUDE SCALES GIVEN MORE THAN ONCE

College Year	Internationalism		Loyalist Spain	
	N	Mn.	N	Mn.
Freshmen	225	47.1	150	44.4
Sophomores	204	43.7	129	40.5
Juniors	127	44.8	96	38.7
Seniors	105	43.6	90	38.4

in Table II; i.e., all freshmen, all sophomores, etc., are grouped together regardless of the year of their college entrance. The scores of Internationalist attitude include all members of each class who responded during three years, excluding 1939; those of attitude toward Loyalist Spain included all who responded in 1936–37, 1937–38, and 1938–39 to the full-length scale.

Thus grouped, the freshman-sophomore, the freshman-junior, the freshman-senior, and the sophomore-senior differences in Internationalist attitude are all statistically significant. For attitude to Loyalist Spain the freshman mean is significantly different from that

[2] The reader will recall what journalists and others referred to as the "upsurge of nationalism" at about this time. Such symptoms as public willingness to spend greatly increased funds for armaments might be mentioned. This trend in public opinion influenced all college classes alike, each of the four mean scores being 5 to 6 points higher than those given in Table II.

of each other class, but no other differences are significant, by the usual statistical criteria.

Attitude to Loyalist Spain, like only one or two other issues included in the study, is peculiar in that it became an issue very suddenly. There was no particular history to this attitude; few students had either interest in or information about Spain prior to the events of 1936. Only a few months after the issue first arose, juniors and seniors are found to be significantly more favorable than freshmen and sophomores. Juniors and seniors had not, as in the case of the P.E.P. scale, been exposed to discussion of the issues for longer periods of time than had freshmen and sophomores. The issue burst on all of them at once. The only possible conclusion to be drawn is that other already existing attitudes and allegiances were responsible for the almost immediate differentiation between the upper and the lower classes.

It is regrettable that this issue was not measured earlier. There was considerable agitation on the campus about it as early as the fall of 1937, and attitudes had become pretty well crystallized by the spring of 1937. The gradually increasing mean scores of the total population reflect the fact that the early months of community concern over the issue were the most influential. During the following two years, as students who had been subjected to that influence departed and others, never having met equally ardent enthusiasm on the subject, entered, the initially high degree of almost unanimous favor toward Loyalist Spain waned somewhat.

The other attitude scales were not repeated.[3] Mean scores, together with the dates on which they were obtained and the critical ratios of differences between freshmen and juniors-seniors, appear in Appendix E. Some degree of freshman-to-senior trend is observable with respect to every attitude measured except that toward Soviet Russia. The direction of the trend in every instance is, as the term was commonly applied to these issues during these years, from more to less conservative. The differences between freshmen and junior-senior scores will be seen to be significant for attitudes toward the CIO, the Supreme Court, the New Deal, and for

---

[3] The scale of attitude toward the CIO was repeated, in much briefer form, after a six-month interval. But in view of the brevity of the interval involved, and of the rather low split-half reliability of the six-item scale, changes in score have not been studied.

Satisfactions. For attitudes toward Soviet Russia, American isolation, the Munich settlement, and Social Distance, these differences are not significant by commonly accepted standards.

The significant differences between freshmen and juniors-seniors all involve domestic issues, whereas those which are not significant involve international issues. The only exceptions to this generalization are attitude toward Loyalist Spain (already discussed) and the Internationalism scale. The latter was administered so many times that, by combining groups which responded in different years, the groups become large enough to make rather small score differences significant. Attitude differences regarding international issues proved not significant, not because such issues were not discussed in the community, but because both of the opposing points of view with regard to these attitude scales were favored by rather active and vociferous groups of faculty and students. Concerning domestic issues, however, the influence within the community (as was also the case with regard to Loyalist Spain) may be said to have been almost unilateral.

★ 5 ★

The Nature and Significance of Attitude Change

THIS CHAPTER DEALS with the question of persistence and change of measured attitudes. Just what does it mean to say, for example, that the average Bennington student's P.E.P. score is twelve points lower on leaving than on entering college? Certain criteria are presented by which the nature and importance of attitude change at Bennington may be appraised. The reader is also invited to turn to Chapter 10 where the question of the persistence of students' attitudes after leaving college is studied.

One measure of student divergence from parents' political attitudes is available. In October of 1936 students were asked which of five presidential candidates they would prefer to vote for, and for which they believed that each of their parents would prefer to vote. One candidate (Lemke) received no votes at all. The Socialist and Communist candidates (Thomas and Browder) received almost exactly the same number of votes in each class, and since votes for either were few, they are grouped together, in Table III. A gradual process of political divergence from parents is here revealed. These results, incidentally, are in almost perfect agree-

TABLE III. PER CENT OF PREFERENCE BY STUDENTS AND THEIR PARENTS FOR PRESIDENTIAL CANDIDATES IN 1936

Candidate	52 Freshmen		40 Sophomores		52 Juniors-Seniors	
	Students	Parents	Students	Parents	Students	Parents
Landon	62	66	43	69	15	60
Roosevelt	29	26	43	22	54	35
Thomas—Browder	9	7	15	8	30	4

ment with those obtained in a straw vote in which nearly every student participated on election day, and are quoted in preference to the latter data because of the more exact comparison which they afford with parents' preferences.

The degree to which attitudes remain stable may be shown by the simple device of correlating scores of the same individuals who remain in college two years or more. These correlations for P.E.P. scores obtained by the same individuals at various intervals are given in Table IV. The lower coefficients, as might be foreseen,

TABLE IV. CORRELATIONS BETWEEN P.E.P. SCORES OF SAME INDIVIDUALS AT VARIOUS INTERVALS OF TIME

Interval	Number of Class Groups	Range of r's	Mean of r's
7 months	8	.81 to .93	.86
1 year	9	.57 to .81	.70
2 years	4	.43 to .73	.60
3½ years	1		.42

are those in which freshman scores are involved. Correlations between freshman and junior or senior scores of the same individuals are uniformly the lowest — in the neighborhood of .4. One can do very little predicting from freshman scores as to what junior or senior scores will be.

This raises the question as to whether individuals whose scores are extreme on entrance tend to have extreme scores on leaving college and, conversely, whether those whose scores on leaving are extreme were also extreme on entering college. Both freshman and junior or senior scores are available for only two classes, data for which appear in Tables V and VI.

The evidence from these tables is clear. Each of the five groupings in both classes maintains the same relative standing in the

TABLE V. MEAN P.E.P SCORES OF CLASSES FOR WHOM BOTH FRESHMAN AND JUNIOR OR SENIOR DATA ARE AVAILABLE, CLASSIFIED BY FRESHMAN SCORES

Freshman P.E.P. Grouping	Class Entered 1935				Class Entered 1936			
	N	Fall '35	Spring '39	Diff.	N	Fall '36	Spring '39	Diff.
Very low	6	56.8	56.8	0.0	6	53.8	47.8	6.0
Moderately low	9	64.4	60.4	4.0	7	62.7	58.6	4.1
Intermediate	15	73.1	62.5	10.6	15	74.9	68.8	6.1
Moderately high	9	80.3	64.8	15.5	7	82.0	75.1	69.
Very high	6	94.3	72.8	21.5	6	88.7	80.5	8.2

TABLE VI. MEAN P.E.P. SCORES OF CLASSES FOR WHOM BOTH
FRESHMAN AND JUNIOR OR SENIOR DATA ARE AVAILABLE,
CLASSIFIED BY FINAL SCORES

1939 P.E.P. Grouping	Class Entered 1935				Class Entered 1936			
	N	Fall '35	Spring '39	Diff.	N	Fall '36	Spring '39	Diff.
Very low	6	65.2	48.2	17.0	6	57.5	46.5	11.0
Moderately low	9	68.6	55.1	13.5	7	64.9	55.4	9.5
Intermediate	15	74.5	62.4	12.1	15	75.2	66.0	9.2
Moderately high	10	75.0	70.5	4.5	7	79.4	78.1	1.3
Very high	5	85.8	81.8	4.0	6	84.7	89.0	− 4.3

junior or senior year that it had in the freshman year. In general
the greatest change in score is shown by groups highest as freshmen and lowest as juniors and seniors, precisely as might be anticipated. It is of interest that the twelve individuals in both classes
whose freshman scores are lowest decline still further in mean
score during their three or four years in college. It is also of
interest that the eleven individuals in both classes whose final scores
are highest show no mean score change whatever from their freshman mean.

Or, if the same two classes are divided into thirds according to
1939 scores, 61 per cent of those in the lowest third in 1939 were
also in the lowest third as freshmen, 32 per cent in the middle third,
and 7 per cent in the highest third. Of those in the highest third
in 1939, 54 per cent were also in the highest third as freshmen,
32 per cent in the middle third, and 14 per cent in the lowest third.
Altogether, 51 per cent of the 86 juniors and seniors responding in
1939 were in the same third of their class that they were in as freshmen; 42 per cent have changed to the next higher or lower third,
and 7 per cent have changed from the lowest to the highest third,
or vice versa. If the college influence upon P.E.P. scores can be
summarized from such data, it can only be said that it serves to decrease the great majority of freshman scores at every level, and
that there are few extreme changes. To this extent precollege influences persist; freshman scores are, by and large, very important
determinants of junior and senior scores.

The attitude changes here reported may be placed in perspective
by comparing them with similar data from other colleges. In the
spring of 1938 the P.E.P. scale was given to 322 Williams College

students, divided among the four college classes as shown in Table VII. Its split-half reliability, as applied to these subjects, was .90. It did not prove feasible to obtain responses from samples of all the major departments of the college. The subjects here involved were largely selected from classes in History, Government, and Economics,[1] and almost certainly are not representative of the entire college. Their mean scores are presumably, therefore, most nearly comparable to those of Bennington majors in Social Studies,[2] which also appear in Table VII.

In April, 1939, 252 students in thirteen classes in the departments of Psychology, Philosophy, and English at Skidmore College[3]

TABLE VII.   MEAN P.E.P. SCORES OF WILLIAMS, SKIDMORE, AND BENNINGTON STUDENTS

	Williams[4]		Bennington[4]		Skidmore[5]		Bennington[6]	
	N	Mn	N	Mn	N	Mn	N	Mn
Freshmen	95	76.1	23	66.1	83	79.9	73	72.8
Sophomores	114	69.4	24	68.1	53	78.1	62	70.0
Juniors	74	70.7	19	61.1	70	77.0	58	68.5
Seniors	36	71.2	12	55.0	46	74.1	45	62.7

returned questionnaires including the P.E.P. scale. Its split-half reliability for these subjects was .82. Mean scores of this total group are compared, also in Table VII, with those of the entire Bennington population obtained at the same time.

The preceding data from Williams are inadequate because the subjects are not representative of the entire college, and because freshman scores were not obtained till several months after college

[1] The writer is particularly indebted to Prof. W. B. Smith for making it possible to obtain responses from nearly all students in the Economics Department, and to Professors Frederick L. Schuman, Enrique De Lozada, and Paul Birdsall for obtaining the co-operation of students in the Departments of Government and History.

[2] Bennington students begin to concentrate in a single major field, broadly defined, immediately on entering college. This concentration is normally to the extent of half the students' work, and during the first two years is considered a "trial major." The comparison of these two total groups is thus not a strictly fair one, as by no means all the Williams students in these classes are majoring in the departments represented. But the educational systems of the two colleges are so different that no strictly comparable Bennington group is available.

[3] The necessary arrangements were made by Prof. Mason Crook of the Psychology Department, to whom the writer expresses thanks.

[4] Social Studies groups; see text. Obtained spring, 1938.

[5] Thirteen classes in three departments; see text. Obtained spring, 1939.

[6] Entire population. Obtained spring, 1939.

entrance. These defects are remedied in part by responses to questionnaires sponsored by the Williams College magazine, *Sketch*. In the fall of 1938, responses were submitted by all freshmen, and in the fall of 1939, by nearly all seniors. Eight items from the P.E.P. scale were included in both questionnaires. Responses by both Williams and Bennington students to these eight items are given in Table VIII. The eight items here included, however, are

TABLE VIII. PER CENT OF CONSERVATIVE REPLIES TO EIGHT P.E.P. ITEMS BY FRESHMEN AND SENIORS AT WILLIAMS AND BENNINGTON COLLEGES [7]

Item No.	*Freshmen*		*Seniors*	
	Williams (N 250)	Bennington (N 55)	Williams (N 164)	Bennington (N 40)
6	34	29	19	5
10	37	22	41	0
11	35	26	29	8
12	52	48	36	5
14	22	21	22	0
18	50	37	27	5
21	35	24	24	5
24	80	62	61	27

not representative of the entire P.E.P. scale. It happens that all of them are stated in conservative form. Bennington students are much less conservative in their replies to such statements than to those stated in opposite form. That is, most of the conservative responses at Bennington, particularly by juniors and seniors, represent disagreements with nonconservative statements rather than agreements with conservative statements. Whether or not this is true at Williams is unknown. It is to be regretted that all the attitude statements included in the *Sketch* questionnaire were of one type.

Conclusions from Tables VII and VIII are fairly clear. Bennington scores are lower in all classes than either Williams or Skidmore scores, and the freshman-senior differences are greater at Bennington than at Williams or Skidmore.

These two colleges were chosen in part because they were near by. Williams had the much more important advantage that a large

[7] For the wording of these statements see the items, numbered as at the left, of the P.E.P. scale in the Appendix. All scores except those of Williams seniors are as of the fall of 1938.

proportion of its students come from families much like those from which Bennington students come; many Bennington students have brothers, cousins, and childhood friends there. It is evident from Table VIII, data for which were obtained in the fall, that initial attitudes of Williams and of Bennington freshmen are much alike. Skidmore was selected as a women's college of approximately the same size as Bennington. It seems likely that the less conservative scores of Bennington freshmen, as compared to Skidmore freshmen, are due to the fact that they were obtained after almost a year of college experience. The community influences, in other words, had already affected the attitudes here measured.

More complete comparative data concerning several college communities, including Bennington, Williams, and Skidmore, are to be published elsewhere. The above citations will suffice, however, to indicate the significance of the freshman-senior changes noted at Bennington. While these changes cannot be described as extreme, they are much more considerable than those observed at any other college. The major reasons for this greater change at Bennington, as will emerge in later chapters, have to do, in the writer's opinion, with the nature of its community life. Not the least important element therein is a relatively homogeneous faculty of predominantly nonconservative social attitudes, who are not only occupants of professorial chairs but also genuine members of a rather closely integrated college community.

Another sort of data reveals the nature of college influences upon attitudes at Bennington. In Appendix B measures of tendency-to-agree and of tendency-to-be-cautious in responding to the Likert type of attitude scale are described. Do juniors and seniors show any more or any less of these tendencies than do freshmen? Two scales, P.E.P. and Internationalism, were responded to by two classes both as freshmen and as juniors or seniors. Mean scores of both these measures appear in Table IX. Agreement score is simply the number of items responded to by "agree" or "strongly agree" minus the number responded to by "disagree" or "strongly disagree." Caution score is the number of items responded to by "?" minus the number responded to by "strongly agree" or "strongly disagree."

The writer's interest in this problem arose from the frequency with which he was told by seniors that they had learned to be more

TABLE IX. DEGREES OF AGREEMENT AND OF CAUTION IN
    RESPONDING TO ATTITUDE SCALES BY INDIVIDUALS RE-
    SPONDING BOTH AS FRESHMEN AND AS JUNIORS OR
    SENIORS [8]

Class Entered	Attitude	N	Agreement Freshmen	Jr. or Sr.	Caution Freshmen	Jr. or Sr.
1935	P.E.P.	42	− 3.3	− 6.6	3.4	1.3
1935	Internationalism	43	− 1.4	− 2.8	− 2.2	3.6
1936	P.E.P.	40	− 5.6	− 6.3	3.5	0.2
1936	Internationalism	40	− 1.8	− 2.9	− 1.8	− 0.7

cautious in their replies. It is clear from this table that this particular
learning was specific to the Internationalism scale, and was limited
to one of these two classes. The freshman-senior tendency in responding to the P.E.P. scale, which dealt with issues much more
vital on the campus during these years, was that of becoming less
cautious in replies. Juniors and seniors are, however, less ready
to agree to attitude statements than are freshmen. The influence
of college experiences might thus be described as that of making
students more critical. They are surer of what they disagree with
than of what they do agree with.

Some seniors explained that they might not have become more
cautious in their responses since freshman days, but that they
certainly had within the last year or two. Caution scores in responding to the P.E.P. scale were therefore calculated for intermediate periods between freshman and junior or senior responses.
At the end of their sophomore year, members of the class entered
in 1936 were intermediate in caution score between freshman and
junior scores. In the fall of their junior year, members of the class
entered in 1935 were very slightly less cautious than as seniors, the
mean junior-year score for 31 individuals who answered all three
questionnaires being 0.9 as compared with 1.4 at the end of the
senior year, and 3.4 for the beginning of the freshman year. There
is little or no substance, then, to the common assumption that
seniors have learned to make fewer extreme responses, either since
freshman or sophomore or junior days.

Concerning the increasing tendency to disagree, there is an in-

_____

[8] See text for method of computing scores. All scores in column "Jr. or Sr." were
obtained in the spring of 1939.

teresting observation to be made. Disagreement is much more pronounced to P.E.P. items conservatively stated than to items nonconservatively stated, particularly by seniors. By chance, the less
conservative scores of seniors would be due to more agreement
with nonconservatively stated items and more disagreement with
conservatively stated items, in equal proportions, than as freshmen.
Both kinds of changes occur, but the class cited in Table X reduces

TABLE X.   PERCENTAGES OF AGREEMENT AND OF EXTREME-
NESS IN RESPONDING TO P.E.P. ITEMS BY 42 INDIVIDUALS
RESPONDING BOTH IN 1935 AND IN 1939

Type of Response	*Items Stated Conservatively*		*Items Stated Non-conservatively*		*All Items*	
	1935	1939	1935	1939	1935	1939
Agree [9]	26	7	37	50	31	27.5
Uncertain	23	19	26	22	25	20.5
Disagree [9]	51	74	37	28	44	52.0
Extreme	13	20	11	10	12	14.5
Moderate	64	61	63	68	63	65.0
Neutral	23	19	26	22	25	20.5

its agreement with conservative items from 26 per cent as freshmen
to 7 per cent as seniors, or 83 per cent of all possible change in this
direction. Or, to state it somewhat differently, the ratio of disagreements to agreements, for conservative items, changes from
2.0 as freshmen to 10.6 as seniors; whereas for nonconservative items
the ratio of disagreements to agreements changes from 1.0 as freshmen to 0.56 as seniors.

These differences in response cannot be attributed entirely to
college influence, since the freshman ratio of disagreements to
agreements is just twice as high for conservative as for nonconservative items. But for seniors this ratio is 18.9 times as high (10.6/0.56)
for conservative as for nonconservative items. To some extent these
results are due to the inclusion in the P.E.P. scale of items stated
in too extremely conservative form. But even so, the change is so
enormous that one can only conclude that college influences are
extremely effective in "debunking" students concerning most of
the conservative beliefs included in the P.E.P. scale, but less effective
in building up the kind of affirmative nonconservative beliefs represented by the items in the scale.

[9] Including "strongly agree" and "strongly disagree" respectively.

Another aspect of the nature of the effects of college experience upon attitudes is that of group homogeneity. In Appendix G are presented the standard deviations of attitude scores, for each class, in order to show whether continued experience in this community tends to result in greater or less uniformity of attitudes. It will be seen that class differences in dispersion are slight, though there is a somewhat smaller dispersion in the senior class. The greater homogeneity on the part of seniors may be due either to selective factors involved in the departure from college of many students before graduation, or it may be due to college influences operating in the direction of uniformity, but it is reasonably certain that the latter of these two considerations is the more important one. There are 10.5 per cent fewer sophomores than freshmen, 30 per cent fewer juniors than sophomores, and 17.4 per cent fewer seniors than juniors. The largest per cent of departures thus occurs between sophomore and junior years, between which periods there is no change whatever in dispersions. To this it may be added that a comparison of the standard deviations, by separate classes, of those who do and those who do not later leave college shows no consistent difference at all.

For the two scales which were repeated (attitudes toward Internationalism and toward Loyalist Spain) there is evidence of slightly increasing homogeneity from the freshman to the senior year. This does not occur without exceptions, but it does appear where the evidence is most complete, i.e., in those years when response was nearly 100 per cent, and for the class entered in 1935, which was followed throughout the entire four years. Response to the scales which were not repeated was unfortunately far from complete, and hence even if distinct trends appeared, they would have to be interpreted with caution. It is likely that for those scales in which junior and senior dispersions are greater than those of freshmen, the differences are to be attributed to the small samples (about half) of the upper classes represented. Where samples are larger in the upper classes, the previously noted trend toward smaller dispersions in the upper classes appears, although it is slight.

By and large, however, it must be said that there is little or no change, from the freshman to the senior year, in degree of homogeneity of attitude. The principal change which occurs, as may be seen rather clearly from the distributions of scores, is as follows:

the great majority of freshmen are rather closely concentrated around the conservative side of the midpoint of most scales, with the remainder ranging between both extremes; while seniors show very little concentration about any point, few or none of them having extremely conservative scores. The calculation of standard deviations, with regard to which freshmen and seniors differ little, obscures these differences. At any rate the results of college experience cannot be said to be those of increasing homogeneity in attitude.

★ 6 ★

Values and Interests

THE MATTER OF VALUES and major interest has a dual bearing on this study. If, in the first place, the rather definite attitude changes of Bennington students are primarily the result of certain kinds of academic interests or of college work pursued, e.g., Social Studies, the significance of those changes is quite different from what it would be if the changes were a community-wide phenomenon.

In Table XI are given the mean P.E.P. scores of juniors and

TABLE XI. MEAN P.E.P. SCORES OF JUNIORS AND SENIORS, CLASSIFIED BY MAJOR DIVISIONS IN COLLEGE

Major	Fall '35		Fall '36		Spring '38		Spring '39		Total	
	N	Mn	N	Mn	N	Mn	N	Mn	N	Mn
Science	10	68.5	6	69.0	6	73.8	15	75.5	37	72.3
Social Studies	24	65.8	18	56.3	30	58.4	28	64.5	100	61.5
Literature	18	66.7	15	61.0	9	61.1	12	59.8	54	62.7
Art	18	68.9	14	64.4	23	63.0	20	64.9	75	65.2
Drama-Dance	16	67.9	8	64.4	12	62.1	12	60.4	48	64.0
Music	7	68.9	4	60.7	11	62.7	16	70.6	38	67.0

seniors in each of the Major Divisions of the college. For each group the latest possible scores in the year are used; the latest ones available for the academic years of 1935–36 and 1936–37 were given in the fall of those years; otherwise spring scores are used. Differences between Major groups are slight. Social Studies and Literature students consistently show somewhat lower mean scores than others; Science students are consistently high, and in two of the four years, Music students are high in mean score. No differences are statistically significant except those between all Literature and all Science students, between all Social Studies and all Science students, and between all Drama-Dance and all Science students. The critical ratios of these differences are respectively 3.8, 5.4, and 3.0. The relatively high scores of Science students are particularly noticeable during the last two years of the study; the mean score of this group becomes higher with each succeeding year, and that of Literature students shows a somewhat similar trend.

As shown by the tables in Appendix D, there are some selective differences in P.E.P. score among freshmen entering different Major Divisions of the college, those in Social Studies being somewhat lower and those in Science and Music being somewhat higher than the average. These differences are slightly increased after three or four years in college; Social Studies and Literature students (whose mean scores as juniors and seniors are lowest) diverge still further from Science and Music students (whose mean scores as juniors and seniors are highest). By and large it must be said that college Divisional influences are less differentiated than might have been anticipated. There are extremely high and extremely low scores in each Major group of each class, with hardly an exception. Attitude change can be predicted far better from such data as prestige score or attitudinal frame of reference in regard to various college groups than from academic Major Division within which the student has concentrated. Whatever the most important of these influences, they operate in community-wide fashion rather than through academic divisions.

Other evidence may be cited in indirect support of this conclusion. A byproduct of this study, not here reported, had to do with information related to measured attitudes, in particular regarding the issue of the Civil War in Spain, which was going on during most of the years of this study. It seems reasonable to assume that interest and information bear some relationship to each other. The evidence referred to above is quite convincing, indeed, to the effect that there is a close relationship between attitude and the kind of information which is acquired and retained; the latter, as might be expected, tends to support whatever attitude is held.

Tests of information about the Spanish Civil War were given

both at Bennington and at Williams. Upperclassmen were better informed in both colleges than freshmen and sophomores, as shown in Table XII. But the more significant fact, for present purposes, has to do with the comparison of those students who are and those who are not enrolled in courses which in some degree dealt directly with the Spanish Civil War. Of the fifteen Williams classes responding, four are known to have dealt with the issue at some length, viz., Contemporary European Government, Modern European History (two sections in each). The mean scores of information in each of these classes are markedly higher than those in any of the other classes. The critical ratio of the difference between the two groups of classes is 5.4. From Table XII, the conclusion

TABLE XII. MEAN SCORES OF INFORMATION CONCERNING THE SPANISH CIVIL WAR AT BENNINGTON AND AT WILLIAMS

	Williams				Bennington			
	4 Classes [1]		11 Classes [1]		Social Studies Majors		All Students Responding	
	N	Mn	N	Mn	N	Mn	N	Mn
Freshmen	0	—	90	13.7	23	14.8	49	13.7
Sophomores	64	20.1	50	13.5	24	16.7	57	15.5
Juniors	45	22.1	29	16.7	19	17.7	39	19.4
Seniors	22	20.1	14	17.8	12	22.8	29	22.7

seems justified that among a very large sample of Social Studies students at Williams, improvement in information concerning this issue is a function of particular courses pursued, rather than of continued community experience. At Bennington, on the other hand, there are no consistent differences between Social Studies majors and other students.

The history of the Bennington college community during this period abundantly confirms the conclusion that interest in this issue was an affair of the community, rather than of courses pursued. Lectures, discussions, movies, and money-raising campaigns for Loyalist Spain were repeatedly held. More than enough money was raised to purchase an ambulance. Only a tiny minority were opposed to the Loyalists, and the favorable attitudes of many students were extreme. Both information and attitudes were of course

[1] The 4 classes dealt specifically with the issue of the Spanish Civil War; the 11 classes did not. See text.

influenced by all these activities, but whatever their relationship, the general conclusion seems unavoidable that interest in the issue was a community-shared one at Bennington and scarcely at all so at Williams. The greater change in attitude toward this issue at Bennington than at Williams is surely related to this fact.

Values may profitably be studied, in the second place, for the purpose of comparing those who are most and least affected by the Bennington community influences upon attitudes. In a given community, attitude change might conceivably be primarily related to almost any of the values included in such a measure as the Allport-Vernon *Study of Values.* The use of such a common measure as this has the additional advantage of yielding some information as to whether Bennington students differ in dominant values from other college groups.

In the spring of 1939 the Allport-Vernon *Study of Values* was given to all members of the graduating class, with nearly complete returns. It should be remembered that this scale is so constructed that numerical values are equivalent, in percentile terms, for all six values. Scores of 28–31 are considered average, and those of 40 or more or 20 or less significantly high and significantly low. Mean scores for the 40 responding seniors were as follows:

Theoretical value 35.7
Economic value 27.5
Aesthetic value 36.7
Social value 32.1
Political value 25.1
Religious value 22.7

As group means, two of these values are very high. The mean theoretical value of 35.7 is higher than that of any group cited by Allport and Vernon,[2] including 26 male students of science, whose mean value is 34.3. The mean aesthetic value of 36.7 for these forty seniors is higher than that of any group cited except that of 40.2 for 24 female students of literature. Two mean value scores of these forty seniors are significantly low. The mean political value of 25.1 is lower than that of all groups cited by the authors except that of eighty missionaries, whose mean score was 21.8. (This value

[2] Allport, G. W., and Vernon, P. E., *A Study of Values*, 1931.

is defined by the authors not as interest in politico-economic affairs, but as interest in *power*.) Women are apt to be somewhat lower in this value than men, just as they are apt to be higher than men in aesthetic value. They are commonly lower than men, however, in theoretical value. And the Bennington seniors are conspicuously low in religious value. Their mean score of 22.7 is lower than that cited for any group by Allport and Vernon, and is approximately as low as any value they cite for any group. Women are commonly higher in this value than men.

Are these value scores related to attitude scores? Differences in mean score between the lowest and highest quarters of the class are given in Table XIII. They are somewhat surprising. Those lowest in P.E.P. score are somewhat higher in theoretical and aesthetic values, and much lower in economic and political values than those highest in P.E.P. score. In short, the least conservative fourth of the class is particularly conspicuous in precisely those values in respect to which the class as a whole tends to be conspicuous. They are like their class, "only more so." The economic value is defined

TABLE XIII. MEAN P.E.P. SCORES OF 1939 SENIORS IN HIGHEST AND LOWEST QUARTERS OF CLASS IN EACH OF SIX VALUES, AND MEAN VALUE SCORES OF THOSE IN HIGHEST AND LOWEST QUARTERS IN P.E.P. SCORE

Values	Mean P.E.P.		Mean Value Score	
	Highest Quarter in Value Score	Lowest Quarter in Value Score	Highest Quarter in P.E.P.	Lowest Quarter in P.E.P.
Theoretical	60.7	65.3	34.9	37.9
Economic	67.9	59.4	30.6	23.6
Aesthetic	64.0	66.1	34.3	37.0
Social	57.3	69.6	31.2	35.7
Political	68.2	60.0	27.3	24.4
Religious	63.4	68.4	24.1	21.5

by Allport and Vernon as interest in what is practical and useful, and the political in terms of power. It may sound perverse that those highest in these values are more conservative and less concerned about public affairs in the politico-economic arena, but such is the fact. The higher value put on power by this group seems to be related to the fact (discussed at greater length in Chapter 14) that many of the most conservative juniors and seniors came to college with ambitions for positions of prestige which were not to be fulfilled. Their continuing or increasing conservatism is directly related to resentment over this failure. Most of those who were more successful in achieving such ambitions do not confess to placing a high value on power — whether because the motive, being more or less satisfied, assumes less importance, whether they are loath to confess the motive, or for some other reasons.

There is no consistent difference between the two groups in religious value. This value offers the one exception to the generalization that nonconservatives are "like their class, but more so." In view of the assumptions commonly held concerning the relationship between conservative and religious attitudes, it is of some interest that those whose P.E.P. scores are at the lowest extreme are not characterized by any lesser degree of religious value than those whose scores are extremely high.

The largest [3] and most important value difference between those high and low in P.E.P. is that of social value. It is defined by the authors in terms of love of people, in terms of prizing persons as ends rather than as means to any other end. The mean score of 35.7 obtained by the lowest quarter of the 1939 senior class in P.E.P. score is exceeded by none of the groups cited by Allport and Vernon, and is approached only by a group of missionaries and a group of Boy Scout leaders. The writer regards this as convincing testimony to his general thesis that nonconservative social attitudes are developed at Bennington primarily by those who are both capable and desirous of cordial relations with their fellow community members.

The mean value scores of these seniors in the major divisions of the college appear in Table XIV. In the main, the differences between the scores of the major divisions are predictable. For example, Science and Social Studies students are relatively high in theoretical value; and Literature and Drama-Dance students are high in aesthetic value. Nor is it surprising that Social Studies students are considerably higher in economic value than are Music or Drama-Dance students, or higher in political value than Art or Drama-Dance students.

What is most significant for present purposes is that the value

[3] This is all the more significant because Allport and Vernon report this value to have the lowest statistical reliability of the six values; extreme differences in this value are therefore rare.

TABLE XIV. MEAN VALUE SCORES OF 1939 SENIORS IN
THE VARIOUS MAJOR DIVISIONS OF THE COLLEGE

Major	N	Theoretic	Economic	Aesthetic	Social	Political	Religious
Science	4	40.5	30.7	26.2	34.7	28.2	15.7
Social Studies	13	38.9	32.1	32.8	33.1	27.7	17.2
Literature	3	32.7	31.0	42.3	33.0	23.0	24.3
Art	9	35.2	25.8	40.9	30.0	22.8	25.3
Drama-Dance	4	29.5	24.2	44.0	31.7	21.0	29.5
Music	7	33.1	24.0	37.3	30.0	24.4	31.7
All	40	35.7	27.5	36.7	32.1	25.1	22.7

score differences between the major divisions bear little relation
to those between high- and low-scoring individuals in P.E.P. Judging by theoretical value, we should expect P.E.P. scores to be highest for Drama-Dance students and lowest for Science and Social
Studies students — which is by no means the case. Or, judging
by economic and political values, P.E.P. scores of Social Studies
students should be higher than those of Art or Drama-Dance students, which again is not the case. Social value, which distinguishes
better than any other between individuals who are high and those
who are low in P.E.P., is about the same for all major divisions.
These data do not permit a weighted comparison, but it is clear
that measured attitudes derive from personal values which bear a
certain relationship to the community, as well as from purely divisional influences of an academic nature.

★ 7 ★

The College Community as a
Frame of Reference

THE DATA ALREADY SUPPLIED provide abundant evidence that the measured attitudes are a function of the particular community in which they were measured. But the community is not a constant for all individuals. If the community-as-a-whole is so important in the development of attitudes, its effect upon each individual will depend upon her relationship to it, how she looks at it. Is it possible to measure such a frame of reference?

It can scarcely be measured regarding the community-as-a-whole, but nothing is simpler than to discover how students look at the community in terms of the attitudes here measured. The Per Cent Estimates questionnaire reproduced in Appendix A was designed for this purpose. The attitude statements therein represent a simplified and abbreviated form of the P.E.P. scale. The statements were simplified because it was desirable to avoid all complexities and ambiguities, to present an issue in its starkest form, even at the risk of oversimplifying it. The number of items was cut down because the task requested is a rather onerous one, and better response could be expected from fourteen than from a larger number of items.

Two kinds of response to each item were requested. The first was an "agree" or "disagree" answer, only those two kinds of response being provided for. The second response was an estimate of what per cent of four college groups (freshmen, sophomores, juniors-seniors, faculty) would agree with the statement. The device is simple, and seems satisfactory except possibly in one respect, viz., the forced yes-or-no responses to somewhat oversimplified attitude statements. But the major purpose of the device was to compare attitude response with estimate response. And if more than two degrees of attitude response had been permitted, the comparison of the two kinds of response would have been not only much more difficult, but also less meaningful. It is more important to know that a student is more inclined to agree than to disagree with a statement with which she believes that the majority of her classmates disagree, than to know that she is uncertain about a statement with which she believes the majority disagrees.

This series of fourteen attitude items has not been listed with the other attitude scales, nor has its validity and reliability been studied. It was designed not for use as a scale, but for comparison of attitude response and estimate response to the same items. It is important, nevertheless, to be sure that attitude response to these items bears a reasonably close relation to P.E.P. response, as it was intended to be a simplified form of the P.E.P. scale. Neither reliability coefficients nor coefficients of correlation with other measures can be computed, except for freshmen, because for other classes distributions of scores are extremely skewed. For 34 freshmen this correlation is .63. The corresponding relationship for seniors can be observed in Table XV, where mean P.E.P. scores are given for those scoring 0, 1–2, 3–6, and 7–14 on this list of fourteen items. There is clearly a close relationship between the two attitude scores.

The complete tabulation of responses to all items appears in Appendix H. From these tables and from the summarized data in Table XV the following observations may be made. First, senior estimates of conservatism (except their estimates of freshman response) are lower, regardless of attitude response, than those of freshmen. The mean percentages of all senior and all freshman conservative estimates are as follows:

Estimates By	Freshmen	Estimates Of Juniors-Seniors	Faculty
Freshmen	52%	43%	38%
Seniors	61%	30%	20%

These differences, in the second place, are largely accounted for by the items answered nonconservatively by the two groups. There is little difference between senior and freshman estimates of items conservatively answered by both groups. Thirdly, estimates both by freshmen and by seniors are lower for items which each group answers nonconservatively than for items which each group answers conservatively; this difference is considerably greater for seniors than for freshmen. Finally, seniors believe that there is a much greater freshman-senior difference than do freshmen.

Before attempting to interpret these findings there is a further question to be raised. Conservative attitude responses are associated with conservative estimates. This might be because *all* estimates of conservative individuals (by whom the great majority of conservative responses are made), including estimates of items answered nonconservatively, tend to be more conservative than *all* estimates by nonconservative individuals, including estimates of items answered conservatively. Or it might be because the majority of all individuals, regardless of conservatism of total response, associate conservative estimates of response to particular items with conservative attitude responses to those items, and nonconservative estimates with nonconservative attitude responses. The data in Table XV indicate clearly that the latter alternative is the cor-

TABLE XV. MEAN PER CENT ESTIMATES OF CONSERVATIVE RESPONSE, CLASSIFIED ACCORDING TO TOTAL ATTITUDE SCORE

Total Attitude Score	Number of Individuals	Items Answered Nonconservatively				Items Answered Conservatively				Mean P.E.P. Score
		N	Fr.	J.–S.	Faculty	N	Fr.	J.–S.	Faculty	
Seniors										
0	9	126	64	24	14	0	—	—	—	56
1–2	9	114	63	23	14	12	79	50	45	63
3–6	8	73	51	29	19	39	68	56	49	70
7–10	4	24	45	25	17	32	63	51	43	81
Total	30	337	59	25	15	83	68	53	46	65
Freshmen										
0	0	0	—	—	—	0	—	—	—	—
1–2	8	101	50	30	23	11	69	58	57	62
3–6	16	153	45	37	34	70	64	63	60	71
7–12	10	54	45	36	32	81	62	53	48	81
Total	34	308	47	35	30	162	63	58	54	72

rect one. Except for estimates of freshmen, there is simply no relation between estimates and total attitude score for items answered in either way. There is a marked tendency on the part of seniors, and a slight one on the part of freshmen, for nonconservatively responding individuals to estimate freshman response more conservatively than do conservatively responding individuals. This is the counterpart of the fact that seniors, in general, estimate freshman responses more conservatively than do freshmen themselves. The generalization seems to be that the less conservative the student, particularly if she is a senior, the more conservatively she estimates freshmen. An indirect confirmation of this is afforded by the correlation, for seniors, of .44 between mean estimate of freshman conservatism and P.E.P. score. The corresponding coefficient for freshman is .12.

How closely do these estimates agree with actual attitude responses? In Appendix H are given both attitude and estimate response to each item; mean estimates and attitude responses are reproduced herewith, in terms of per cent of conservative response.

Estimated By	Freshman Response		Jun.-Sen. Response		Faculty Response	
	Actual	Estimated	Actual	Estimated	Actual	Estimated
Freshmen	34	52	20	43	10	39
Seniors	34	61	20	30	10	21

These data are among the most revealing of the whole study. They point, first, to the widely shared belief by both freshmen and seniors (particularly seniors) that freshmen are more conservative than juniors-seniors who, in turn, are more conservative than faculty. This belief is justified by actual responses,[1] in the second place. The *relative* degrees of conservatism of freshmen, juniors-seniors, and faculty are rather well estimated by seniors but not by freshmen, who underestimate the differences. The absolute degrees of conservatism of the three groups, thirdly, are considerably overestimated both by freshmen and by seniors. Seniors overestimate freshman conservatism more than freshmen overestimate

[1] Only 26 of 42 questionnaires submitted to faculty were returned, in spite of a personal plea, and though anonymity was emphasized. Faculty members were asked, however, to indicate departments in which they taught, and some individuals may have feared "detection" from this source. Questionnaires were not submitted to a few faculty members who had been at the college only a few weeks at the time. Judging from many individuals who later informed the writer that they either had or had not returned questionnaires, he is inclined to believe that the responses received represent a reasonably good selection of the full-time faculty of several years' tenure, i.e., those likely to have been most influential during the past four years. It is probable, however, that a slightly larger proportion of the less conservative than of the more conservative faculty responded (the term being used as previously defined).

it themselves, but overestimate junior-senior conservatism less than do freshmen.

The degree to which actual responses agree with estimated responses may also be shown by coefficients of correlation. Spearman rank-order correlations between actual and estimated responses to each of the 14 items are as follows:

	Estimates of Freshmen	Estimates of Juniors-Seniors	Estimates of Faculty
Estimates by freshmen	.75	.79	.65
Estimates by seniors	.82	.81	.58

To what degree do either freshmen or seniors assume that the various groups will agree as to relative conservatism on the fourteen items? Intercorrelations (Spearman) of estimates by freshmen and by seniors for the three possible pairings of the three groups are as follows:

	Estimates by Freshmen	Estimates by Seniors
r Freshmen. juniors-seniors	.88	.75
r Freshmen. faculty	.85	.64
r Juniors-seniors. faculty	.97	.87

The corresponding intercorrelations among actual responses are .85, .75, and .81. It is thus assumed by freshmen that there are only slight differences among the three groups in absolute degree of conservative response, and almost none at all in relative degree of conservative response to the several items. Seniors, on the other hand, see greater differences both in relative and in absolute degree of conservative response.

All groups show an amazing tendency to assume that their own attitude responses correspond to those of the majority of their classmates. As seen in Table XVI, no less than 76 per cent of all senior item responses are in agreement with majority estimates, and only 14 per cent in disagreement, the remainder of the items being estimated at 50 per cent for their class. For freshmen, 52 per cent of item responses are in agreement with majority estimates, and 30 per cent in disagreement. It is highly significant that where there is disagreement on the part of seniors, in nearly every case it represents the individual's belief that her class is less conservative than herself.[2] This is true for all classifications of total attitude score, but particularly of the high-scoring group; among the eight seniors whose total score is 6 or greater, only one of 55 nonconservative responses is believed to represent a minority position.

TABLE XVI. PERCENTAGES OF ITEM RESPONSES IN AGREEMENT WITH AND IN DISAGREEMENT WITH MAJORITY ESTIMATES [3]

Total Score		34 Freshmen						30 Seniors				
	N	Disagreements			Agreements	50% Est.	N	Disagreements			Agreements	50% Est.
		Non-cons.	Cons.	Tot.				Non-cons.	Cons.	Tot.		
0	0	—	—	—	—	—	9	7	0	7	84	9
1–2	8	41	1	42	45	13	9	1	9	10	84	6
3–6	16	21	3	24	52	24	8	2	20	22	67	11
7–12	10	17	14	31	53	16	4	0	27	27	54	19
Total	34	23	7	30	52	18	30	2	12	14	76	10

Disagreements on the part of freshmen, however, represent individuals' beliefs that they are less conservative than their class about twice as often as they represent the contrary belief. Thus we have a sort of regression toward the mean: most disagreements on the part of seniors, who know their class is less conservative than are freshmen, reflect most individuals' beliefs that the class is also

[2] There is an apparent contradiction here. In the second paragraph above it is stated that all groups (including seniors) tend to overestimate the conservatism of all groups (including seniors). Since actual responses, in this case, are made by the same individuals who make the estimates, this seems to be equivalent to saying that the average senior considers her class *more* conservative than herself. This conclusion, however, is not justified. It is based upon the fact that the average senior estimates that (averaging all 14 items) 30% of her classmates respond conservatively, whereas actually only 20% so respond on the average. The more exact statement would be that the average senior underestimates the magnitude of the nonconservative majority with which she is in agreement (see Table LVII). There is thus no question of the average senior's considering her class, as a whole, more conservative than herself; she merely overestimates the size of the minority.

Thus the average senior may not fully appreciate the near-unanimity with which her classmates agree with many of her frequent nonconservative responses, though she believes herself (correctly) to be with the majority in making them. When she does believe herself in the minority she almost invariably believes herself more conservative than the majority, and not vice versa. In short, she either believes herself in the majority (in responding nonconservatively) or (in responding conservatively) more conservative than the majority.

[3] Columns headed "Non-cons." indicate nonconservative responses associated with estimates of conservative class majorities; those headed "Cons." indicate conservative responses accompanied by estimates of conservative class majorities. Estimates of exactly 50% are neither agreements nor disagreements.

less conservative than they themselves; most disagreements on the part of freshmen, who also know that freshmen are more conservative than seniors, reflect individuals' beliefs that their class is also more conservative than themselves.

It is no surprise to learn, from Table XVII, that senior attitude responses are little like seniors' estimates of freshman responses. But it was not to be expected that, as may be seen from the same table, freshman attitude responses actually agree more closely with freshman estimates of seniors than with their estimates of their own class. This table is like Table XVI except that freshman attitude

TABLE XVII. PERCENTAGES OF ITEM RESPONSES OF SENIORS IN AGREEMENT WITH AND IN DISAGREEMENT WITH THEIR MAJORITY ESTIMATES OF FRESHMEN, AND THOSE OF FRESHMEN IN AGREEMENT WITH AND IN DISAGREEMENT WITH THEIR MAJORITY ESTIMATES OF SENIORS

Total Score	Freshmen Estimates of Seniors						Senior Estimates of Freshmen					
	N	Disagreements			Agreements	50% Est.	N	Disagreements			Agreements	50% Est.
		Non-cons.	Cons.	Tot.				Non-cons.	Cons.	Tot.		
0	0	—	—	—	—	—	9	71	0	71	21	8
1–2	8	10	2	12	77	11	9	60	0	60	30	10
3–6	16	17	6	23	61	16	8	26	4	30	45	25
7–12	10	9	24	33	53	10	4	13	5	18	53	29
Total	34	13	10	23	64	13	30	48	2	50	34	16

responses are compared with their estimates of seniors, and senior attitude responses with their estimates of freshmen. All but the most conservative freshmen consider themselves much more like seniors than like freshmen, and all but the most conservative seniors believe they are in complete disagreement with freshmen. Perhaps nothing could show better than do these two tables the community pull in what is believed to be (and, by and large, actually is) the direction of junior-senior attitudes. And it should be remembered that this is also the direction of what is believed to be (and actually is) the majority faculty attitude.

The Per Cent Estimates questionnaire was also responded to by the 252 Skidmore students (cf. Chapter 5). The complete tabulation of responses appears in Appendix H. It is interesting to note that freshman-senior differences in conservatism more nearly resemble those at Bennington according to this measure (obviously a cruder one) than according to the P.E.P. scale. Mean freshman-senior difference at Bennington is 44 per cent of all possible difference in the nonconservative direction; the corresponding percentage at Skidmore is 23. In terms of P.E.P. score the corresponding percentages are 10 at Skidmore and 22 at Bennington.

The significant finding from the Per Cent Estimate responses is that Skidmore students do not believe that seniors are very different from freshmen in response to these items. Skidmore freshmen also consider faculty responses to be about the same as those of students, though Skidmore seniors believe faculty to be somewhat less conservative than students. Skidmore seniors are much like Bennington freshmen in the degree to which they consider faculty less conservative than themselves.

How accurate are these estimates? Actual responses are compared with estimates in Appendix H, in terms of freshman-senior difference. At Bennington, as we have seen, seniors tend to overestimate actual differences between freshman and senior response, while freshmen tend to underestimate it. At Skidmore both freshmen and seniors underestimate the difference — in fact, reduce it almost to zero. This single fact, perhaps, best reveals the differences in community mores between the two institutions. Seniors do respond less conservatively than freshmen at Skidmore, but apparently the fact is not advertised. It seems to be overadvertised at Bennington. The longer one remains at Bennington the more one is convinced of the magnitude of this difference. At both institutions the degree and direction of error in estimated attitudes provides a useful indicator, if not an accurate measure, of community influences at work in modifying those attitudes.

The question of the validity of the Skidmore estimates must be faced, since there appears to be rather little discrimination among estimates of response to the several statements, either by freshmen or by seniors. Were these estimates made nearly at random? The task required was an unusual one, and Skidmore students may have felt it unreasonable or impossible, but nevertheless gone through the motion, since they had been asked to do so. Not entirely at random, certainly, for the rank-order correlation coefficient between actual freshman responses and freshman estimates of freshman responses is +.54. That between actual senior responses and senior estimates of junior-senior response is +.59. The corresponding coefficients at Bennington are +.75 and +.81. The smaller coefficients at Skidmore do not necessarily mean that the task was performed any less conscientiously than at Bennington. All other evidence indicates that Bennington students are more aware than Skidmore students of what the dominant attitudes in their own community are. This alone could, and probably does, account for the superiority of the Bennington coefficients.

The Per Cent Estimates thus afford us certain glimpses into the community, a picture of attitude toward attitudes, as it were. It is commonly believed that the Bennington pattern includes a considerable sloughing off of conservative attitudes. Freshmen overestimate the actual degree of junior-senior conservatism, and thus underestimate the trend. Seniors overestimate the actual degree of freshman conservatism, and thus overestimate the trend. The majority of freshmen believe that they are more like seniors in attitude than like freshmen. Most seniors believe that they are far less conservative than ʼ_eshmen, but more conservative than the majority of their classmates. Nevertheless both freshmen and seniors, and particularly seniors, consider themselves in agreement with their class majorities, for both conservative and nonconservative responses. It is as if the typical freshman said to herself, "I'm in general agreement with my class, but I tend to be more like juniors and seniors than most of my classmates do"; and as if the typical senior said, "By and large I agree with my class, of course, but I haven't shifted quite as far from the freshman position toward the faculty position as have most of my classmates."

★ 8 ★

Personal Status

ENOUGH HAS ALREADY been said about the importance for individual attitudes of community relationships to make imperative a study of individual interrelations within the community. There appears to be a community pull in the direction of what are believed to be typical junior-senior social attitudes. But such social forces are not sheer abstractions. They are mediated by individuals. It seems an obvious prediction that in this community, prestige-endowed individuals, particularly in the upper classes, should be characterized by less conservative social attitudes.

This did not become obvious to the writer until two of the four years included in the study had passed, although a sociometric study had been made during the first year. In the late spring of 1938, therefore, and again one year later, an attempt was made to measure individual prestige. Considerable care was taken in the wording of the directions. It was necessary to get at *community-oriented prestige,* rather than mere personal charm. Directions were therefore as follows:

Suppose there was to be an important gathering of representative students from every type of American college this summer. Each of the colleges selected is to be represented by five students. They are to be chosen not for ability to speak in public, nor for any other special ability, but merely as worthy representatives of their institutions. The only purpose of the gathering is that of informal association of students with each other. It is fair to assume that Bennington College will be judged, to a greater or less extent, by the students who represent it.

What five students, now in college, would you choose as most worthy of representing Bennington College? The order in which you name the five is of no significance. Please consider only individuals' characteristics, capacities, achievements, etc., and not their major fields in college.

The somewhat different manner in which these questionnaires were gathered is described in Chapter 2. Response was virtually 100 per cent complete.

The range of frequency of choice as representative, in answer to this question, was from 0 to 89 in 1938, and from 0 to 90 in 1939. Mean P.E.P. scores for six classifications of frequency of choice appear in Table XVIII. It will be seen that P.E.P. scores

TABLE XVIII. MEAN P.E.P. SCORES, CLASSIFIED ACCORDING TO FREQUENCY OF BEING CHOSEN AS REPRESENTATIVE

Frequency of Choice	Freshmen		Sophomores		Juniors-Seniors		Entire College	
	N	Mn	N	Mn	N	Mn	N	Mn
1938								
40–89	—	—	3	60.3	5	50.4	8	54.1
12–39	—	—	5	65.6	15	57.6	20	59.7
5–11	—	—	5	65.3	18	62.2	23	62.7
2–4	10	64.6	18	68.6	19	61.6	47	65.3
1	12	63.4	17	68.6	15	62.1	44	65.0
0	61	72.8	39	71.3	14	69.0	114	71.7
Total	83	70.5	87	69.2	86	61.5	256	67.1
1939								
40–90	—	—	—	—	6	59.5	6	59.5
12–39	—	—	2	48.0	16	63.1	18	61.5
5–11	2	60.5	4	57.2	15	63.8	21	62.4
2–4	8	69.5	2	74.5	16	64.4	26	66.7
1	10	71.0	20	68.9	15	69.9	45	69.3
0	53	74.1	58	72.8	34	70.0	145	72.5
Total	73	72.8	86	70.6	103	66.0	261	69.5

become progressively higher as frequency of choice becomes lower, not only for juniors and seniors, but for freshmen and sophomores as well. The comparable mean scores for the two years are very similar, with two exceptions: groups composed of very few subjects, and the group of 1939 juniors-seniors chosen but once. In 1938 the significant line of demarcation for juniors-seniors is that between being chosen once and not at all, whereas in 1939 it is between being chosen twice or more and once or not at all. Otherwise, results for the two years are similarly consistent in the relationship shown between conservative attitude and frequency of choice as worthy to represent the college.

These data may be reinforced by a few observations about extreme scores. Among the group of 1938 juniors and seniors, the mean P.E.P. score of the three individuals most frequently chosen is 47.7; for the three most frequently chosen juniors and seniors in 1939 the mean is 57.7; each of these means is two to three points below that of the entire group of juniors-seniors chosen forty times or more. In 1938 only three of twelve individuals chosen more than fifteen times exceed the mean of the entire class in P.E.P. score, and each of the three by only a very few points. In 1939 only one of fifteen individuals chosen more than fifteen times exceeds the mean P.E.P. score of the entire group of juniors-seniors, and that by only four points. Among fourteen juniors and seniors not chosen at all in 1938, four are below the mean P.E.P. score of the entire group — and two of them by considerable amounts. Among 34 juniors and seniors not chosen in 1939, eleven are below the mean P.E.P. score of the entire group, three of them by as much as one standard deviation of the distribution of scores for the entire group. The relation between attitude and prestige is thus clearer at the "popular" than at the "unpopular" extreme. Perhaps the reason is that, in any given community, a more or less fixed pattern of characteristics is invariably associated with prestige, whereas there are many patterns associated with the lack of it.

Are *changes* in prestige associated with attitude changes? Not for the 1938 juniors, for during the ensuing year there are hardly any significant changes either in frequency of choice or in P.E.P. scores. Among 1938 freshmen, those who were chosen once or more included every one of those chosen more than once a year later; thus early does "leadership" begin to emerge. It can only be said that there is some slight tendency for those who increase in prestige to decrease in P.E.P. scores, and vice versa.

Perhaps it is a more significant question whether prestige-endowed individuals make lower P.E.P. scores on first arriving at college. The pertinent data, for these earliest responses, appear in Table XIX. The numbers of subjects in each grouping are small in this table, but the trends are remarkably consistent. Except for the very small groups scoring highest in frequency of choice as representatives, the trend toward higher mean P.E.P. scores with lower representative scores is of about the same magnitude as that which appears in Table XVIII. Individuals who, as much as three and a half years later, are believed to be most worthy representatives of the college

TABLE XIX. MEAN P.E.P. SCORES OF ENTERING FRESHMEN, CLASSIFIED ACCORDING TO FREQUENCY OF LATER CHOICE AS COLLEGE REPRESENTATIVE

F. of Choices	Year Chosen	Class Entered In							
		1935		1936		1937		1938	
		N	Mn	N	Mn	N	Mn	N	Mn
40–90	1938	4	75.0	} 6	74.7	—	—		
12–39	1938	7	62.4			—	—		
5–11	1938	8	66.1	3	67.0	—	—		
2–4	1938	10	73.0	13	72.7	8	69.9		
1	1938	10	73.9	12	73.6	11	64.3		
0	1938	12	79.8	25	77.8	45	74.1		
40–90	1939	3	75.0	} 8	76.4	—	—	—	—
12–39	1939	9	69.0			2	67.5	—	—
5–11	1939	6	72.3	7	65.4	4	65.5	2	70.5
2–4	1939	8	73.1	5	76.4	2	69.5	6	73.0
1	1939	3	73.7	8	73.0	17	71.8	8	74.4
0	1939	14	77.7	18	74.6	39	72.9	39	76.9

are, as early as their second month of college experience, less conservative in terms of P.E.P. score than others (with the exception of the very highest scoring group in representative scores).

It will not do, however, to conclude that because this trend already exists in the first few weeks of the freshman year, it merely continues for four years as it was in the beginning. The fact is, as shown in Table XX, that the relationship between freshmen attitudes and later prestige increases. That is, greater prestige is

TABLE XX. MEAN P.E.P. SCORES OF ENTERING FRESHMEN AND CHANGES THEREFROM IN 1938 AND 1939, CLASSIFIED ACCORDING TO FREQUENCY OF CHOICE AS REPRESENTATIVES

F. of Choices	Year Chosen	Entered 1935			Entered 1936			Entered 1937			Entered 1938		
		N	Fresh. Mn	Change	N	Fresh. Mn	Change	N	Fresh. Mn	Change	N	Fresh. Mn	Change
12–90	1938	11	67.0	− 12.5	6	74.7	− 10.4	—	—	—	—	—	—
2–11	1938	18	70.0	− 10.2	16	71.6	− 5.0	8	69.9	− 7.6	—	—	—
0–1	1938	22	77.1	− 6.9	37	76.4	− 7.4	53	72.1	− 1.2	—	—	—
12–90	1939	12	70.5	− 12.5	8	76.4	− 9.9	2	67.5	− 19.5	—	—	—
2–11	1939	14	72.8	− 9.1	12	70.0	− 6.9	6	66.8	− 3.7	8	72.4	− 5.3
0–1	1939	16	76.9	− 8.9	26	74.1	− 2.6	42	72.9	− 0.9	43	75.5	− 3.0

not only associated with lesser conservatism as early as the second month of college, but it is also associated with greater decrease in conservatism.

The trend toward lesser conservatism on the part of entering freshmen who are later to achieve greater prestige demands explanation, as does also the exception to the trend on the part of those destined to achieve the very highest prestige. The trend is conceivably a result of the influence of the first few weeks of college life, for not until the last year of the study were the first fall questionnaires distributed before the seventh week of college.[1] This accounts in part for the trend, beyond doubt, but it can scarcely account for all of it.

It seems both reasonable and necessary to assume considerable persistence in those personality characteristics associated with community prestige (or the lack of it), so that even on first entering college those characteristics were presumably more or less important components of the freshmen personalities. What were these characteristics then, which were so consistently associated with social attitudes, and why the association? Whatever they were, they already had a history, and were presumably associated in some rather consistent manner with precollege prestige. It must also be remembered that freshmen do not come to college as to a closed book — and particularly not to this college. The decision to come to Bennington (in view of the common belief that it is a unique institution) nearly always has more than the usual significance. Part of this significance has to do with rather widely shared beliefs concerning the "progressivism" of the institution, and the latter term is often interpreted in politico-economic as well as in educational terms. Not all prospective students (nor their parents) believe this, nor do those who believe it necessarily approve of it. Certainly the college does not select freshmen who are particularly "liberal" in social attitudes.

The conclusion toward which the writer is driven is simply that the histories and personal characteristics of entering freshmen are such that they are impelled, with varying degrees of awareness, toward varying degrees of leadership and prestige. The more they are so impelled, the more it is necessary for them to fit in to what

---

[1] The writer now believes this to have been a mistake in experimental procedure. Until the fourth year of the study he felt it to be important to wait until the bustle of the first few weeks had subsided. In the fall of 1938 the P.E.P. scale was given to freshmen only during the second week of college. This change in procedure may have something to do with the fact that the attitude trend shown by this class is less marked than that of others.

they believe to be the college pattern. As entering freshmen they are in a particularly weak position to flaunt it. And the less they are so impelled, of course, the less necessary for them to fit the pattern. We may, indeed, go farther than this: the less they are so impelled, the less likely it is that they are even aware of what the pattern is; it is less important for them to know than for those who are so impelled.

All this hinges upon the assumption not that all freshmen have come to look upon politico-economic "progressivism" as an institutional folkway of the college, but rather that there are differences among entering freshmen as to the degree to which they thus look at it. We know from the Per Cent Estimates (see Chapter 7) that this is true some six months after entering college, and it seems likely that the first two months of college experience are more crucial in creating these frames of reference than the next four months. Having made this assumption, we need further assume only that there is a fairly close relationship between the degree of considering such progressivism to be an important institutional folkway and the degree of being impelled toward positions of leadership and prestige. The nature of this interrelationship is elsewhere discussed.

But why the reversal of the trend among the very highest scoring group in prestige? Numbers of subjects in these groups are so small that the reversal could be dismissed as accidental — did it not occur so regularly. A ready and reasonable answer is at hand, although it cannot be stated with certainty. These individuals, judging from interview data, were with hardly an exception already experienced as prestige-endowed personalities on first entering college. They were individuals who took their leadership hard. Most of them came from conservative preparatory schools, i.e., in the politico-economic sense; the conspicuous exceptions make conspicuously *low* P.E.P. scores as entering freshmen, which only confirms the ensuing argument. In other words, the same characteristics of institutional loyalty which made them very nonconservative as college juniors and seniors made them very conservative in their conservative preparatory schools. It also made them sufficiently tenacious in their attitudes to persist as long as the second month in college. Case Q61, described in Chapter 13, is a beautiful illustration of this.

The writer has gathered all the pertinent data concerning positions and responsibilities held by students in college. Such data are notoriously difficult to quantify. There is a very obvious and apparently almost perfect relationship between the prestige score here described and the number and importance of college positions held. It seems wiser, therefore, to treat only the prestige scores in this section of the study devoted to quantitative approaches, and to use the other data for individual purposes, in Part III.

It has been pointed out that the representative scores were designed to measure community prestige rather than desirability as a friend. But the latter is also of significance in such a study as this, and particularly in a community small enough and intimate enough for nearly every one to know nearly every one else. In the fall of 1935, therefore, and again in the spring of 1938 questions of the type designated by Moreno [2] as "sociometric" were asked of all students in college. The wording of the questions was not the same on the two occasions, and freshmen were not included in the earlier administration.

The 1938 results are more valuable not only for the latter reason, but because they can be directly compared with choices for representative students, obtained at the same time. The wording of the 1938 directions was as follows:

Suppose that, after leaving college, there were to be exactly five students with whom you would keep in close touch. Assume that geographical and other accidental considerations can be ignored. What five students now in college would you choose to keep in close touch with if you could?

That there is a close relationship between frequency of being chosen as representative and frequency of being chosen as a personal intimate is shown by the following scatter diagram.

Frequency of Choice as Representative	Frequency of Choice as Friend						
	0–1	2–3	4–5	6–7	8–10	11–15	16–21
40–90				1	2	2	1
12–39			3	5	3	1	1
5–11			5	6	4	4	
2–4		7	6	3	4		
1		4	8	2			
0	4	9	6				

[2] Moreno, J. F., *Who Shall Survive?* 1934.

The degree of relationship is indicated by a coefficient of contingency of .70, a Pearson r not being calculable in view of the distribution of representative scores.

A relationship between P.E.P. score and frequency of choice as friend is therefore predictable. This is shown, in different ways, in Tables XXI and XXII. The former table is designed to show that

TABLE XXI. MEAN P.E.P. SCORES OF THOSE CHOOSING AND THOSE CHOSEN AS FRIENDS BY INDIVIDUALS HAVING MOST AND LEAST PRESTIGE

Choice Relationship	Class	Eight Students Chosen as Representative 40 Times or More			Nineteen Juniors and Seniors Not Chosen at All as Representatives		
		Mn Choices per Person	% of All Choices	Mn P.E.P.	Mn Choices per Person	% of All Choices	Mn P.E.P.
Those who choose them	fr.-soph.	3.1	29	64.7	0.8	31	67.0
	jr.-sr.	7.7	71	59.5	1.9	69	67.8
	all	10.8	100	61.0	2.7	100	67.6
Those chosen by them	fr.-soph.	0.6	13	60.0	1.6	34	61.1
	jr.-sr.	4.3	87	55.5	3.2	66	63.1
	all	4.9	100	56.0	4.8	100	62.4

the most representative students, whose P.E.P. scores are much below the average, belong to friendship groups (or would-be friendship groups) whose mean P.E.P. scores are also below average, and below those of the friendship groups of the nonrepresentative students. (Juniors and seniors only are considered in the right-hand half of this table because nearly half of the entire student body would have been included had all classes been considered; and also because the consideration of juniors and seniors only makes the contrast the sharper. Three sophomores were included among the eight most representative students.) The fact that mean scores, for both representative and nonrepresentative groups, are lower for those chosen than for those choosing is of considerable interest. It indicates that the hierarchy of friendship-desirability is related to P.E.P. score. Whether one is possessed of great or little prestige, those whom one considers desirable as intimates are less conservative, in P.E.P. terms, than those by whom one is considered desirable.

This is due in part, of course, to the fact that prestige-endowed individuals tend to be chosen by freshmen and sophomores more frequently than they choose freshmen and sophomores. This is not true, however (as might be anticipated), of juniors and seniors without prestige; i.e., mean P.E.P. scores of those chosen by non-representative juniors and seniors are lower than mean scores of those who choose them, even though the same proportions of upper and lower classes are involved.

Table XXII confirms and supplements this. The extreme groups in P.E.P. score from all classes are compared with regard to friendship choices. The 23 students in each of the extreme groups represent 9 per cent of the entire student body, and the P.E.P. scores above and below which they are selected represent about 1.5 standard deviations above and below the mean score of the entire group.

TABLE XXII. MEAN P.E.P. SCORES OF FRIENDSHIP GROUP-INGS OF GROUPS EXTREME IN P.E.P. SCORE

Class	N	23 Students Scoring 49 or Less				N	23 Students Scoring 85 or More			
		Those Who Choose Them		Those Chosen by Them			Those Who Choose Them		Those Chosen by Them	
		Mn Choices per Person	Mn P.E.P.	Mn Choices per Person	Mn P.E.P.		Mn Choices per Person	Mn P.E.P.	Mn Choices per Person	Mn P.E.P.
Fresh.	6	3.0	55.4	5.0	53.4	9	2.9	78.4	4.4	75.5
Soph.	4	6.0	61.2	5.0	64.8	8	5.7	75.0	4.9	69.5
Jr.-Sr.	13	6.7	60.3	4.8	57.0	6	4.2	67.6	4.7	62.5
Total	23	5.6	59.8	4.9	57.6	23	4.2	74.0	4.7	69.9

One of the points of interest in this table is that the freshmen who choose and who are chosen by the low-scoring group are lower in P.E.P. score than those members of all other classes who choose or are chosen by the low-scoring group. The probable reason is as follows: the low-scoring group is composed largely of nonfreshmen of considerable prestige. Some particularly close bond must be assumed to account for this connection between freshmen and individuals who are older and possessed of greater prestige. *The attitudes here measured provide that bond,* or at any rate are very closely related to it. This assumes nothing as to the priority of either friendship or similarity in attitude, for their relationship is surely a circular one. Whether or not conservative attitudes similarly serve as a bond between freshmen and others of the high scoring group is not apparent; if so, it is true to a much lesser degree, as mean scores of freshmen in this table are about what would be expected without any such assumption.

Data concerning the frequency of choice within various groups, both in 1935 and in 1938, appear in Table XXIII. The columns headed "chance" in this table indicate the number of choices which

TABLE XXIII. FREQUENCY OF CHOICE AS FRIEND OR AS REP-
RESENTATIVE WITHIN VARIOUS GROUPS

Nature of Group	Year	Size of Group	Total Choices Received	Choices Received within Group				Total Choices Given	Choices Given within Group			
				Actual		Chance			Actual		Chance	
				N	%*	N	%*		N	%*	N	%*
Most chosen as friend	1935	26	241	45	18.7	37	15.4	125	45	36.0	19	15.4
P.E.P scores 54 or less	1935	21	105	22	21.0	13	12.4	100	22	22.0	12	12.4
P.E.P. scores 80 or more	1935	21	88	11	12.5	11	12.4	98	11	11.2	12	12.4
Most chosen as represent.	1938	19	166	38	22.3	12	7.3	92	38	41.3	7	7.3
P.E.P. scores 49 or less	1938	23	129	25	19.4	11	8.8	112	25	22.3	10	8.8
P.E.P. scores 85 or more	1938	23	98	14	14.3	9	8.8	110	14	12.7	10	8.8

* That is, per cent of all choices received or given by the group involved

would have been received or given by any group of the same size and receiving (or giving) the same number of choices, on a probability basis. That is, the 26 individuals in the first group in Table XXIII include 25/168, or 14.9 per cent, of all those to whom or from whom choices might be given or received by members of the group. (There were 169 students in the three classes responding, among any of the other 168 of which a given individual's choices might be distributed, just as there are 25 others within the group of 26 among whom any member of it might distribute her choices.) These 26 individuals received 241 choices altogether, and gave 125; by chance, therefore, they would receive 14.9 per cent of 241 (i.e., 37) choices and would give 14.9 per cent of 125 (i.e., 19), from and to this group, respectively. They actually received and gave 45 within the group.

The most conspicuous superiority of actual over chance choices in this table is that of choices given for the "popular" groups of 1935 and of 1938. They are, so to speak, inbred groups. The superiority of actual over chance choices received is almost as great as for choices given in 1938, but not in 1935. This 1935 difference is small, because the group is so selected as to receive maximum choices from all groups, including itself; the chance frequency of choices received is therefore very high. In 1938 the "popular" group was selected on the basis of representative choices, not choices as friends, and hence the chance frequency of choices received as friends is much lower.

It is evident that there is some friendship cohesiveness within both extreme attitude groups in 1938, and for those extremely low in P.E.P. score in 1935. In both years this cohesiveness is considerably greater for the extremely low-scoring than for the extremely high-scoring groups. In terms of per cent of possible choices received, the extremely low-scoring groups are, in fact, much like the "popular" groups. In summary it may be said that there is little or no evidence for cohesiveness among the extremely high-scoring group, and considerable evidence of it among the extremely low-scoring group. The nonconservatives, in other words, are not only more desired as friends by the entire student body than are the conservatives, but are more desired by each other than are the conservatives. This seems to the writer only another way of saying that politico-economic progressivism, as defined by the P.E.P. scale, is a desirable trait in this community.

Certain supplementary data concerning attitudes and personal status are included in Appendix I. Of principal interest are data regarding P.E.P. scores and the holding of various college positions at Skidmore and at Williams. These data show that prestige, as thus measured, is only slightly related to nonconservatism for juniors and seniors. Although the relationship is less marked than at Bennington, it is in the same direction.

Friendship groupings at Bennington, in summary, are thus clearly related to social attitudes. The relationship is clearer for those who are less, than for those who are more, conservative in P.E.P. score. The attitudes matter, to the former group, and are largely a matter of indifference to the latter. There are, of course, exceptions to both these generalizations; they are discussed in the section of the study dealing with individuals.

★ 9 ★

Community Reputation

IN VIEW OF THE ANNOUNCED purposes of this study, some measurement of personality characteristics was demanded. It was the most difficult of the measurement problems faced. The use of the "standard" measures [1] of personality traits simply did not fit into the writer's gradually developing set of hypotheses. Nearly all of the available evidence suggests that there is no reason to expect to find significant statistical relationships between such traits and social attitudes. It is possible, even probable, that in a given culture setting, personality measures may be developed which will be so related, but it seems quite futile to apply standard measures and expect to find linear relationships.

The hypotheses here developed demanded, in other words, that the personality measures be community-oriented. Rating scales seemed feasible; but who should be asked to rate whom? All other questionnaires had been given to all students, or at least to entire classes. But no student would be willing to rate so many individuals, nor would the ratings have much validity, granted the willingness. Each student might have been asked to choose a few others to rate, but there were several objections to this; there would be some resentment at the request; some individuals would not be chosen to be rated; and worst of all, those chosen would in most instances be friends concerning whom the ratings would have little objectivity.

The following scheme was therefore hit upon. In the spring

[1] The single exception was the Allport-Vernon Study of Values; see Chapter 6.

of 1939 the writer chose four students who had been frequently chosen as worthy to be college representatives, who had held several college positions, who were very widely acquainted, whose friendship groupings were largely different, and who understood and sympathized with the purposes of this study. Each of them was asked to make out such a list of twelve junior and senior students that all important friendship groupings and all academic majors were included — in other words, an inclusively representative list. The four lists included twenty-four names, every student house being represented. A personal note was written to each of these twenty-four students in which she was invited to the writer's home on a certain evening for the purpose of carrying out a task essential to the present study. They were warned that about two hours would be required, and asked to remain for a "party" afterwards. All but one of the twenty-four actually came; there was good reason to believe that the groups represented by this absent student were adequately provided for by the others. No one present that evening would have doubted that the requested task was carried out conscientiously.

The task consisted of filling out the "Guess Who" blanks as they appear in Appendix A. Complete mimeographed instructions were provided, and also a list of names of all students in the classes entered in 1934, 1935, and 1936. These were the three classes for whom attitude data for three or more consecutive years were available.

The "Guess-Who" technique was decided upon in preference to a rating scale for two reasons. First, data concerning all the 150 members of these three classes could not have been obtained by the latter method, even under the favorable conditions presented on this occasion. And the writer believed, in the second place, that a few *extreme* instances of the characteristics described were of more value than statements concerning the degrees to which many individuals were thus characterized. Even when the to-be-measured traits are selected with maximum reference to the particular culture in which they are found, and even under the best possible conditions of rating, the writer's hypotheses do not call for a close relationship between all degrees of attitude and all degrees of the personality characteristics here included. The most that can be expected is to find a relationship at the extremes. And the "Guess-Who" technique is the best so far devised for isolating individuals extreme in such traits.

The reader will note that a very few strands run through all the items of the Guess-Who list. They involve areas where interest is absorbed, areas where attitudes of criticism and resentment are felt, areas of susceptibility, etc. All of them are directly related to the college community, or to areas which conceivably conflict with interest in the college community. The hypothesis upon the basis of which they are chosen is simply that those most completely involved in the college community will prove to be those whose social attitudes are most like those commonly believed to characterize juniors and seniors, especially those with prestige, and faculty — in other words, those with relatively low P.E.P. scores.

The data were obtained primarily for purposes of individual study, but certain group findings may be presented. In Table XXIV are presented Guess-Who data for three groups in each of the two classes for whom both freshman and junior or senior scores are available. Group A includes those whose P.E.P. increased or failed to change from the freshman score: Group B includes those whose P.E.P. scores decreased markedly from freshman scores. Each of the groups included roughly one-third of the class as of 1939, the middle third being excluded in this table.

For some of the 28 items there are no differences between Group A and Group B in either class, and for others there are no differences in one class or the other. For no item is there a marked difference between the two groups in one class which is in opposite direction to the difference shown for the other class. For roughly one-half of the 28 items there are marked differences between Group A and Group B in both classes, and in the same direction. In every instance these differences are in the predicted direction.

There are, however, difficulties involved in the statistical study of attitude *changes* of small groups of subjects. Group A, in Table XXIV, includes students whose freshmen scores were almost as low as that of any senior, so that change was almost impossible. Group B includes students whose freshmen scores were so high that even after a considerable drop their senior scores were relatively very high indeed. Groups A and B by no means correspond to the very extreme in P.E.P. score. Guess Who data for such groups are offered in Table XXV, where individuals from the three classes followed three years or more are grouped together. The 22 individuals included in each group in Table XXV represent approximately the lowest-scoring and the highest-scoring sixth of their respective classes; 1939 scores are used for classes entering in 1935

TABLE XXIV. PER CENT OF STUDENTS NOMINATED MORE THAN ONCE FOR EACH GUESS–WHO ITEM, CLASSIFIED BY DEGREE OF CHANGE FROM FRESHMAN P.E.P. SCORE

Item #	Class Entered 1935				Class Entered 1936			
	Group A (N 15)		Group B (N 15)		Group A (N 13)		Group B (N 13)	
	%2+	%5+	%2+	%5+	%2+	%5+	%2+	%5+
1	27	7	13	13	69	15	8	8
2	27	0	7	0	8	0	8	0
3	20	0	33	7	38	8	31	8
4	0	0	27	20	0	0	38	15
5	0	0	27	20	8	0	31	8
6	13	7	13	7	16	0	0	0
7	33	7	20	0	38	8	8	0
8	20	7	20	0	38	8	8	0
9	47	0	20	0	38	8	8	0
10	47	7	33	0	31	0	8	0
11	33	13	60	7	8	0	23	8
12	13	7	27	27	8	0	38	15
13	13	7	20	0	38	15	0	0
14	33	0	27	13	0	0	38	15
15	27	0	53	7	16	0	23	0
16	27	7	27	0	8	0	38	0
17	13	0	33	13	31	0	16	0
18	20	0	20	7	8	0	23	0
19	27	7	13	0	54	0	16	0
20	33	0	7	0	23	8	38	0
21	7	0	27	20	16	0	46	16
22	13	7	27	0	54	8	16	0
23	20	7	33	20	8	0	46	8
24	27	7	20	0	54	16	0	0
25	47	13	13	0	31	0	0	0
26	20	13	47	27	8	0	31	0
27	27	0	7	7	23	0	16	0
28	13	0	47	7	8	0	16	0

The headings "%2+" and "%5+" indicate the per cent of individuals nominated twice or more and five times or more, respectively.

See text for descriptions of Groups A and B.

and in 1936, and 1938 scores for the class entering in 1934. In view of the difficulties mentioned above, Table XXV is probably a more significant one than Table XXIV.

TABLE XXV. PER CENT OF STUDENTS NOMINATED MORE THAN ONCE FOR EACH GUESS–WHO TIEM, FOR INDIVIDUALS EXTREMELY HIGH AND EXTREMELY LOW IN P.E.P. SCORE AS JUNIORS OR SENIORS IN 1938 AND 1939

Item #	Low-Scoring Group (N = 22)			High-Scoring Group (N = 22)		
	$\%2^+$	$\%5^+$	Weighted	$\%2^+$	$\%5^+$	Weighted
1	0	0	0	41	18	59
2	23	5	27	27	0	27
3	23	9	32	14	0	14
4	27	9	36	0	0	0
5	50	32	82	5	0	5
6	23	9	32	18	9	27
7	18	9	27	45	9	55
8	14	5	18	14	5	18
9	9	9	0	50	14	64
10	18	0	18	50	14	64
11	27	0	27	23	9	32
12	36	18	55	5	5	9
13	5	0	5	23	14	36
14	32	9	41	14	0	14
15	18	0	18	23	5	27
16	45	5	50	14	9	23
17	23	5	27	18	0	18
18	36	14	50	14	0	14
19	14	5	18	32	0	32
20	36	14	50	23	0	23
21	32	18	50	9	0	9
22	23	0	23	36	5	41
23	27	18	45	18	0	18
24	0	0	0	41	18	59
25	14	0	14	45	23	68
26	59	14	73	14	0	14
27	18	5	23	27	0	27
28	32	0	32	9	0	9

The headings "$\%2^+$" and "$\%5^+$" indicate the per cent of individuals nominated twice or more and five times or more, respectively. The heading "weighted" indicates a summation of the two percentages in the preceding columns, which is equivalent to a double weighting of those nominated five times or more.

There are no differences of importance between the low-scoring and high-scoring groups, in this table, for eight or nine of the 28 items. These items have to do, in the main, with characteristics regarded as undesirable, and the student judges were somewhat loath to suggest names for these items. Very few individuals were named as many as five times for any of these items. For most of the remaining items the differences between the two groups are marked. For five of them the difference in unweighted percentages of all individuals nominated twice or more is 40 per cent or greater.

The significance of these findings seems great to the writer. These Guess-Who responses represent *extremes* of the characteristics described in the 28 items. The student judges could not have been more than remotely aware, if at all, of the relationship between these characteristics and social attitudes — except, perhaps, for item #5. And yet, considering item #1 for example, not a single student in three classes who is extremely low in P.E.P. score is mentioned as being "most absorbed in social life, week-ends, etc." while almost half of all these extremely high in P.E.P. score are mentioned twice or more in the same connection. More than a quarter of the low-scoring group are mentioned twice or more as being "most absorbed in college community affairs" while not one of the high-scoring group is so mentioned. More than a third of the low-scoring group are mentioned as "most anxious to hold positions of community responsibility" while only one of the high-scoring group is so mentioned. Almost half of the high-scoring group, and none of the low-scoring group, are mentioned as "least likely to engage actively (after leaving college) in pursuits related to college interests." Almost two-thirds of the low-scoring group, and only one-seventh of the high-scoring group, are mentioned as "least likely to lead a life of sheltered leisure" after college.

Item #5 is particularly revealing. Half of the low-scoring group are mentioned twice or more, and one-third of them mentioned five times or more as "most absorbed in national and international public affairs," while only one individual among the high-scoring group is so mentioned as often as twice. The student judges may or may not have been correct in their choice of students for this item; in the writer's opinion they were. But at any rate the fact that this cross-section group of student judges mentioned so many individuals extremely low in P.E.P. score and only one student extremely high in P.E.P. score reveals what they thought the situation to be. Extreme interest in public affairs is associated with non-conservative attitude, while conservative attitude is asociated with indifference.

In Tables XXVI and XXVII certain Guess-Who items are grouped together and their relationship to P.E.P. scores noted. In the former table the total frequency with which each individual is nominated for five items involving "negative community attitude" (items #9, 10, 13, 15, 22) is subtracted from the total frequency with which she is nominated for five other items involving "identification with the college community" (items #4, 12, 14, 16, 21).

TABLE XXVI. MEAN P.E.P. SCORES, ACCORDING TO REPUTA-
    TION FOR IDENTIFICATION WITH THE COLLEGE COM-
    MUNITY

Reputation Score

Class Entered	+ 15 or More		+ 5 to + 14		+ 4 to − 4		− 5 to − 14		− 15 or Less	
	N	Mn P.E.P.	N	Mn P.E.P.	N	Mn P.E.P.	N	Mn P.E.P.	N	Mn P.E.P.
1934	5	49.2	6	53.2	12	60.4	12	61.5	3	68.7
1935	4	55.2	8	61.2	21	63.2	9	67.7	5	69.0
1936	6	58.2	9	65.1	30	68.7	11	75.0	2	65.0
Total	15	54.4	23	60.6	63	65.3	32	67.9	10	68.2

Thus we see that the reputation score in this table indicates the degree to which individuals are believed to have identified themselves with the college community. For each of the three classes studied, mean P.E.P. score increases steadily as this reputation score declines. The single exception consists of a group of two in the class entered in 1936 with reputation scores of −15 or less; one of these two individuals was a notorious recluse who came to college with an extremely low P.E.P. score which did not change during the three years in which her class was studied. Hence the mean of this group of two is relatively low. Otherwise the relationship between reputed community identification and P.E.P. score is clear and definite.

In Table XXVII, Guess-Who responses to the last six items of the list are similarly treated. Total frequency of mention on items #24, 25, and 27 is subtracted from total frequency of mention on items #23, 26, and 28. The latter items indicate reputation for active and enthusiastic pursuit of interests, and the former just the opposite. Reputation score in this table thus refers to qualities of energy and enthusiasm rather than preference for sheltered leisure. The relationship between this and P.E.P. score again is clear for

TABLE XXVII. MEAN P.E.P. SCORES, ACCORDING TO
REPUTATION FOR ENERGY AND ENTHUSIASM

Reputation Score [4]

Class Entered	+ 8 or More		+ 3 to + 7		+ 2 to − 2		− 3 to − 7		− 8 or Less	
	N	Mn P.E.P.	N	Mn P.E.P.	N	Mn P.E.P.	N	Mn P.E.P.	N	Mn P.E.P.
1934	3	69.3[2]	13	54.2	9	57.1	8	65.5	5	68.8
1935	7	59.4	5	58.0	16	64.2	15	65.9	4	67.5
1936	3	52.0	14	63.1	27	67.0	9	75.6	5	80.8
Total	13	60.0	32	59.3	52	64.4	32	65.4	14	72.7

each of the three classes, although there is one glaring exception. Three students in the class entered in 1934 whose reputation scores are +8 or more have a mean P.E.P. score *higher* than that of any other group in the class. Two of these three individuals were the active leaders of a small coterie of rebels against what they regarded as the current overconcern and overemotionalism about public affairs. Their P.E.P. scores were high. They represented a reversal of the general trend reflected in Table XXVII, and they were a phenomenon which did not recur.

The relationship between P.E.P. score and other traits included in the Guess-Who items may be judged, roughly at least, from Tables XXIV and XXV. One of them is of particular interest. In most communities "liberals" and "radicals" are thought of as being the more critical individuals. Several items in the Guess-Who deal with this or allied traits. Items #6, 7 and 8 all refer to "critical" attitudes, but only on item #7, dealing with criticism of faculty, is there a difference between those who score extremely low and extremely high on the P.E.P. scale. *And it is the high-scoring group which is more critical.* Items #13, 15, 17 and 19 all refer to "resistant" attitudes; two of these show moderate differences and two show no differences between those extremely high and extremely low in P.E.P. score. Those resistant to community codes and resistant to faculty authority tend to have *higher* P.E.P. scores than those not mentioned as resistant. Similarly, as shown by item #20, those most influenced by faculty authority tend to have *lower* P.E.P.

[2] See text for comment on this score.

scores than others. Nothing could show more clearly that in this community at this time behavior commonly associated with "liberal" and "radical" social attitudes in other communities had somehow become associated with "conservative" social attitudes. And, more significantly, nothing could show more clearly that the nature of the relationship between social attitudes and such personality characteristics as these depends upon the nature of community forces.[3]

[3] A problem not treated above is the relationship between reputation and P.E.P. scores three or four years earlier, on first entering college. Such a relationship was found for representative scores, as reported earlier in this chapter. Freshman scores were available for only two of the three classes for whom reputation scores were obtained. In one of these two classes it happened that freshman response was poor. Calculations were nevertheless made for all possible members of these two classes, for attitude of identification with the college community. For the class entered in 1936, whose freshman responses were incomplete, there was no relationship to P.E.P. score. For the class entered in 1935 *degree* of positive or of negative reputation score was not related to P.E.P. score, but there was a difference of 12 points in mean freshman P.E.P. score between those whose mean senior reputation score was +5 or more and those whose mean senior reputation score was −5 or less. This difference is about the same as for senior P.E.P. scores.

* 10 *

Former Students and Graduates

WHAT HAPPENS TO the social attitudes of Bennington students no longer at the college? In the spring of 1939 questionnaires were mailed to every student who, since the fall of 1935, had participated in any part of this attitude survey and who was no longer in college. This included about 97 per cent or more of every class in college since 1935. The first three classes to graduate from the college were all included.

The questionnaire included the P.E.P. scale and nine of the agree-disagree items from the Per Cent-Estimates questionnaire described in Chapter VII. The latter was included as the most recent list of attitude items given to contemporary students, whose responses might thus be compared with those of former students. These items are reprinted in the Appendix.

Responses are tabulated in Tables XXVIII to XXXIII. The first of these tables includes responses of all students leaving college after three or four years,[1] mean P.E.P. scores being given for 1935 and the spring of 1938 (for those in college at those times) as well as the 1939 scores obtained by mail. Percentage of response is indicated for each class. For all students leaving in 1936, 1937, and 1938 and after three or four years in college, response was 83 per cent complete. For those leaving in the same years, after two years in college, re-

---

[1] Comparatively few students leave college at the end of the third year, and examination shows that they are much like those who remain four years. They are too few to include in a group by themselves, and they clearly belong with the four-year rather than with the two-year group.

sponse was 63 per cent complete, and 53 per cent for those leaving after one year.

In Table XXVIII, the last available P.E.P. scores are also given for those who did not reply in 1939. A comparison of last scores while in college of those who did and those who did not reply in

TABLE XXVIII. MEAN P.E.P. SCORES OF STUDENTS HAVING SPENT VARIOUS PERIODS IN COLLEGE [2]

| | Leaving 1936 | | | | Leaving 1937 | | | | Leaving 1938 | | | | |
	N	% of Total	P.E.P. 1935	1939	N	% of Total	P.E.P. 1935	1939	N	% of Total	P.E.P. 1935	1938	1939
A. *Three or four years in college*													
Replying 1939	42	71	66.7	68.0	39	93	66.7	60.5	43	86	66.8	59.2	57.2
Not replying 1939	17	29	68.0	—	3	7	69.3	—	7	14	72.9	64.0	—
Total	59	100	67.1	68.0	42	100	66.9	60.5	50	100	67.6	59.9	57.2
B. *Two years in college*													
Replying 1939	16	67	71.0	72.7	8	47	73.6	66.1	19	70	—	70.0	72.2
Not replying 1939	8	33	71.6	—	9	53	80.3	—	8	30	—	72.0	—
Total	24	100	71.2	72.7	17	100	77.3	66.1	27	100	—	70.5	72.2
C. *One year in college*													
Replying 1939	10	71	71.8	85.2	0	—	—	—	8	62	—	67.3	68.5
Not replying 1939	4	29	77.2	—	7	100	76.	—	5	38	—	68.4	—
Total	14	100	73.4	85.2	7	100	76.	—	13	100	—	67.7	68.5

1939 shows that the former members of each group made slightly lower P.E.P. scores while in college than the latter. This indicates some tendency for those higher in P.E.P. score while in college (and presumably later also) to be more hesitant about replying by mail. Comparison of scores obtained before and after leaving college should therefore be made only for the groups responding in 1939. It is not surprising, of course, that there are no large changes in mean P.E.P. score during the one, two, or three years between leaving college and the spring of 1939. It is somewhat unexpected, however, that only one group of those spending three or four years in college increased its mean score during the interval (in this case, three years), and that by only one point. The other two three- and four-year groups decreased in mean score, the decrease of the two-year interval group being six points. Of those spending two years in college, two groups increase in mean P.E.P. score by two points each during the interval, while one group decreases by seven points.

[2] The P.E.P. scale was not given in the spring of 1936 or of 1937, so that scores on leaving the college are not available for these groups. For the group leaving in 1937, scores are as of the fall of 1936, not 1935.

Similar data are given in Table XXIX; numbers of subjects are smaller in this table because only those are included who responded to the P.E.P. scale each time it was given, thus making possible a comparison of several mean scores. It is regrettable that numbers of subjects not replying in 1939 for whom all previous scores are available are so small. Failure to reply in 1939 seems to be compounded of two factors: general disinclination to answer such ques-

TABLE XXIX.   MEAN P.E.P. SCORES OF FORMER STUDENTS
RESPONDING TO ALL QUESTIONNAIRES

| | | Leaving 1937 | | | | | | Leaving 1938 | | | | |
| | | Replying 1939 | | | Not Replying 1939 | | | Replying 1939 | | | Not Replying 1939 | | |
Scores Obtained	Years in College	N	% of Total	P.E.P.	N	% of Total	P.E.P.	N	% of Total	P.E.P.	N	% of Total	P.E.P.
Fall 1935	3–4	31	91	67.5	3	9	69.3	36	84	64.7	7	16	72.9
Fall 1936	3–4	31	91	62.1	3	9	60.0	36	84	61.8	7	16	67.1
Spring 1938	3–4	—	—	—	—	—	—	36	84	59.7	7	16	64.0
Spring 1939	3–4	31	91	60.5	3	9	—	36	84	57.0	7	16	—
Fall 1935	2	6	43	76.3	8	57	79.7	—	—	—	—		
Fall 1936	2	6	43	68.3	8	57	70.3	14	74	81.1	5	26	76.6
Spring 1938	2	—	—	—	—	—	—	14	74	70.1	5	26	73.8
Spring 1939	2	6	43	64.2	8	57	—	14	74	73.9	5	26	—

tionnaires, as indicated by nonresponse during college, and somewhat higher P.E.P. score while in college. The first of these factors does not seem to be related to P.E.P. score, as previously shown. Table XXIX confirms the previous table, in general. It shows that the trend toward decreasing P.E.P. scores shown in college continues after college for all groups leaving college in 1937 or later, except for one group spending only two years in college. It also shows that those who failed to reply in 1939 were also characterized by decreasing scores while in college, and are thus not a selected group in this respect.

Degree of change in P.E.P. score after leaving college is thus a function both of time spent in college and time spent since college. This is shown in Table XXX, in which last available scores in college and 1939 scores are given for various groups.

What characterizes those whose scores decrease after leaving college, as compared with those whose scores do not decrease? All evidence indicates that it is primarily a matter of personal experiences. Data concerning such experiences of former students are not available, and could not be treated statistically if they were. It is

TABLE XXX. MEAN P.E.P. SCORES OF FORMER STUDENTS, CLASSIFIED ACCORDING TO TIME SPENT IN COLLEGE AND SINCE COLLEGE

| | 3–4 *Years in College* | | | 1–2 *Years in College* | | | *Total* | |
Years since College	N	Last Score in College [3]	1939	N	Last Score in College	1939	Last Score	1939
3	42	66.7	68.0	26	71.3	77.5	68.4	71.6
2	39	62.1	60.5	8	68.3	66.1	63.1	61.5
1	43	59.2	57.2	27	69.2	71.1	63.0	62.6
Total	124	62.6	61.9	61	70.0	76.4	65.1	65.6

of some interest, however, to note what happens to those whose P.E.P. scores are very high or very low on leaving college. Such data are given in Table XXXI, in terms of P.E.P. score change for groups low, high, and intermediate in score just prior to leaving college. The low and high groups are so small that trends are upset by one

TABLE XXXI. MEAN P.E.P. SCORES OF FORMER STUDENTS, IN COLLEGE 3 OR 4 YEARS, CLASSIFIED ACCORDING TO SCORE ON LEAVING COLLEGE

Last Score in College

| | | 50 or Less P.E.P. | | | 51 to 74 P.E.P. | | | 75 or More P.E.P. | |
Years out of College	N	In College	1939	N	In College	1939	N	In College	1939
3	6	41.5	55.9 [4]	21	65.3	64.2	14	79.4	78.4
2	6	39.2	37.3	19	63.5	62.9	7	78.3	73.4
1	9	42.4	38.8	30	61.7	60.6	4	81.5	72.0 [5]
Total	21	41.2	43.3	70	63.2	62.3	25	79.4	76.0

or two extreme changes. Except for one very large drop among those highest in score while in college, the mean change of the initially high group was the same as that of the initially intermediate group — one point. Except for two individuals showing very large increases, in the initially low group, the mean change for the entire group is almost exactly the same, not quite one point. That all three groups would so nearly maintain their college levels was scarcely

[3] I.e., scores obtained at last possible opportunity; all scores included for each group, except in "total" column, were obtained at the same time.

[4] Two individuals in this group made increases of 30 points or more; all others are increases of 11 points or less.

[5] One individual in this group decreased in score by 53 points; one other increased by 16 points, the other two changing two points or less.

predictable. One might have anticipated that all three groups would have tended to revert to home and family standards, which were presumably reflected in their freshman scores of several points above scores on leaving college. According to the principle of regression toward the mean, the low-scoring group should change most, since home and family standards pretty uniformly suggest high P.E.P. scores. But, judging from evidence already adduced to the effect that the social attitudes included in the P.E.P. scale really matter to the low-scoring individuals, the group intermediate in scores on leaving college might be expected to change most, since they have diverged somewhat from family standards but have little firm conviction.

The question inevitably arises: do these responses represent *real* attitudes or are they just "Sunday School" answers? The immediate question, of course, is whether the 1939 responses, submitted by mail, are any less "real" than those given while in college. It is hard for the writer to see why they should be. While there is conceivably something to be gained, while in college, by responding in terms of what are believed to be faculty preferences, students no longer in college have little to gain thereby. On the other hand the extraordinarily high percentage of responses received indicates a considerable degree of loyalty to the college, since there was nothing to gain by returning the mailed questionnaire. It is certainly not impossible that "loyalty to the college" was associated, in the minds of many students, with the willingness to stretch every possible point to answer as faculty members would like to have them answer. If so, it was true while in college as well as later; and it is doubtful if feelings of fond nostalgia, insofar as they occurred, would increase this tendency very greatly.

In Tables XXXII and XXXIII are given percentages of conservative replies, by former and by present students respectively, to the nine agree-disagree attitude statements included in the mailed 1939 questionnaire. (The statements are reproduced in Appendix A.) The same factors of time spent in college and time spent since college, noted in connection with P.E.P. scores, are clearly evident here. Table XXXI is so arranged that the left-hand column of each pair should include more conservative responses than the right, insofar as these two factors are operative. This is actually the case for every item for each of the three pairs of groups. Table XXXIII is included

TABLE XXXII. PER CENT OF CONSERVATIVE RESPONSES TO AGREE–DISAGREE ITEMS BY FORMER STUDENTS

Item #	In College 1–2 Years	In College 3–4 Years	Out of College 3 Years	Out of College 1–2 Yrs.	In College 1–2 Yrs., Out of College 3 Yrs.	In College 3–4 Yrs., Out of College 1–2 Yrs.
	(N 61)	(N 122)	(N 63)	(N 120)	(N 25)	(N 84)
1	62	48	60	49	68	45
2	66	31	59	30	72	23
3	43	20	35	22	44	15
4	43	18	40	19	60	14
5	23	16	27	13	20	8
6	57	49	67	43	72	43
7	15	7	14	7	12	2
8	16	12	17	12	28	13
9	48	36	56	31	56	27
Median	43	20	40	22	56	15
Mean	41.4	26.3	41.7	25.1	48.0	21.1

in order that comparisons between contemporary and out-of-college students may be made. Roughly, those longest out of college and those who spent least time in college correspond to present college freshmen, while those most recently out of college after spending the most time there correspond to present seniors.

TABLE XXXIII. PER CENT OF CONSERVATIVE RESPONSE TO AGREE–DISAGREE ITEMS BY PRESENT STUDENTS

Item #	47 Freshmen	51 Sophomores	47 Juniors	40 Seniors
1	64	63	55	52
2	57	43	32	20
3	49	43	34	17
4	50	33	26	18
5	28	23	11	5
6	68	63	55	50
7	15	20	4	2
8	38	22	34	27
9	55	22	38	27
Median	50	33	34	20
Mean	47.1	36.9	32.1	24.2

Two or three of the issues involved in these nine items had become critical since most of the former students had left college. The Civil War in Spain, for example (item #5) began in the summer of

1936. Students who left college in 1936 after three or four years in college are considerably less favorable to the Spanish Loyalists than are comparable groups leaving college one or two years later. Nor is this merely due to the fact that all responses of this group are relatively conservative. In terms of conservatism, this item ranks fifth for this group, while ranking seventh or eighth for all other groups. Those who left college in 1936 after only one or two years, on the other hand, do not differ in this respect from comparable groups leaving one or two years later. The most likely explanation of this is that none of the one-year and two-year groups were very significantly influenced by their college experience regarding this or any other specific issue.

The Munich agreement (item #6) was made in September, 1938, after the departure from college of all those here included as former students. Considering the "agree" response to this item as conservative for present purposes, conservative response to it does not differ in rank for former students as compared with present students. But it is unquestionably significant that those who spent most time in college, and those most recently in college are those who answer least conservatively, even though the issue was never discussed while they were in college. One must conclude that certain more or less generalized attitudes are built up by long and recent college experience. The generalized attitudes are reinforced by feelings of loyalty and identification, either with the college as an institution, with certain individuals in the college, or with individuals or institutions toward whom they were led as a result of college experiences.

PART THREE:

Individual Studies

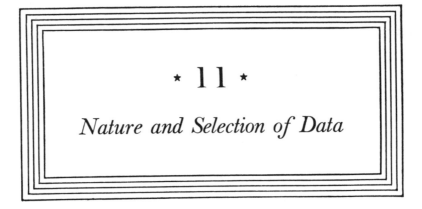

★ 11 ★

Nature and Selection of Data

ALMOST COMPLETE INDIVIDUAL data are at hand for about 140 students who spent three or more years in college between 1935 and 1939. This includes almost every student who graduated in 1938, 1939, or 1940. Considerations of space make the inclusion of individual data concerning all these students impossible. The method of selection thus becomes crucial.

Only the class entered in 1935 submitted questionnaire responses both as entering freshmen and as graduating seniors. It is therefore from this class that it is most important to present as nearly as possible a complete sample. Individual summaries, identical in form with those which appear on pp. 108–109, have been prepared for each individual in this class for whom four-year data are available; ideally all of them would be presented by way of documentation, but space forbids. Many individuals in this class appear in Chapters 12 and. 13, the bases of selection being explicitly stated. The data from the class entered in 1934 are least valuable, since their attitude status as freshmen is unknown. Certain sources of information not obtained from other classes are available for some or all members of the class entered in 1936, whose freshman, but not whose senior, attitude status is known. Since there is comparatively little attitude change between junior and senior years, the absence of senior scores is not a serious matter. Individuals from this class are therefore selected for study for two purposes.

In Chapter 12 a very few individual studies, chosen from this class, are presented; they are selected as somewhat extreme cases about whom unusually complete data are at hand. They are presented as contrasts in respects known to tbe significant for attitude change. And about half of the subjects presented in Chapter 13 for purposes of describing certain personality patterns are members of this class.

Both quantitative and nonquantitative data are included in the individual summaries. Nothing new will be learned from the individual studies concerning quantitative relationships; they can neither add to nor detract from the already known findings, but they can do much by way of illuminating them. The purpose of the quantitative data is to show how the individual stands relative to her class. The purpose of the nonquantitative material is to throw into relief such factors as are presumably relevant to the acquiring of the quantitative scores.

For the sake of balancing brevity against completeness and significance, not all quantitative data are included in the summaries. Attitude scores are limited to those most relevant to issues emphasized in the community during this period. Information scores and values scores are verbally summarized rather than presented in terms of standard deviation units. The method of obtaining scores of prestige, per cent estimates, and Guess Who ratings is described in Chapters 7, 8, and 9.

The excerpts labeled "college records" are the writer's selections. The "most frequent descriptive phrases" are taken from the semi-annual reports of counselors and instructors. Ideally, for the sake of objectivity, these selections should have been checked and corrected by one or more other judges. The experimenter, however, had at his disposal neither financial nor other incentives by means of which he could appeal to anyone entitled to inspect these confidential records to go through the highly laborious procedure of selecting the most frequent descriptive phrases. He does not believe that they would be greatly altered, had this been done.

The other notations from official college sources are from students' counselors, from other teachers who knew them well, and from the college physician. Some of them are from written records, and some were obtained in interviews between the writer and counselors, teachers, or the college physician. The latter. of course. are not subject to check. The writer can only say that they are verbatim, and from individuals best in a position to obtain evidence.

The interview data will not be clear without a full description of the interview situation. Individual appointments were made with each member of the graduating class in the spring of 1938 and in the spring of 1939, and with nearly all members of the graduating class in the winter of 1939-40. They were informed that the interview concerned the attitude study in which they were participating. No pressure was applied; they were simply asked if they would be willing to come, and no one declined. The interviewer was at first somewhat apologetic in asking busy seniors for their time — one-half hour at first, later increased to one hour. He soon discovered that nearly all of them were anxious to come; many of them stopped him on the campus to ask when their turn would come. After filling out several questionnaires a year for three or four years, they had a considerable vested interest in the study. Even if they had no further interest, they wanted to see their scores.

The interview was semi-standardized. The writer now feels that the first year's interviews are relatively valueless. He did not discover the most revealing questions to ask until late in the first year, and one very significant question was not asked until well along in the second year of interviewing. During the second and third years the questions were as follows — though in the heat of pursuing one question, under pressure of time, one or two others were occasionally omitted:

1. Forget, for the moment, that I have ever been interested in your opinions on public issues. I want to know what has happened to you as a person, not as a political creature, since the first day you came to Bennington. I want to know the important ways in which you have changed; whether the changes were due to Bennington or to some other influences I don't care. For example, some students tell me, with obvious sincerity, "I'm completely revolutionized; I'm just entirely made over; I'm so different that my best friends of four years ago would hardly know me for the same person." Others say, with equal sincerity, "Oh, not much has happened. I'm exactly the same person that I always was. I'm four years older, and I guess that's about all the difference." Tell me where you would come with regard to these two extremes, and then describe the nature of whatever change there has been.

2. Now let's turn more specifically to public affairs. Tell me what has happened to your information, to your interest, and to your opinions about public issues since you first came here.

3. What would you say about your parents' interest in and opinions about such issues? Do you have discussions about them at home? If so, what is the nature of these discussions? Have your parents ever been worried about any opinions that you have acquired in the last four years?

4. How do you suppose you compare with other seniors in regard to information, interest, and opinions about public affairs?

5. Now tell me something about the students who are known as being prominent in college community affairs; let's refer to them as "leaders," for want of a better term. As a group, do they differ from other students of their own classes in regard to information, interest, or opinions about public issues? How well do you know this group of students? Do you have any particular personal feeling about them?

6. Have you ever heard it said that there is a sort of social pressure on students to become more liberal in their opinions on such matters? What is your opinion as to whether any such pressure exists?

7. Now let's look at your scores of the past four years. (They are shown and explained.) You see that you were (or were not) more or less correct in comparing yourself with other members of your class, according to these scores.

8. Now we have all the evidence. Let's see if we can jointly arrive at an explanation which will be satisfactory to both of us as to why your attitude scores have been exactly what they are. No matter what the scores are, you see, there must be some explanation for them, and that explanation must fit into all the other things that we know about you. You, of course, are in a better position to see all the factors than I am.

9. Just one other question: you've been in a college where the general influence, as far as the issues included in these questionnaires is concerned, is pretty definitely in the direction of causing students to become less conservative. You have (or have not) more or less followed the general trend. What do you suppose would have happened to your attitudes if you'd gone to a college where the influence was predominately conservative? Would you have been in the majority (or in the minority) as you have here?

10. (included only in about one-half of all interviews) Now I want to ask something about your precollege experiences. The three or four years before coming to college are often pretty critical for a girl's personality. You must have had some experiences — successes and failures — which more or less set the stage for your most important hopes and fears on first coming to Bennington. Suppose that, on the day you first came to college, you had put into words the things that you most wanted to do and most wanted to avoid in the coming years in college. What were the most influential precollege experiences, and what were the hopes and fears to which they led?

The summarized interview statements follow this outline very closely. The writer has had to use his judgment in selecting the brief statements which appear. In some cases there is almost no problem of selection, but in other cases somewhat contradictory statements make it a difficult task. In the latter sorts of cases the attempt has been made to retain the apparently conflicting statements, rather than to oversimplify them by eliminating one of the conflicting phrases.

Only one other comment concerning the interviews is necessary. The interviewer was literally astonished at the whole-hearted manner in which almost every student rose to the challenge of making a joint interpretation of all the evidence. With extremely few exceptions, they caught the nature of the problem and attacked it with considerable objectivity. For some of them it was the first experience of putting themselves in the test-tube. Several students later volunteered additional contributions which they had not thought of at the time of the interview. Many of them later spoke of self-insights which they had first obtained during the interview.

Twelve of the students graduating in 1940 agreed to write autobiographical sketches, following a mimeographed outline given to them. All the seniors in this class who had shown either considerable attitude change or almost no attitude change were asked to do so, after being warned that the task would require three or four hours, or perhaps more; the twelve who agreed to do it represent about one-half of those asked. Only eight of the twelve were actually submitted, and it has seemed wiser to quote four of them at considerable length rather than to quote all of them more briefly.

Considerable care has been taken to disguise the identity of the students of whom individual studies are presented in the following chapters. Identifying data such as major in college and father's occupation have in most, but not all instances, been altered. An entirely new set of code numbers has been assigned. Quotations are either verbatim or only slightly reworded for the sake of brevity.

Quantitative data have in no instance been altered. Attitude scores are given in terms of standard deviations from the class average, raw scores being given only for the P.E.P. scale in order that freshman scores may be compared with later ones. Class averages are not the same from year to year, so that standard deviation scores indicate only the individual's position with reference to her class at a given time. It should also be remembered that high scores represent conservative attitudes. The significance of standard deviation scores is as follows:

0	....	exactly average
− .4 to + .4	....	in average group
− .5 to − .9	.. ..	somewhat below average
+ .5 to + .9	....	somewhat above average
−1.0 to −1.9	....	significantly below average
+1.0 to +1.9	... .	significantly above average
−2.0 to −3.0	....	very low — extreme
+2.0 to +3.0	....	very high — extreme

CASES Q63 AND Q73 are selected as being alike (as nearly as possible) in respect to prestige. Q73 is the only good example of a student who as a senior maintained the high P.E.P. score of her freshman year and who received a relatively high number of choices as college representative. She ranked seventeenth in the college in this respect, but no one ranking higher, either in 1938 or in 1939, maintained as a senior a significantly high freshman P.E.P. score. Q63 ranked sixth in prestige. She is chosen in preference to several others who might have been contrasted with Q73 because autobiographical data are available for both of them, and because they are intimate friends whose friendship groups very largely overlap. Their attitude scores are as follows:

	Q63			Q73		
	1936–1937	1937–1938	1938–1939	1936–1937	1937–1938	1938–1939
P.E.P. (raw)	71	61	58	80	77	81
P.E.P. (s.d.)	− .3	− .7	− .7	+ .4	+ .7	+ .9
Internationalism	.0	+ 1.4	+ 1.2	+ .2	+ .8	− 1.4
C.I.O.	− .3			+ 2.1		
Supreme Court	.0			+ .6		
New Deal			− 1.4			− .7
Spanish Loyalists	.0	− .7	− .4	.0	+ .6	+ .3
Soviet Russia		− .3			.0	
Social Distance			− .7		+ .8	
Satisfactions			− .3		+ .5	

(Scores of attitude toward the Munich settlement, and toward American isolation are omitted here, as in other case summaries. They are not very clearly related to conservatism as otherwise defined.)

With very few exceptions, the scores of Q63 are below average while those of Q73 are above average. The only significant exception is in international attitude, and it is noteworthy that Q73 decreases in this score at a time when the class average is increasing. As freshmen these individuals differ significantly only with regard to the C.I.O. As college juniors they diverge considerably in almost every attitude. As freshmen, Q73's information scores are considerably better than those of Q63; within the next two years both have improved, both absolutely and relatively to the class, to a point where both are slightly above the class average.

Other comparative data are as follows. Q73 majors in Social Studies, Q63 in Art. Each of them describes both parents as Republicans. Q63 has held two major and several minor positions in college, and Q73 two subordinate positions. They are mentioned twice or more, in the Guess-Who questionnaire, as outstanding in the following characteristics:

Q63	Q73
absorbed in studies	
*absorbed in community affairs	
*anxious for college positions	anxious for college positions
influenced by community codes	
influenced by faculty authority	
enthusiastic college supporter	enthusiastic college supporter
likely to continue college interests	not likely to continue college interests
	wants life of sheltered leisure
	does not want life of sheltered leisure
	likely to be deterred by family disapproval

    * Mentioned five or more times

With regard to self-community estimates, Q63 believes that the majority of her class agrees with her response to 13 of 14 items (no item being estimated at 50% conservative response by the class), while Q73 believes that her class agrees with her response to 7 of 12 items not estimated at 50% conservative response by the class. In Q63's one disagreement with her estimate of the class response she considers herself less conservative; Q73, in 4 of her 5 disagreements with estimated class majority, considers herself more conservative. Q63 estimates the mean conservative response of the class to all 14 items as 22%, while the corresponding estimate of Q73 is 32%. Comparing these estimates with those of the entire class, it is as if

Q63 said, "I consider the class pretty liberal, and so am I," while Q73 is saying, "I am definitely more conservative than a moderately liberal class."

Q73 shows no sense of majority appeal when responding a second time to attitude items to which alleged per cent responses of her class are now appended, her second responses being identical with her first. Q63, however, makes 4 of 5 possible changes in the direction of conforming with the alleged class majority, and no changes in the opposite direction.

These students are also characterized somewhat differently in the college records, though they have much in common. The following descriptive phrases are found repeatedly in the records of each of them: eager, lots of energy, enthusiastic, impetuous in discussion, conscientious, hard working. During their first two years both are frequently described as superficial, confused, routine rather than brilliant, more interested in practical than in theoretical points. Both are mentioned as very willing to accept faculty criticism. But here the similarities end. Q63 is described as actively seeking criticism and trying earnestly to profit by it. Q73, on the other hand, is reported to accept it sweetly enough, even to ask for it, but to be relatively little affected by it. This difference seems to be related to another: Q63 is repeatedly reported, especially during the first two years, as lacking in self-confidence, while one instructor's phrase concerning Q73 neatly sums up the almost universal faculty opinion of her: self-confident but not self-critical. The record gives a fairly clear picture of Q73 as one who is blithe and unobsessed with doubts of self.

Certain differences also appear in the interview data. Q73, while asserting that she has changed since her freshman year, particularly in respect to aggressiveness toward contemporaries, says she has changed "rather less than more." Q63 says she is almost revolutionized" personally; "I wasn't an individual till I came here; I never asserted myself against the family, or in any other situation. Now I consider my life my own." She estimated her own attitude scores very accurately, and believes that the scores of most of the college leaders are about like hers. "If I'd gone to a college where the leaders were very conservative I'm sure I wouldn't have gotten any more conservative than I was as a freshman — probably less, because just finding out about the world would have made me more liberal. I have a definite susceptibility for liberalism — I guess I've always had a complex about being richer than my friends. I've been much happier here than I ever could be at a conservative college, because here I can be liberal and be in harmony with the leaders at the same time."

Q73 had not expected her P.E.P. score to be as high, relative to the class, as it was, though a few minutes later she says, "I guess I've really always been a conservative." She believes that the typical Bennington student is radical her sophomore year and then gets over it, but ends up less conservative than as a freshman. "Freshmen and sophomores are radical because they think it's smart. . . . I like to think I'm more of a liberal than my scores would show, and probably because I know I ought to stand on my own feet and be more independent of my family. I'm really too much attached to my mother, and I'm worried about it. . . . I have felt that there's social pressure here to become a liberal. I haven't exactly resented it, but I doubt the common assumption that it's intellectually superior to be liberal." She believes that student leaders are a fair cross-section of all students in social attitudes. "Leaders include conservatives as well as liberals. I, for example, definitely belong with the leader group; they're all my friends. . . . I think I differ from my liberal friends chiefly in that I don't consider my mother beneath me intellectually, as so many of them do. She's satisfied with things as they are, and I'm loyal to her."

These differences are confirmed and amplified by autobiographical data. The following citations from Q63's account are either verbatim or only slightly condensed:

Father is a retired bank president, jovial and loved by every one. Mother is more "dignified," and doesn't enjoy meeting people so much. My older brothers teased the life out of me, especially about my unattractiveness to boys, and were a source of inferiority complex to me. My governess had much more to do with bringing me up than my mother did. I never really confided in Mother. . . . My first school was small, and I was a sort of leader. At 13 I was sent to a boarding school where I was pretty young and not especially cute, and so I had to work on my personality consciously. I developed a loud, raucous clown personality. I met some boys, became more attractive, and had a good time. Then I went to another boarding school where my mother thought I would meet a "higher type of girl." I was homesick, and became unattractive again. It was very strict, no one liked me, and I was miserable. But I was a dumb animal, and didn't protest. In fact, I see

now that I never would admit my unhappiness or hurt feelings or pain
to any one. We had an "honor system" at this school, and I always reported my own misdeeds even though my friends didn't. It was "honor,"
and my father had always emphasized honor; if I tell him everything I
do he never scolds me severely, because "I have been honest with him."
As a matter of fact, he spoils me, and I seem to be recognized as his
favorite. I am really more like Father than any of the others. I have
always had the feeling, till recently at least, that Mother liked my sister
better than me. . . . At school, after weeks of tears, it was impressed on
me that my sister had been school president and that my brothers were
big shots, while I was none of these. So I set to work to be recognized.

I found friends, and by the end of three years had held all the positions
I had set my heart on. I never got the top positions, but was satisfied.
I hit the medium of being genuinely interested in everybody, including
lemons, but only giving my friendship to a chosen few. . . . I suppose
I came to college partly to escape being a debutante. I would not have
been very successful at this. I was determined not to be the typical
boarding-school product at Bennington. Typical debutante girls always
make me feel uncomfortable, and I have been known to feel jealous of
them. I am most unhappy when I feel lonely, when I feel that I am not
as popular as other girls. Some years ago my greatest unhappiness was
not going out with boys as much as other girls, but now I go out about
as much as other girls. . . . My family do not hold me back from anything I want to do. They think I have been very enterprising but very
queer in some of my summer activities, but they didn't stop me. They
don't like my being the "family red"; in fact, they were pretty worried
at one time. We used to fight or else keep very quiet on such subjects;
now we just agree to differ and be friends. They are shocked that some
of my friends work for the C.I.O., and would die if I did.

The following excerpts are from Q73's autobiography:

Father was a not very successful manufacturer. He was raised by his
grandmother, who spoiled him abominably. He had few friends as a
child. He did no athletics in college, but was voted the best dancer in
his class. Mother was the daughter of a raiload president, and was always very popular. My only sibling is a brother three years older. He
was named after my father, but couldn't stand the name, and changed it.
I was bigger for my age than he, and brighter than he in school, altogether disturbing to his self-esteem. I knew how to wangle myself into
what seemed a favored position, though our parents didn't consciously
play favorites. He was stubborn and hard to discipline; I was not. He
didn't play his cards to his own advantage, as I did. . . . Our house was
bigger than those of my friends, and so we usually played at our house,
and I more or less ruled the roost. I was popular with the boys, and

always carried off the scholastic honors. I was captain of the big athletic team, and hero in the plays we gave. This went on till I was 13. . . .

Then we moved. I missed my friends; I wasn't popular at dances, and had a generally miserable time. Mother and Father weren't getting along so well. She still adored her father, who was successful and universally respected. Father was neither, and he drank to excess. So Mother took up all sorts of community activities. My brother was away at school, and so she turned to me for companionship and stimulation. She talked me into being way above my years intellectually. We talked over books, all my personal problems, and I told her everything. Our humor clicks to perfection, and our respect and love for each other is mutual. She never had to punish me much. She became an amateur psychologist, and helped me in every problem. She tried to keep her disagreements with Father from me, but I had no respect for him. My closeness to my mother irritated him. . . . Mother is a born psychologist, but she did make one mistake. She instilled in me the belief that I was a born leader. She told me I had a strong personality, immense energy, and a good mind. . . . When I was thirteen I went away to boarding school. I made friends easily and liked it the first year. I received two elective honors that year which were almost unheard of for a freshman. My roommates, who were my age but in higher grades, resented this. The next year I developed some very unpleasant personal relationships. I noted in my diary that I was afraid another girl would turn out to be the leader, though I couldn't see what she had that I hadn't. It was a matter of life and death to me whether I was leader or not. By this time I was beginning to loathe the petty restrictions of the school, even though I was a favorite of the headmistress (whom I despised), which didn't make me popular with the girls. I had some very unhappy periods. During one of them Mother called to say, over and over, that she still believed in me. I wrote in my diary, "I'm not a hit because I'm so conceited and puffed about myself being a leader that I can't see over myself." . . . Then Mother decided that I should change schools. I adored the new school. I made friends fairly fast and did well in work. I began to discover that I was having good times with boys.

Then I had to decide whether to go to college or come out, but I didn't really want to come out, and so I came to Bennington. . . . My special friend of my freshman year had one idea in life — to have fun — and it didn't take me long to agree with her. I made several other close friends and had a marvellous time. At the end of the year I wasn't surprised to find that my work was considered just fairly good, and some of it not even that. Mother was horribly disappointed, but I said I wanted to come back and try again. The next year I didn't see so much of my fun-loving friend, but I let myself be monopolized by a girl who wanted only one or two close friends, and pleased that she needed me. My work improved, and everything went smoothly. . . . That summer I went abroad with three other girls, and I learned one tremendously important thing. Before, I had always been the one to take charge of arrangements, but now I decided to be the clinging vine. We met some boys. I found that I could make my way with the best of them. I hated to come back to college, but I did, made more friends, and learned more than ever before — and had fun doing it. But I had one sad disappointment. My monopolizing friend was elected head of the house and I wasn't. It hurt. I think the trouble was my self-confidence and arrogance. I have a tendency to look down on every one else and to think I see through them. If I do say so myself, I have a rather quick mind; I catch on to inuendos, and I love to talk in them. I wrote a long letter to Mother, and went home that week-end. She straightened me out. I was elected to a position which has never been held in very high esteem. I set to work tooth and nail. From all reports I have made good at it. . . . I have often wondered if I am being smothered by my mother's love. I dislike thinking I am not completely self-made and independent. . . . As for people I've admired and tried to imitate, I guess I hold my mother on as high a plane as any one. I respect her mind and her ideas on everything.

Here we have two individuals with many similarities. Both are enthusiastic, full of energy. Each has had her difficulties in making friendships. Each is anxious to hold college positions, and each has been more or less successful. Each admires and is very close to one parent, of conservative opinions. Yet one of them has openly broken with that parent's opinions while the other has not. Q63 believes her social attitudes to be much like those of the majority of her classmates, while Q73 knows that she is more conservative than most of them. Q63 is willing to change her attitude responses in the direction of what she believes to be class conformity; Q73 is not. Q63 states, with light in her eyes, that she is "almost revolutionized" personally since entering college: she has now become a person in her own right. Q73 says she has changed "rather less than more," and worries about her dependence on the admired parent. Q63 is described both by herself and by faculty as lacking in self-confidence, till recently at least. Q73 describes herself as self-confident, and faculty agree with her. Q63 has been chosen for two of the most important college positions, Q73 for second-string positions only.

To which of these, or to what combination of them, shall we attribute the differences in social attitudes? Certainly Q63 has lower thresholds for community influence than Q73, and certainly this threshold difference is related to personality characteristics here described in terms of self-confidence. Q73's self-confidence may perhaps better be termed mother-self-confidence. Perhaps the best summation of the differences between these girls is that Q73's final reliance in her struggles for social adjustment is an extra-college influence — her mother; while Q63's earlier experiences had been such that her lot was cast entirely with that of friends within the community.

One other difference between them is probably relevant. Each refers in her autobiography to living in a house bigger than those of friends. To Q63 this is a source of "embarrassment and shame"; to Q73 it is a source of power, because she is able to lord it over the others playing at her house. There is some reason to believe that each of them persists in these characteristics ways of looking at social situations. They are both anxious for college positions, but positions are seen somewhat more in terms of power by Q73, and rather as an indication of being liked by Q63. This is illustrated by comments in the autobiographies concerning deepest wishes. Both mention marriage and children, to which Q73 adds, "If my dream castle could come true I would spend all my time helping other people with their problems." And Q63 adds, "My idea of a heaven-like existence is something like a large-scale producers' and consumers' co-operative in which every one is liked by lots of other people and every one is sensitive as to what other people need." Perhaps these comments are not so different, but they seem to the writer characteristic of the greater part of the respective autobiographies. Q63's dominant need to be in and of a group has led her to a sense of identity with the college; this in turn has led her to a certain degree of feeling of identity with larger groups who are deprived and suffering — and hence her social attitudes. Q73's dominant need to lead has brought her to seek to rise to the top of the college rather than to be in and of it — and hence she never adopted its dominant social attitudes.

This sort of difference is, after all, much like the difference in self-confidence. Q63 is deeply aware of how her fate depends upon others; Q73, to use her own words, likes to think she is independent and self-made. These are not all-or-none differences, of course, but they seem to be some of the pebbles which have caused the streams to diverge.

Q61 and Q81 are chosen for contrast as being "typical" in almost every measurable characteristic of those whose attitudes do and do not change, respectively. Q81, like Q73, is atypical in that she has been a member of one important committee, while Q61 has held three important positions. Their attitude scores on entrance are about the same, and each describes both parents as Republicans. Q61 majors in Social Studies, and Q81 in Science. They differ greatly in prestige, Q61 ranking fifth in the entire college in 1939, while 60 students were chosen equally or more often than Q81. They are also very different in reputation, the characteristics for which they are mentioned twice or more being as follows:

Q61	Q81
*absorbed in community affairs	
*absorbed in public affairs	
⋅*anxious for college positions	
*influenced by community codes	
influenced by crowd enthusiasms	
influenced by faculty authority	resists faculty authority
*enthusiastic college supporter	
	absorbed in college work
	critical of educational policies
	*critical of faculty
	critical of student committees

* mentioned five or more times

Attitude scores are as follows for freshman, sophomore, and senior years:

	Q61			Q81		
	1935–1936	1936–1937	1938–1939	1935–1936	1936–1937	1938–1939
P.E.P. (raw)	91	75	66	85	91	85
P.E.P. (s. d.)	+ 1.5	+ .5	− .1	+ .9	+ 1.9	+ 1.4
Internationalism	+ .8	− .7	− .4	.0	+ .4	+ 1.5
Loyalist Spain		− 1.2	− .5		+ .8	+ .7
Social Distance			+ .1			+ .3
Satisfactions			− .5			+ .6
C.I.O.		+ .5			—	
Supreme Court		+ .1			—	
New Deal			− .7			+ .9

As seniors, they diverge very consistently in attitudes. All of Q81's information scores are below her class average, significantly so in her last two years. Q61's information scores are slightly above her class average as a freshman, and very much above average during her last two years.

These two students differ considerably in their estimates of the conservatism of their own class. Q81's mean estimate of conservative response by her class to all items is 53% — almost the highest estimate in the entire class. (The actual response is 20% conservative.) Q61's mean estimate is 20%, below the mean class estimate. Q61 believes that the majority class response to every one of the 14 items is non-conservative, though she answers four of them conservatively. Q81 estimates that the majority of her class responds conservatively to 7 items and non-conservatively to 4, the other 3 being estimated at 50%; she answers ten of them conservatively herself. Two of her disagreements with the estimated class majority are conservative and the other two are non-conservative responses. Q81 is saying, in effect, "The class answers most of these items conservatively, and so do I, though I am more conservative on some items and less on some." And the significance of Q61's estimates is, roughly, "The class is consistently liberal, while I am not quite consistently so."

When presented with what are stated to be per cent responses of the class to 8 of the 14 items previously responded to, Q61 makes only one change in response — in non-conservative direction, but contrary to the alleged majority response. Q81 makes three changes, two in non-conservative and one in conservative direction; two of them are changed to agreement and one to disagreement with the alleged class majorities.

Q61 thus believes herself in general agreement with her class, though a little more conservative except when persuaded that the class is more conservative than she had thought. Q81, who is neither as consistent in her estimates of the class nor as persistent in her own responses, also considers herself in general agreement with it. Q61 may thus be contrasted with Q63, whom she resembles in many ways (including attitude change), but who considers herself a little less conservative than the class. Q81, similarly, may be contrasted with Q73, whom she closely resembles in attitude syndrome, but who considers the class far more conservative than herself.

The most often repeated faculty judgments concerning Q61 are as follows: enthusiastic, conscientious and somewhat tense, over-anxious to please, thoroughly dependable, helpful and cooperative, thoroughly dependable, self-critical. Early comments such as "too dependent on faculty approval" are gradually replaced by such notations as "more self-dependence, growing in intellectual independence." There are also several references to the demands on her time by community activities. The evaluations of Q81 which appear in the records are quite different: too limited notions of what she wants, rigid and dogmatic, rebellious and negative, belligerent, accepts criticism only if it fits into her scheme of things, not receptive to new ideas. Both are described as being industrious and ambitious, but Q81's industry is nearly all directed toward the single goal of becoming a research physiologist, and there are many references to her resentment of advice to obtain a broader background, and preferring laboratory work to conferences with faculty, which were often skipped. One instructor comments as follows concerning her: "her rigidity is a defense in an environment which stresses independent thought." Her counselor comments, during her first year, that she has no friends except those known in high school. Much of Q61's industry has been spent in community activities of non-academic nature. She achieved some notoriety during her freshman year by her activities in support of the Republican presidential candidate.

The following excerpts are from Q61's senior interview:

I've changed a lot since coming here, but I'm not revolutionized. A year or two ago I was pretty scared at how much I had changed, but now I guess I've swung part way back, or else I've become more used to myself. I've developed an attitude toward attitudes. I believe in acting on your present attitudes, but realizing that they are tentative. I met a whole body of new information my sophomore year. I took a deep breath and plunged. I became much less conservative, then swung part way back, then found more evidence for the new opinions, and am more liberal again. I was teased and criticized at home for my extreme opinions. My father criticizes me for lack of experience, and I him for the limited nature of his experience. . . . When I came here I decided to make up for the shortcomings of my previous school life. I had put sports and work above personal contacts. I had put leadership above group membership. I always wanted to be head, though I tried not to dominate. In previous schools I wanted terribly to be prominent, and I wasn't too successful. I didn't make a secret club that was very important to me. This was partly because I wouldn't play up to people.

On coming here I wanted to make good socially, whether I was leader or not, and I decided that the way to do it was to be nice to people

whether you really liked them or not, and that this wasn't really hypo-
critical. . . . As to the college leaders, they tend to be more liberal than
others, but they aren't really leaders; they are followers. Students don't
choose leaders here; they choose individuals that they trust, who are
approachable, genuine. That's all it really means to have college positions
here, that students like you and trust you. I think any one, whether a
"leader" or not, who really exposes herself will get liberal here. Those
who don't can't get away from dependence on their families.

And from Q81's senior interview:

I'm more to the side of not changing at all since I came here. My biggest
change, I guess, is realizing how conventional my family is. I spent my
first two years trying to fit Bennington to my pattern, and now I realize
you can't do it. Now I can see my teachers' point of view at least part of
the time. When I was on the —— Committee I discovered how extreme my views were, but I still think Progressive Education needs more
external discipline. . . . As to public affairs, I'm just as uninterested as
ever, and really less well informed than when I came, because then I
could at least echo my family. What opinions I had before have been
neutralized. I'm still as conservative as my family, who think Roosevelt
is *really* insane, but I haven't their strength of conviction. I think I'm a
pretty typical student that way: most students lose what opinions they
had and don't replace them with anything. But I wasn't typical in one
respect: I was one of a group of about 20 freshmen who were wild — we
smoked, drank, swore, and everything. About half of us, including me,
got over it. . . . I guess, after seeing my scores, that I'm not so typical
after all. Probably I was judging from my own crowd, who just aren't
interested. My lack of change you'll have to put down to lack of interest.
It couldn't be a general resistance to what is new, because after a while I
got to like modern art and modern music which are so prevalent around
here. That makes it look as if I had built up some sort of resistance to
the political ideas you get around here, but that isn't the case; it's just
laziness. I read enormously as a child; then at 13 or 14 I got intellectual
and attacked learned tomes. Then I reacted against it. Now I hate text-
books, and never read voluntarily except fiction, and little of that. . . .

As a matter of fact, I'm not so sure that most juniors and seniors have
changed their political ideas so much. Maybe they're just giving the
expected answers. I'm not the kind who would ever give the expected
answers. I'll bet that's why most of the college leaders are so liberal —
if they are, and they'd be pretty sure to answer that way. I know it's
considered the proper thing for us to get more liberal here, and I've always resented community expectations of all sorts. That doesn't sound
as if I cared much for Bennington, but I'm honestly 100% for it. I went
to a very conservative high school, so that I was terribly happy to come
here — the only college I wanted to go to.

Supplementary notes from Q81's autobiography include the following:

My father is a corporation lawyer. He's shy and very quiet, even with his own family. Sometimes he worries a lot about the office, but he doesn't talk much. His hobby is birds and bugs and flowers, etc., and he's president of several wild-life societies. He is also active in many community affairs. He leaves all the family discipline to Mother. I am the one who understands Father best — I know how to drop ideas gently as a hint, so that later he thinks they were his own. Whenever there's a family argument, it's almost always Father and I against Mother and younger sister. (But there are many things we would never think of arguing about. For instance, he openly thinks that anything radical is simply crazy, and he cannot be shaken in the slightest way in any of his opinions.) Mother is the daughter of a medical research man who is very famous. She and her family always had an extremely congenial life, and she likes to contrast it with the constant bickering in my father's family. I resent her constant discipline. Sometimes I refuse to do things I really want to do, because she nags me before I get a chance to do it. Neither my sister or I have ever been punished much — not that we were such ideal kids, but never since I can remember has any great opposition to adult opinion ever been considered in my family. My sister is eight years younger, and so I have never competed with her very much. She's terribly bright and terribly conceited, and sometimes I try to take her down a peg. Mother is easier with her than she was with me. . . .

I was pretty miserable, I remember, when I first went to kindergarten, and when I complained about it I was put in a different room. In fact, I hated the next four years of school pretty generally. I made some friends, but can still remember the general attitude of fear I had. The children seemed merciless and tough, and for some reason I couldn't hold my own. Then a new school was built, and I went to it and was in seventh heaven. Teachers were young and lively, and we were proud of the brand new school, and we felt free to tell the teachers absolutely anything, even if we thought they were lousy we told them so. It was really cooperative, and the children ran the school as much as the teachers, and we learned a lot. My own position with the children changed overnight, and I was class president the only two times we had one. I was leader of the gang and teacher's pet at the same time. I hated leaving there and got a bad start in high school because I was sick. The high school was huge; my old crowd was dissolved in the big new crowd, and all the old friendships were broken practically overnight. I hated it from start to finish. I had grown too tall, was awkward, and had a perfectly terrible complexion. I couldn't make friends, and so I gave up and became a recluse. I was elected to various school committees, etc., but it didn't lessen my general agony. . . . I had helped my Dad with his wild-life collections since I was a kid, and I hated it. About the time I pulled out of social life in high school, he got me a sort of scholarship at the —— Museum. The kids in school were amazed. It must be I was going to be a real scientist. I didn't bother to enlighten them. It was fun to impress them with how hard I was working. So I broke off all my high school life except the academic, and started to build up the atmosphere of the great scientist about me. I met a very handsome laboratory assistant at the Museum, and I worked ferociously to impress him. There were some other kids at the Museum, and we got to seeing more and more of each other in over-time work. I couldn't draw as well as they could, and that spurred me to work harder to catch up with them. I was spending from four to seven hours a day on this biology work at the Museum. None of it was because I liked it, but I found it interesting to develop a superior attitude toward the other kids. . . .

When it came to deciding about where I would go to college, Bennington looked to me like a pleasant life and good-bye to biology, and in that mood I came. I knew I needed the social development that would be possible here. But I had to major in something, and Science was just about the only possibility. Now I see the reason why I'm in it, and I wish I'd never had the idea. But I've given up the idea of being a brilliant research physiologist. I'd rather be a measly teacher in some hick-town school where I can lead the merry life that my teachers used to in the school I loved. My problem is how to be interested and active in biology without being a biologist. . . . My approach to boys is definitely inhibited by lack of experience. My most intimate friends are varied; they were selected by just knowing a few from home who knew others in their dormitories, and with girls from my own house. Thus our group has grown, or rather my three groups have grown, as I belong to three pretty distinct groups. . . . If I had a magic wand I would probably wish to go on being a Bennington student forever without getting sick of it or having Bennington change. Maybe it would be more fun to have a home and family. . . . I am most unhappy when I feel inadequate, or when my behavior is misinterpreted. I am most tense and uncomfortable with a crowd of my own age, particularly if it includes men. I have no ability at light, general conversation. But I don't have trouble making friends once I'm past the light-conversation stage. Getting along with people normally — not by demanding attention or by being "great" or famous — is most important to me. The only role I honestly care to play is just to be successful in winning the friendship and admiration of the people in any community I happen to live in.

The following selections are from Q61's autobiography:

We have all sorts of dusty diplomas around the house to indicate the superior standing of my paternal ancestors: there was less money and a

great deal less snobbery on my mother's side. Daddy has inherited a
fairly sizeable income, but he works hard at writing. He is always
home for lunch and tea, and consequently sees a good deal of us children when we are home. Mother occupies herself with four children
and civic and social engagements; she is the kind of person who needs
other people, while my father is not; she is inclined to be more socially
snobbish than Daddy. I went to five different schools, first to please one
parent and then the other. I am the oldest child, and next is a sister
two years younger. When we were little I used to be the boss. We had
terrible fights, but I wasn't very strong, and when I was about twelve
she began to beat me, so I began to use my tongue to get back at her.
But I was never really jealous of her, because for a long.time I excelled
her at everything. The fourth child was born when I was thirteen, and
I went away to school and camp, and the friendship of girls my own age
became a conscious aim. Daddy is a strict disciplinarian, sometimes
placing discipline above friendship. Our mother and father have seldom
been the kind of parents we take all the little things to, and almost never
do we discuss problems we aren't acutely aware of. Tom and Alice follow my mother's aristocratic tendencies. The rest of us side with my
father. On the whole, our family has not been the close, emotionally
knit group that others seem to be, but through careful nurturing we
seem to have common objectives. In each of us there is a tremendous
drive for prestige which I sometimes deprecate because of the limitations
on friendships which it unconsciously imposes. . . .

My position in the family was secure until I went away to school.
Mother began to feel that I wasn't growing up fast enough; I didn't take
enough interest in feminine things like high heels and fastidious dress.
My affection came more surely from Daddy than from her. I had always
been his favorite in ways, though he was never ostentatious about it.
All of us really like each other, but we don't know each other very
well. We seldom discuss the things that really mean a great deal to us.
It is more or less understood that we inhibit emotional behavior. One
of the strongest feelings that I think each of us has is a sense of
responsibility to Father and Mother. The biblical parable of the talents
has always in various forms been repeated to us. If one of us fails in this
respect the rest of us continually rub it in. . . . In school I never had
any difficulty. I started late, then skipped a class, and later skipped
another class, which made me seem inordinately bright. I could usually
make the honor roll if I wanted to. At one school it seemed important.
At the next school I placed all my energies in another direction. In
going away to school I lost contact with my childhood friends, with
whom I had always measured up very favorably. Now I had to make
new friends. I entered in the middle of the year a cliquy school, and it
was terribly difficult. I felt terribly inferior, because up to this time a
little group of friends had kept changing schools along with me. At
boarding school I never stood out as good or bad, but my scholastic

record didn't suffer. I lacked the imagination or initiative to think up awful things to do, but I rebelled against the two-faced-ness of most of the leaders. The hypocricies of the students and teachers made me boil. I hated to see what could be gained by what seemed "playing up" to people even though you disliked them. I must have been played up to also because I would do almost anything for anyone. I had few good friends and none whom I felt I could turn to for the first year and a half. I was preoccupied with work and sport. I wanted like anything to be among the popular, among the leaders and the chosen. I religiously carried hockey sticks and balls one year to get the hockey managership for the next. One of the aims was to get as long a list as you could to put under your name in the yearbook when you graduated. I missed one of the two most secret groups. It indicated to me that I lacked certain standing. I had become somewhat scared of people. It was hard to get to know them. I could pass the time of day with any number, but I could not know more than two intimately. The unhappiness caused by this was overcome a year later, when I made several lasting friends at school abroad whom I still keep up with. I was always apparently self-assured and cheerful from the outside, but socially I lacked self-confidence. I took rules and regulations for granted; they weren't worth fighting. My ambitions were to be acknowledged friend and leader. These I never felt I had realized. . . . I am generally happiest now when there is complete understanding between me and the person I am with. I consistently inhibit the emotional, and can know someone from the outside for a long time before I can ever break down some barrier I place between us. I have very few good friends, but I know hundreds of people fairly well. There are many whom I would give anything to know better, both boys and girls. I have never been at a loss for men, though I have only known one well at a time. If I could have anything I wanted I would desire above all else more really good friends. Heaven would be a community of personalities all dressed in their true colors.

. . . My conflicts arise from leading two lives just now, one with my family and one at college where people are judged not by the standards of society but for their "true" worth, where artificiality is at a minimum. When the two lives create friction, I am tense and upset. I cannot argue against a rooted faith of Mother's or Daddy's. I simply hold my tongue and behave in accordance with their wishes if and when a crisis occurs. It's simpler now; I don't feel so much like a hypocrite. I am merely following the only course open to me rather than needlessly rebelling. It makes me despondent to have the family unjustly annoyed with me or lose faith in me through misunderstanding. I'd give a great deal if within the family there were more complete understanding of aims and difficulties, if we were closer. . . . The world thinks of me as civic minded, somewhat socially conscious, and as willing to do a lot of dirty work. I don't object to these as long as they don't obstruct valuable friendships. But at times I'm afraid they do. Personal relationships are absolutely necessary for me.

In spite of the differences between these two students in regard to the quantitative data, their subjective statements of what they most want seem much alike. Both resemble Q63, whose attitude scores are like those of Q61 but not like those of Q81. Q61 and Q81 are alike, in other words, in one major respect concerning which Q63 and Q73 were considered very different. Does this mean that the subjective data are not to be trusted, or that they have little relevance to attitude change? Before drawing such a conclusion let us stop to summarize some of the important differences between Q61 and Q81.

Q61 is popular with students, and considered cooperative and enthusiastic about college. Q81 has very little prestige among students, being considered highly critical of the college. By faculty Q61 is considered anxious to please, and Q81 belligerent. Q61 has thrown herself into college affairs, while Q81 has mainly devoted herself to academic work. Q61 accurately estimates class conservatism as being rather low, and in the main she agrees. Q81 greatly overestimates class conservatism, and in the main she agrees. Both by her own testimony and by reputation, Q61 is concerned about public affairs; Q81 gives every indication of being indifferent. In short, Q61 is swimming in the very center of the community current, while Q81 is in a back-eddy which she seems to consider representative of the entire stream — perhaps because she has spent so much energy combatting the current which she found there.

In terms of personal factors, the question becomes that of why one student has entered the main stream and one has not. The factors responsible for Q61's doing so seem very similar to those which brought Q63 into the stream — so much so, indeed, that we shall come to speak of them as typical of one group who show considerable attitude change. But it cannot be said that the factors responsible for Q81's failing to enter the main stream are the same as those operative for Q73. At the risk of over-simplifying, the relevant differences between the latter two may be described as follows:

Q73 stopped short of complete immersion in the community stream because her mother stood on the bank, downstream, beckoning to her. She swam with the current, but it was more important to reach a given point than to dally or bask in the water. Getting her head wet might cut off the line of vision to her mother, and obstruct progress. She was aware, moreover, that she was not permitting her head to get wet. But Q81 never ventured so far from the shore. She had done so, years before in a quieter pool, and it was satisfying. But meanwhile fate had snatched her into a deep, swift river, and earlier skills were not enough. So she had scooped out a little pool for herself. It was deep, but it had very little current, and she learned again to keep afloat. Then college offered her another chance to navigate a flowing stream. It was more like the gentler one of her early years. But she had lost the necessary skills, and while she was developing them she must, to keep afloat at all, take refuge again in a little side-pool of her own construction. Whenever she turned from this pool to the main stream she met a current which must be fought, lest she be swept beyond her depth. So she never got inside the fringes of the current.

The differences, to abandon the figure, are that Q81 simply lacked the skills with which to enter into full-fledged community life. She had to use what skills she possessed to keep her self-respect at all, and these kept her apart from all but small sub-groups. Q73, who had the skills to all appearances, needed them for purposes other than full community participation.

Q61 and Q63 differ in social attitudes from Q81 not because they wanted full community participation more, but because they possessed a better kit of tools. All our evidence seems to indicate that attitude change at Bennington depends chiefly upon rather full community participation. And this depends upon skills which make it possible as well as upon motives which make it subjectively desirable.

J22 and K42 are presented together for purposes of contrast.[1] J22 is the only senior whose freshman score was extremely low but whose senior score was not low. K42 is the only senior whose freshman score was extremely high but whose senior score was not high. They represent extreme changes in opposite directions. K42's total attitude picture as a senior is actually less conservative than that of J22.

[1] Objective data for these two subjects are summarized on pp. 108–109, and selected statements from senior interviews appear on the opposite page. For reasons of space, the questions to which the interview statements are responses do not appear; they will be found on pp. 84–85.

K42 is the daughter of extremely conservative parents; J22's are not only very liberal, but one of them is widely known as such. Both are about average for the class in their estimates of class conservatism. J22 indicates, both in her disagreements with estimated class majorities and in her interview responses, that she still considers herself less conservative than the average college senior, while K42 is very accurate in her estimate of her attitude position, relative to the class. The Guess Who characteristics of both are such as to suggest a considerable degree of insulation from college influences. The combination of extreme freshman conservatism with such community insulation should have predestined K42 to a very conservative senior score. What accounts for her unexpectedly low score?

K42's early insecurity and her partial emancipation from it seem to provide the answer. Her attitude changes stem from two sources: her deep loyalty to a few teachers and a few older students who helped her in her hour of need, and her basic preference for being with the majority ("I'm no non-conformist"). While the Guess Who ratings would not seem to indicate any such preference, it is almost certain that the two mentions she received for each negativistic characteristic are to be attributed to her close association with a small group regarded as exclusive. This group affiliation represented for her, however, a still needed security rather than a barrier against the rest of the community, in the judgment of those teachers who knew her best. She served, indeed, as a sort of "outer contact" for this group, according to one member of it.* By and large, however, it must be said that K42 is an exception to the general rule. She became less conservative primarily because of accidents of personal loyalty rather than because of any very deep involvement with community influences.

J22 is no exception to the general rule. Her college history is one of progressive withdrawal from community influences regarded by most other students as "typically Bennington." She gives her instructors the general impression of being "fed up" with concern

* It is probable. of course, that similar Guess Who ratings of other students also reflect reputation for clique-membership rather than actual preference for shutting out other students. There are few other cases, however, in which such reputation is accompanied by non-conservative attitudes. Doubtless the general rule would have held for K42 also had it not been for the personal loyalties to individuals regarded as non-conservative.

over public issues, whether from home influences or from somewhat precocious high school activities concerning them. She, too, has a history of insecurity, but not in intellectual areas, as with K42. She frankly describes her present major ("and almost my only") aims as those of having a home of her own and developing easy personal relations with her own friends. These friends, significantly, had in the main been acquired outside of college.

In summary, these two individuals traveled in opposite attitudinal directions because one of them came to find greater security in college and one apart from college. J22 had long since tasted the fruit of intellectual success, with its assumed correlate of liberalism. She now discarded it for plainer fare beyond the college walls. K42 found the fruit almost beyond her grasp, but once having attained it, found that it tasted of new beliefs as well as of social acceptability.

C12 and G42 [2] are presented as conspicuous exceptions to the general rule previously offered. Both are very high in prestige, but their attitudes are conservative. They are the only conspicuous exceptions in their class to the general finding that prestige-endowed students show a considerable decrease in P.E.P. score.

Both C12 and G42 make high estimates of the conservatism of their class. Neither considers herself conservative, judging from disagreements with estimated class majorities, and according to their interview statements. G42's Guess Who ratings are almost perfectly typical of those whose conservatism decreases considerably in college. Those of C12 are similarly typical in some respects, but are characteristic of those who remain conservative in others. C12 is described by faculty as conscientious, hard-headed and independent but not stubborn or resistant. G42 is reported to be eager to please, but more concerned with community than with academic success. There is thus every reason to predict that G42 should belong with the non-conservative in attitudes, and some reason to predict that C12 should belong with them.

C12, as a "partial exception" only, may be briefly dealt with. One point is particularly relevant. She is one of the few seniors

[2] Data for these two subjects are summarized on pp. 110–111, in the same manner as for J22 and K24,. See footnote p. 105.

	J22	K42
MAJOR	Art	Social Studies
P.E.P. (raw)	fresh. 55 sen. 69	fresh. 90 sen. 61
P.E.P. (s.d.)	fresh. −1.5 sen. + .5	fresh. +1.2 − .2
OTHER ATTITUDES	Loyalist Spain +1.0 C.I.O. + .4 New Deal −1.1 Social Distance + .5 Satisfactions + .8	Loyalist Spain +1.1 C.I.O. +1.8 New Deal −1.5 Social Distance − .5 Satisfactions − .2
VALUES significantly high or low	high in aesthetic	high in theoretic low in aesthetic high in social
INFORMATION general specific	fresh. av.; sen. low av. average	fresh. very low; sen. low av. low average
PRESTIGE rep. choices positions held	2 in 1938; none in 1939 none	4 in 1938; 6 in 1939 1 minor committee
PER CENT ESTIMATES	average in estimate of class conservatism . . . disagrees with estimated class majority in 3 of 14 responses, one of which is conservative.	average in estimate of class conservatism . . . no disagreements with estimated class majority
GUESS WHO characteristics mentioned twice or more times	absorbed in family affairs . . . influenced by community codes . . . resists faculty authority . . . will not continue college interests . . . seeks sheltered leisure	indifferent to student committees . . . wants to be left alone . . . resistant to crowd enthusiasms
COLLEGE RECORDS most frequent descriptive phrases	highly independent; unobtrusive; works better alone than in groups	timid and insecure; no interest in ideas (early years); great improvement in intellectual independence; still somewhat dependent upon faculty approval
miscellaneous		has achieved some independence of pampering parents; deep loyalty to a few teachers who helped her during freshman-sophomore insecurity

J22

Not much has happened, though I'm definitely changed. I'm much less sure as to fundamental values.

I scarcely have any opinions now, whereas I used to be very sure what the world needed. But this is not a change which would show on the questionnaires.

My parents have always been liberals. I'm not interested enough to talk to them much about public affairs any more.

I suppose I'm still less conservative than most seniors, but definitely less interested now.

I have little contact with the group of leaders. I don't think they differ from other students in general conservatism.

I used to think there was a lot of social pressure here to be radical. But I haven't felt it, and I guess it was mostly freshman wishful thinking.

What's happened to me is that part of my former interest in public affairs has shifted to domestic interests, and the rest has shifted to scientific understanding rather than caring about outcomes.

K42

I'm nearer the revolutionized end of the scale. My ideas have changed more than my personality.

I'm more interested in public affairs, more tolerant, and more liberal.

My parents just take the status quo for granted; they have everything they want. We never argue. Maybe they've changed, too. We know how to change the subject if disagreement threatens.

Every girl here likes to think she's liberal, and so do I. I don't know how I compare with others, but I know I'm not conservative. I know I'm the most liberal in my particular gang.

The college leaders should be liberal, and I imagine they are. They're not close friends of mine. I like them, with reservations. They're a bit too efficient.

I've never resented any social pressure here. I'm easily influenced by people I respect. I was terribly insecure as a freshman, and without really knowing it I came to accept the opinions of two or three faculty members, also some older students. who put me on my feet again.

In a conservative college I'd be conservative. I'm no rebel or non-conformist. I couldn't be in a minority unless I was terribly secure in other ways.

whose claims to increasing caution of response are justified. Between the end of her junior and senior years her P.E.P. score changed from 66 to 63. But in terms of *direction* of response to the same items (regardless of strength of agreement or disagreement)

	C12	G42
MAJOR	Science	Literature
P.E.P. (raw)	fresh. 69 sen. 63	fresh. 73 sen. 69
P.E.P. (s.d.)	fresh. —.4 sen. .0	fresh. .0 sen. +.5
OTHER ATTITUDES as junior or senior	Loyalist Spain +1.0 C.I.O. + .6 New Deal — .6 Social Distance + .1 Satisfactions — .1	Loyalist Spain + .8 C.I.O. — .3
VALUES significantly high or low	high in economic low in social very high in political	no scores
INFORMATION general specific	fresh. av.; sen. signif. high high average	fresh. & sen. average significantly low
PRESTIGE rep. choices positions held	67 in 1938; 65 in 1939 2 major, 2 minor positions	32 in 1938; 39 in 1939 1 major, 1 minor position
PER CENT ESTIMATES	high av. in estimate of class conservatism . . . disagrees with estimated class majority in 3 of 14 responses, 1 of which is conserv.	high in estimate of class conservatism . . . disagrees with estimated class majority in 1 of 14 responses, which is non-conserv.
GUESS WHO characteristics mentioned twice or more (* 5 times or more)	absorbed in college work, *in community affairs, in public affairs . . . *anxious for positions . . . *influenced by community codes . . . resistant to crowd enthusiasms, *to moving appeals . . . *enthusiastic college supporter . . . seeks sheltered leisure . . . *apt to be deterred by family disapproval	absorbed in studies, in college affairs, *in public affairs . . . anxious for positions . . . resists crowd enthusiasms . . . influenced by faculty authority . . . *enthusiastic college supporter . . . *will continue college interests . . . *does not seek sheltered leisure . . . not deterred by family disapproval
COLLEGE RECORDS most frequent descriptive phrases	responsible, dependable, persistent; immense growth in independence and self-criticism; best in her class; considered group leader, but shows no need to dominate; eager for criticism, but takes it in independent manner	serious, hard-working, reliable; level-headed, even and consistent; profits by criticism, but overdependent upon authority; cooperative group member; undertakes too much
MISCELLANEOUS	strongly developed executive sense	outstanding as committee chairman; excellent personal adjustment

C12

I'm nearly revolutionized. I only knew about my own little world, when I came.

Some of my attitudes have changed, but I'm skeptical about others that too many students accept uncritically, and so I haven't changed much in those areas.

My parents would generally be considered conservative, though really my father is pretty liberal, considering what he's up against.

I'm liberal, but not too liberal. Moderation is one of my major characteristics. The average student takes on liberal attitudes too lightly. This only increases my native caution.

I know some students become defensive because of what they think is pressure to become liberal. So they never find out that it isn't really so. except in the sense that faculty expect you to learn both sides of important questions.

I'd never heard of social science before I came here, and getting to know about it has become vital to me, more vital than trying to change things. But I think I'm more liberal than my questionnaire answers show, because so many of the statements are unacceptable in some part of their wording — maybe just one word — that I refuse to agree.

G42

I am pretty nearly 100% a new person. I hate to think of what a timid child I was when I came.

I've woven a good deal of new content into the generally liberal point of view I had when I came.

My parents are definitely liberal. My father has taken a good many beatings for his liberalism. We don't discuss specific issues much at home; it's just taken for granted that we're all liberal.

I certainly belong with the more liberal group of my class, though I probably would not be considered extreme.

It's hard to say about the student leaders, because we discuss college affairs rather than public affairs when we get together, which is practically all the time. In the main I'd say they are like me, unexcited liberals.

There's plenty of wholesome influence, but no pressure that I would consider undesirable. I can see how students with a conservative background might resent it, but they're just the ones who need it.

I'm amazed at my scores. I guess I've simply taken it for granted that my father gave me all the liberalism I would ever need. The fact is that I've been so blissfully happy here that I haven't really cared about a single thing except developing further and further the characteristics that gave me, for the first time in my life, a little prestige and belief in my own social possibilities.

her preponderance of non-conservative over conservative responses increased from 3 to 14 during this period. During the same period her caution score (number of neutral minus number of extreme P.E.P. responses) increased from -8 to $+3$. In terms of direction of response, in short, her conservatism decreased during her four years in college more than that of the average student (from a freshman standard deviation score of .0 to a senior standard deviation score of —.5). What seems to have happened is that, during her fourth year in college, her hard-headed, cautious, independent tendencies were transferred from direction of response to degree of response. In respect to direction of response, at least, she turns out to have been influenced by community forces to about the degree expected in view of her rather active participation in community affairs.

G42, however, makes no claim to increasing caution, nor do her responses show it. Her only change in response to the P.E.P. items, during the entire four years, is a slight increase in disagreement to items conservatively stated. Yet she is one of the most active and enthusiastic participants in community affairs ever seen in the college. Her own analysis of the reasons, as given in the last paragraph of the interview summary, seems pretty accurate. For many years, before coming to college, she had been the victim of a lingering illness which was likely to prove fatal. Her education had been received almost entirely at the hands of tutors at home. She had had almost no give-and-take with her own age group. Her "social success" in college was as amazing to her as to the faculty and to her parents. The liberal atmosphere of the college represented nothing new to her (one of her parents is widely known as a liberal); its opportunities for social intercourse meant everything. Almost from the first she seems to have concluded that her social attitudes were already running in the approved course. Other students might have to change their opinions if they were to be in the swim; she had already been "liberalized" at home, and her task was rather that of achieving success in community affairs, to which she probably gave more time and energy than any one else in her class. One of the major college currents swept past her without her knowing it. It cannot be said that she was insulated from college influences, but her college frame of reference simply did not include liberalizing influences as something which applied to her.

⋆ 13 ⋆

Some Personality Patterns Related to Modes of Community Adaptation

INDIVIDUAL INTERPRETATIONS have been made, in the preceding chapters, largely in terms of motives and abilities which serve to impede or to facilitate all-around assimilation into the community. This chapter is concerned with the question whether, in a single community, certain sets of personality factors are associated with certain attitudes with sufficient frequency so that we may speak, with some significance, of patterns of personality as related to attitudes.

The days when psychologists attributed either liberal or conservative attitudes toward a given issue to any single set of personality factors are happily gone. There is some danger, however, of jumping to an opposite conclusion which is equally erroneous, viz., that personality factors involved are completely unique for each individual, in the sense that similarities among individuals whose attitude scores are similar are far less significant than differences among them. Certainly each individual has his points of uniqueness in arriving at a given attitude position, but it is the thesis of this chapter that in a given community certain significant classifications of personality factors, closely related to attitude scores, may be made. They are not the only personality factors involved, of course, but they are significant enough to have some predictive value.

The discussion which follows is based upon the phenomenon, previously documented, that in this community not only is the prevailing attitude trend in a nonconservative direction, but this prevailing trend is commonly known. The major hypothesis is that whatever personality patterns are to be discovered will be related to degree of general community assimilation. The minor hypotheses have to do with sets of personality factors which render more or less likely the inclusion, in the subject's perception of the community to which she must adapt in one way or another, of the prevailing attitude trend. More specifically, certain sets of personality factors may be presumed to be associated with awareness of one's own conservatism, relative to that of one's classmates, and certain other sets to be associated with a lack of awareness of one's own conservative position. Similarly, we shall attempt to discover whether there are certain more or less consistent differences between those who are and those who are not aware of their own nonconservative positions. Are there differences which appear to be significant among groups which knowingly accept, knowingly reject, unknowingly accept, and unknowingly reject the prevailing attitudes?

It has previously been indicated that a large proportion of the most conservative juniors and seniors are considered, both by faculty and by Guess Who raters, as resistant or overtly indifferent to the college as a community. Nothing could seem more logical than to assume that the conservatism of such students is itself an aspect of this community negativism. Such a conclusion, however, can only be based upon the assumption that these individuals have somewhat the same habits of viewing the community as a place where dominant attitudes are nonconservative as do other students who are not conservative. If, on the other hand, these conservative individuals tend to view the community as a place where their own attitudes are dominant, they can scarcely be considered community-resistant in respect to measured social attitudes. To put it somewhat differently, habits of community negativism are not necessarily directed against all of the community mores, and perhaps not in every case against the prevailing attitude trend. It must be remembered, moreover, that some conservative students appear to be not at all community-negativistic.

Most of the least conservative students, it has been pointed out, are reputedly community-co-operative. Whether or not their nonconservative attitudes are to be considered merely an aspect of going along with the community trend must depend, as with the conservative individuals, upon how they view themselves in relation to the community. Those who consider themselves far less conservative than most of their classmates can scarcely be said to be merely going along with the trend. Neither can the nonconservatism of those not considered particularly community-co-operative be attributed merely to going along with the majority.

We shall attempt, then, to assemble such personality data as are available for groups of seniors classified as follows:

most conservative
1. most community-negativistic
   considering selves most conservative relative to class
2. most community-negativistic
   considering selves least conservative, relative to class
3. least community-negativistic
   considering selves most conservative relative to class
4. least community-negativistic
   considering selves least conservative relative to class

least conservative
1. most community-co-operative
   considering selves most conservative, relative to class
2. most community-co-operative
   considering selves least conservative, relative to class
3. least community-co-operative
   considering selves most conservative, relative to class
4. least community-co-operative
   considering selves least conservative, relative to class

These eight groups selected for somewhat intensive study were drawn from the two graduating classes for whom most data were available. The procedure of selecting them was as follows. A preliminary list was made out, including all seniors whose final P.E.P. scores were .5 standard deviations or more above the class average or .5 or more below the class average. Those who did not fill out the Per Cent Estimates questionnaire, or for whom no interview could be arranged, were eliminated. Three for whom the Guess Who ratings were conflicting were also eliminated. The remaining subjects, classified as either conservative or nonconservative, were then arranged in the order of their estimated divergence from majority class attitudes, as described below. Two conservative and three nonconservative subjects who were intermediate in this estimated divergence were finally eliminated, in order that groups as distinct as possible in this respect might be obtained. In two cases subjects who had not been interviewed were added, in order that each of the final eight groups might be of approximately the same size.[1]

Degree of divergence from estimated class majorities was calculated as follows. Total conservative divergence was taken as the sum of the estimated percentages of nonconservative response by juniors-seniors to all items answered conservatively by the subject. Total nonconservative divergence, similarly, is the sum of the estimated percentages of conservative response by juniors-seniors to all items answered nonconservatively by the subject. Final score equals total conservative minus total nonconservative divergence, divided by the total number of items (14 in most instances). This score represents the average degree to which the subject believes her item responses are more conservative than those of her class.

Conservative subjects who are mentioned by two or more Guess Who raters as resistant or indifferent on two or more items are here considered "negativistic," provided they are not also considered community-co-operative by two or more raters on more than one item. (In the latter case they were eliminated from consideration here.) All other conservative subjects are herewith labeled "non-negativistic." Similarly those nonconservative students named by two or more Guess Who raters on two or more of the following items are labeled "co-operative," provided they are not also named by two or more raters as being negativistic on one or more item: "absorbed in college community affairs," "influenced by community expectations" or "by enthusiasms of the crowd," "enthusiastic supporters of the college." All other nonconservative students are labeled "non-co-operative." Conservatives who consider themselves conservative in relation to their class are labeled "aware" and those who do not are labeled "unaware." Nonconservatives who consider themselves nonconservative in relation to their class are labeled "aware," and those who do not are labeled "unaware."

---

[1] Two individuals were later eliminated when it was discovered that their interview statements were in flat contradiction to the degree of divergence from the class majority, as described below. Except for these two, there was exact or substantial agreement, in every case, between interview statements and divergence as estimated from Per Cent Estimate responses.

Conservative Subjects

Negativistic and Aware		Non-negativistic and Aware	
Q10	+ 26.8	F32	+ 27.9
Q12	+ 23.9	Q28	+ 22.1
G32	+ 12.9	Q35	+ 21.4
F22	+ 11.1	Q78	+ 18.9
E22	+ 10.7	Q73	+ 10.7

Negativistic and Unaware		Non-negativistic and Unaware	
Q47	− 0.7	Q68	0.0
Q19	− 0.7	Q70	− 1.1
L12	− 2.1	D22	− 6.1
Q81	− 4.2	M12	− 10.0
Q60	− 13.6		

Nonconservative Subjects

Non-co-operative and Unaware		Co-operative and Unaware	
Q25	− 7.9	Q61	+ 8.2
E22	− 8.6	Q57	− 12.9
Q 6	− 11.8	Q72	− 13.2
Q62	− 12.1	E12	− 13.9
D52	− 15.7	Q63	− 15.0
		Q75	− 16.7

Non-co-operative and Aware		Co-operative and Aware	
C32	− 27.7	Q83	− 21.4
Q71	− 27.7	E72	− 21.8
Q 7	− 28.6	M42	− 21.9
Q 9	− 30.0	H32	− 23.2
Q21	− 30.2	Q22	− 34.3
K42	− 30.7	B72	− 34.7
		Q43	− 35.7

CHART I. MEAN PER CENT ESTIMATES OF CONSERVATIVE DIVERGENCE, FOR SELECTED GROUPS OF SENIORS

Space does not permit the presentation of the full body of data for all of these subjects; fuller citations concerning some of them are to be found in earlier chapters. Selection of data has therefore been made in terms of the factors already found to be related to attitude change. For present purposes brief summaries seem adequate.

Most of the data which follow are taken from written reports by instructors or counselors, and from the files of the college physician. The phrases "is considered" and "is described" indicate agreement by three or more instructors. "Self-interpretations" are taken as nearly as possible verbatim from interviews with seniors, particularly in response to the following questions by the interviewer:

1. What do you suppose would have happened to your attitude scores if you had gone to a college where the prevailing trend was in a conservative direction?
2. Everyone has certain experiences during the years just before coming to college which leave him with certain hopes, fears, ambitions, etc. Suppose that, when you first came to college, you had stopped to review such experiences, and had put into words the things that you considered most important to do or not to do during the coming college years. What would these hopes, fears, ambitions have been?
3. (Toward the end of the interview) Now let's see if we can put together everything that we've talked about, and come out with a theory as to just why your attitude scores during these years have been exactly what they are. (In some cases the formulation of the answer was offered, in part, by the interviewer, but in every instance the final product received the assent of the interviewee.)

THE CONSERVATIVE GROUPS

NEGATIVISTIC AND AWARE

Teacher relationships: Four of the five are considered stubborn or resistant in some degree, and this is considered a major trait in the case of three of them. Two are described as overtly timid, but in the case of two others traits of independence, stubbornness, etc. are interpreted by instructors or by the physician, or both, as compensation for basic timidity. None is named by Guess Who raters as particularly resistant to or influenced by faculty authority.

group relationships: two of the five are described as suffering from strong feelings of inferiority; three are considered aloof, reticent, ill at ease in the classroom.

Only two of them receive any representative choices, neither of these receiving either in 1938 or 1939 more than five choices. The numbers of "friendship" choices received by the members of this group in 1938 were 9, 8, 8, 2, and 1; of these (naming the students in the same order) 3, 4, 3, 2, and 0 were mutual, or reciprocated choices.[2]

personal stability: None of the five is considered by the physician to be among those least stable emotionally in these two classes, though two are noted as manifesting somewhat neurotic tendencies. None is included among those considered most stable in these classes.

[2] The total range of representative choices in each year was from 0 to approximately 7.5 each year, and for sophomores approximately 3.6. The range of "friendship" choices was 0–21, and the mean 4.8, the difference between sophomores and junior-seniors being negligible. Of these choices slightly less than half, on the average, were reciprocated for both sophomores and juniors-seniors.

parental relationships: Four of the five are considered by instructors or physician, or both, to be overdependent upon one or both parents. Three describe their parents as dominating, and one of these three does not hesitate to say that she has preferred to accept this dominance, never having had any reason to rebel against it.

self-interpretations: Two of the four in this group who were interviewed state that in a college where the prevailing attitude trend was conservative they would tend to become more "radical." The other two say they would still be conservative, because they take their political opinions from their fathers.

All of the four describe their major hopes, on entering college, in terms of making their own way in a new community, although each varies the theme in her own way. All seem to have been definitely insecure about it. E2 had attended the same "cozy little school" in her small home town for twelve years, and though she had achieved a certain prestige there, college seemed very big and distant. G32 felt that such small social successes as she had achieved had always been outshone by those of her siblings. F22 had earned considerable status through academic achievements, but had remained aloof, "a highbrow," and had determined not to repeat this experience. Q10 had been a rather conspicuous leader in high school; she hoped to be equally successful in college, but felt little assurance that she would: "I knew I'd have lots more competition here."

The degree of success which these ambitions were to meet provides a clue for the understanding of their reputed community negativism. All met some measure of defeat. E2 was "more or less successful with other students" (her representative choices are highest in this group), but feels rejected by her instructors. "Probably the feeling that they didn't accept me led me to reject their opinions." (Her Per Cent Estimates show that she considers the faculty far less conservative than juniors-seniors.) G32 speaks with some bitterness of "liberal" student leaders "with whom I wouldn't care to be intimate," but claims to be satisfied with a small group of friends. (She is chosen as a "friend" only twice, and reciprocates both choices.) F22, who is chosen but once as a "friend" and does not reciprocate that choice, gave up the struggle after a brief attempt, and turned toward home for her satisfactions. "I wanted to disagree with all the noisy liberals, but I was afraid and I couldn't. So I built up a wall inside me against what they said. I found I couldn't compete, so I decided to stick to my father's ideas. For at least two years I've been insulated against all college influences." Q10 rather early concluded that she had no chance of success in college. "It hurt me at first, but now I don't give a damn. The things I really care about are mostly outside of college. I think radicalism symbolizes the college for me more than anything else."

NEGATIVISTIC AND UNAWARE

teacher relationships: All are described by instructors as being in some degree stubborn, resistant, or insistent upon having their own way. All but Q19 are also described as timid or shy and retiring, this being described as a major trait in the cases of L12 and Q60. Both Q19 and Q81 are named by more than one Guess Who rater as resistant to faculty authority.

group relationships: All but Q19 are considered very insecure in their social relationships; they appear to have come to college with almost no capacity for normal social relationships, though Q81 made considerable improvement in this respect in college. Only one of them received any representative choices either in 1938 or 1939, Q81 having received two and three choices, respectively. The numbers of choices as "friend" received by the members of this group were 14 (by Q81), 6, 3, 2, and 2; of these choices exactly one was reciprocated by each of the five.

personal stability: Three are recorded in the medical files as suffering from definitely neurotic traits, and the other two are described as of questionable stability. Such phrases as "pathologically belligerent," "extremely narcissistic," and "periodically incapacitated by internal conflicts" appear in the records of the three. Another is there described as insecure in relations both to authority and to her peers. Every one of them is described as "inhibited" or "afraid to let go," particularly by instructors in the arts.

parental relationships: Each of the five is considered to be extremely dependent upon parents. In the case of two of them, there is no evidence of conflict about this, the dependent relationship never having been questioned, apparently.

self-interpretations: Of the four who were asked how their attitudes would have changed in a conservative college, two replied instantly that it would make no difference, as they would go their own ways in any event. L12 and Q81 replied that if they were made to feel that pressure was being applied in the conservative direction, they would certainly react against it.

All but Q19 describe, with considerable depth of feeling, precollege experiences of rebuff, ostracism, or isolation. Three describe their hopes, on entering college, in negative terms, i.e., merely to avoid a repetition of the previous experience. Q47 is somewhat more affirmative: "I came here without any idea of how to make friends, and yet I suppose that is what I wanted more than anything else." Even Q19's statement is somewhat similar: "In high school I was always thought of as my parents' daughter. I never felt really accepted for myself, except with my own special group. I wanted to make my own way here." Characteristic phrases used by the others are: "What I most wanted was to get over being a scared bunny"; "I was made to feel an outcast in high school, and above all I didn't want that to happen here"; and "I hated practically all of my school life before coming here. In high school I had the perfect inferiority complex, and I finally pulled out of school social life, deliberately. Of course I did it out of fear, and it was a mistake — one which I didn't intend to repeat here."

As judged by self-reports every one of these five met with a considerable degree of success. "I've made all the friends I want," reports Q47. Characteristic statements, in the same order, of the last three quoted in the previous paragraph are: "I'm over my fears, almost; I'm ever so much more confident and independent"; "I feel much more socially facile now. If I can continue to have happy social relationships, that's all I really care about"; and "I've just begun to be successful in winning friendships, and I've been blissfully happy here."

Every one of the five denies building up any resistance to the acceptance of "liberal" or "radical" opinions. Three of them believe that only small, special groups in college have such opinions, while the other two describe themselves as the kind of persons who just go their own way, paying no attention to anything but their own little circles, and their college work. Q47's typical statement is: "I'm a perfect middle-of-the-roader, neither enthusiast nor critic. I'd accept anything if they just let me alone."

A few comparisons may now be made between these two groups of reputedly community-negativistic students. They resemble each other in that all or nearly all of each group are considered negativistic also by instructors, and in that a majority of each group is considered timid. Timidity, however, is more overt in the case of the unaware group. The majority of each group is considered pretty insecure in social relationships, although the social skills acquired by the aware group before coming to college seem definitely greater than those of the unaware group. The average number of choices as "friend" received by the two groups is almost identical (5.6 and 5.4, respectively) but 43 per cent of these choices are reciprocated by the aware group, as compared with only 18 per cent of them which are reciprocated by the unaware group. This suggests that the two groups are about equally "popular" as friends, but that members of the aware group tend to be considerably more satisfied with little friendship groupings.

As a group, the unawares are considered to have more characteristics of neuroticism and instability than the awares. In particular the former group is described as more inhibited.

But the major distinction between these two groups seems to be in subjective estimation of the degree of social success attained. The unawares feel definitely more successful. It is of particular interest to recall that this group seems to have come to college with lesser ambitions for social success, due largely to precollege experiences of rejection.

The psychological concept which seems most relevant here is that of level of aspiration. The precollege experiences of most of the aware group had led them to hope for more social success than those in the aware group dared to hope for. The same objectively modest degree of success which brought considerable gratification to the unawares brought something more closely resembling frustration to the awares. The latter, merely by virtue of aiming higher than the former, were forced to become more aware of what was involved in aiming high — i.e., that attitude change was one of the factors involved with prestige. The group which aimed lower faced no such necessity; their aim, in fact, was expressed less in terms of community prestige than in terms of personal friendships.

Experiments have shown that levels of aspiration tend to rise with increased success. Our data provide one interesting bit of confirmation for this finding. The unawares tended to choose as "friends," in 1938, individuals with considerably more prestige than did the awares. The mean prestige score[3] of all the individuals chosen by the unawares was 6.0, and of the individuals chosen by the awares, 3.1. If choosing as friends those who have prestige may be said to indicate a relatively high level of social aspiration, this would tend to confirm the hypothesis that the unaware group was achieving more social success, subjectively, than the aware group; i.e., because their presumably lower initial level of aspiration had risen above that of the aware group.

One question remains: why do these relatively "satisfied" unawares have the reputation of being community-negativistic? They do differ slightly according to the Guess Who ratings from the aware group: two of the latter and none of the former are mentioned by two or more raters as "anxious to be left alone"; and four awares and no unawares are mentioned twice or more for one or more of the items containing the word "resistant." In all other respects the two groups are rated alike. To the interviewer, however, they did not seem at all alike, particularly in attitude toward the student leaders. Not one of the unawares expressed more than the faintest degree, if any, of resentment against them, while each of the five

---

[3] That is, the mean number of choices received as representative; the scores of the five individuals chosen as friends by each member of each group were averaged.

awares who were interviewed did express considerable or extreme resentment of this kind. The explanation of the partially undeserved reputation for community-negativism of the unawares seems to be that they resembled the awares in so many ways that they were fitted by raters into the same stereotype.

NON-NEGATIVISTIC AND AWARE

teacher relationships: Instructors' reports for Q35, Q73, and Q78 are studded with such adjectives as "co-operative" and "eager." For Q28 there is but one reference, during her freshman year, to resistant attitudes. F32 is described as "opinionated" and "sometimes argumentative," but never as stubborn or resistant, though oversensitive to criticism. None is described as timid.

group relationships: Such terms as "inferiority feelings" or "insecurity" are nowhere met except in the case of F32, who went through a period of near-failure and quite lost confidence in herself for the time. There are repeated references to F32 as being conceited and haughty. The others, and Q78 in particular, are described as having a natural and co-operative manner with other students. In 1938 they received 9, 3, 3, 3, and 1 representative choices, and in 1939 (mentioned in the same order) 15, 16, 6, 0, and 5. Numbers of choices as "friends" were (in the same order) 5, 8, 4, 7, and 5, of which 3, 4, 3, 2, and 4, respectively, were reciprocated.

personal stability: All but F32 are considered by the physician to belong within the "normal" range; F32 is described as insecure in many ways, but not among those least stable emotionally in her class.

parental relationships: Q73, Q28, and F32 are considered to have too strong ties to one or both parents. There has been little evidence of conflict about it, except for F32, who appears to have resolved the conflict by returning to parental authority. Three of the five are considered to have spent too many week-ends away from college, the chief reason for this in each case being, apparently, social activities planned with parents. The same three are named by two or more Guess Who raters as "likely to be deterred from some interesting pursuit because of family disapproval." In addition, Q78 is named as "most absorbed by home and family affairs."

self-interpretations: The three who were questioned as to their attitude development in a conservative college replied in very similar terms, that if they were made to feel that conservatism was a mark of intellectual superiority they would tend to react against it, just as they had reacted against the contrary notion here.

All four of those interviewed describe more or less definite ambitions for leadership on coming to college. This appears rather pronounced in the case of Q73, following considerable precollege competition for prestige. Q78 reports, somewhat less ambitiously, "In a way I was sick of receiving scholastic honors. I had never been much of a leader in high school, and I naturally wanted to develop that side of myself." F32's statement is as follows: "The only thing that made me doubt my ability to make my own way in college was the suspicion that I would be known just as my older sister's younger sister. That's just what happened. But I got over that, and then when my work began to go really well I felt that I could honestly hold my head up." Q35's hopes were expressed rather in terms of friendship than of prestige: "I always got along all right, but I had to change schools so often that it was hard to make my way in so many new places. I'm really pretty timid, as a result of all that, but I wanted to prove to myself that with four years in one place I could make as many friends as I wanted."

All were rather successful, subjectively. Q78 appears genuinely satisfied with her degree of success, while Q73 admits a little disappointment at never having attained the "really top-notch positions. But," she adds, "I've made the positions I have held more important than they ever were before." "I really feel very secure and happy now," states F32; "I feel that I'm liked and respected, at least by those who matter to me." Q35's statement is: "I've made much more rewarding friendships here than ever before. I've sacrificed a good deal to keep some of them."

Their summary statements are as follows. Q73: "I'm all my mother has in the world, and my succeeding means as much to her as to me. It's considered intellectually superior here to be liberal or radical. This put me on the defensive, as I refuse to consider my mother beneath me intellectually, as so many other students do." Q78: "I've come to realize how much my mother's happiness depends on me, and the best way I can help her is to do things with her at home as often as I can. This has resulted in my not getting the feel of the college in certain ways, and I know my general conservatism is one of those ways. But it has not been important enough to me to make me feel particularly left out. If you're genuine and inoffensive about your opinions, no one really minds here if you remain conservative." F32: "Family against faculty has been my struggle here. As soon as I felt really secure here, I decided not to let this college atmosphere affect me too much. Every time I've tried to rebel against my family I've found out how terribly wrong I am, and I've very naturally kept to my parents' attitudes." Q35: "I've been aware of a protective shell against radical ideas. When I found several of my best friends getting that way, I either had to go along, or just shut out that area entirely. I couldn't respect myself if I had changed my opinions just for that reason, and so almost deliberately lost interest — really it was out of fear of losing my friends."

NON-NEGATIVISTIC AND UNAWARE:

teacher relationships: All four are consistently described as conscientious and co-operative. All but M12 are considered overdocile and uncritical of authority. No overt resistances of any sort are mentioned, although D22 is emotionally disturbed by criticism. All but Q70 are named by two or more Guess Who raters as "most influenced by faculty authority," and none as "most resistant to faculty authority."

group relationships: Definite feelings of inferiority characterize all four; they are very extreme in the case of D22. Q68 showed considerable improvement in this respect during her years at college. None received any choice as representative in 1938 or 1939, except that M12 and Q70 each received two in the latter year. Q70, M12, Q68, and D22 received, respectively, 3, 2, 1, and 0 choices as "friend"; of these, 2, 1, 1, and 0, respectively were reciprocated.

personal stability: D22 is given to severe emotional upsets, and was considered among the least stable students in college. M12 was considered to have many areas of insecurity, but to have handled her conflicts reasonably well. The other two are described in the medical records as rather well-adjusted individuals.

parental relationships: Conflict over parental and sibling relationships seem to be at the basis of D22's and M12's difficulties. D22 frankly states, in her interview, that her parents mean more to her than anything else in the world. The other two are apparently dependent and contented, but not to an extreme degree. Both state, in very similar language, that they have never felt the necessity of differing with their parents on any important issue.

self-interpretations: All four assert that their scores, in a college where the prevailing attitude trend was conservative, would be about the same. The following typical statements are from D22 and Q70, respectively: "I'd still be conservative in view of my family background"; and "I might react against it as a freshman or sophomore, but then I'd forget about it and settle down to my own affairs."

All four recall considerable anxiety as to whether they would fit into the college community, but for different reasons. "Somehow," says D22, "I've never been really accepted. What I seem to remember most before coming to college was being laughed at. That hasn't been true here, but I still have hardly any real friends." "I just took it for granted," states Q68, "that everybody in college would know that I came from a very simple and unpretentious home. But gradually I've come to forget about that, and I've had a grand time here." M12 simply says that she had always been timid: "I was really scared at the prospect of being so far from home." Q70's anxiety, however, is described as being centered about intellectual rather than social success. "I had always had lots of friends, mostly casual, and my teachers always liked me, but I always had the feeling that they were passing me because I was pleasant rather than because I had any brains. I almost failed here, but I suddenly discovered a field that I could work in, and have fun too. And through my work I've found the best friends I ever had."

Q68 and Q70, as seen from the above citations, feel themselves far more successful than they had expected to be. It should be noted, however, that Q70's success came through what she herself describes as withdrawing from the community as a whole, and concentrating both her work and her friendships within rather narrow confines. M12 is also almost exuberant about what she considers personal improvement, but she attributes this improvement exclusively to experiences undergone away from the college. "I had to develop poise and confidence down there, and I made my really close friendships there. It was more important to me than college." Even D22 expresses a surprising degree of satisfaction with her social relationships in general, but again, it is a satisfaction born of turning away from college to home and family friends. "My family's friends are more important to me than any friends I've made here. I've got what I wanted out of college, and now I'm glad to go home."

Final statements are as follows: D22: "I'd like to think like the college leaders, but I'm not bold enough, and I don't know enough. So the college trend means little to me. My family influence has been strong enough to counterbalance the college influence." M12: "It isn't that I've been resisting any pressure to become liberal. The influences here didn't matter enough to resist, I guess. All that's really important that's happened to me occurred outside of college, and so I never became very susceptible to college influences." Q68: "If I had had more time here I'd probably have caught on to the liberal drift here. But I've been horribly busy, what with working to make money and doing the necessary college work to keep up. I guess I've always thought of college as a place where I worked and where I made some wonderful friendships, but politics and that sort of thing I've always associated with home and family instead of with the college." And Q70: "Most juniors and seniors, if they really get excited about their work, forget about such community enthusiasms as sending telegrams to Congressmen. This was particularly true of me, because it was so important to me to be accepted as a person in my own right, I mean intellectually. I naturally came to identify myself, in every way, with the group which gave me this sort of intellectual satisfaction."

The two groups of reputedly non-negativistic seniors may be briefly compared. As to teacher relationships, they differ chiefly in that the awares are more eager and enthusiastic, while the unawares are more plodding and conscientious. Inferiority feelings are conspicuous in the unaware group, though they are not entirely lacking among the awares. All of both groups are still closely attached to parents, with more evidence of conflict about it in the unaware group.

The unawares have almost no prestige, while four of the five awares receive more than the average number of such choices. The unawares are chosen as "friends" with considerable less frequency than the awares, but there is little difference in the proportion of reciprocated choices.

All but one of the interviewed awares interpret their atypical conservatism in terms of loyalty to parents, while all of the unawares state that they have never (for different reasons) entered completely enough into college community life so that they had to fit public affairs into a college, rather than into a home, frame of reference. The various reasons for this which are offered by the unawares all have to do with their areas of insecurity.

The two groups do not appear to differ much, as do the two groups of community-negativistic seniors, in respect to the degree to which ambitions were attained. In general, both of the non-negativistic groups are pretty well satisfied.

Conservative subjects are, in general, characterized by far more community-negativism than other subjects. Negativistic traits appear to be generalized, at least to the extent that nearly all seniors considered negativistic by the Guess Who raters are also so considered by instructors. They are not sufficiently generalized, however, so that they are necessarily directed against the prevalent attitude trend. There are, indeed, about as many reputedly non-negativistic as community-negativistic seniors who have consciously opposed the prevailing trend. We must, therefore, instead of considering opposition to the trend as merely an aspect of general negativism, inquire why some negativistic subjects are and some are not negativistic in this particular respect, and why some non-negativistic students are and some are not negativistic in this respect, i.e., aware of their own relative conservatism.

Our data suggest that behavior which results in reputation for community-negativism is determined not only by relatively persistent personality characteristics, but also by the nature of experiences undergone in college. Students who were negativistic and aware had higher levels of social aspiration, on entering college, than did those who were negativistic and unaware. It seems reasonable to suppose that the negativism of the former group was in part created by their failure to achieve these high aspirations.

Community-negativism is most likely to be directed against the prevailing attitude trend, according to our data, under the following conditions: (1) if the individual possesses sufficient social capacities, and (2) is sufficiently free from absorption in her own personal conflicts to be able to respond to the college community as a community; and (3) if she has fallen short of her social aspirations. The last condition suggests that the "sufficient social capacities" should be amended to read, "just barely sufficient social capacities," for scarcely one of the negativistic and aware subjects reached the level of her aspirations.

Students regarded as non-negativistic may become negativistic in regard to prevailing attitudes under the following conditions: (1) if they possess sufficient energy and (2) confidence in their own social capacities to be able to respond to the college community as a community and at the same time maintain their home and family relationships more or less intact; and (3) if they feel considerable pull from dominating or demanding parents.

Community-negativism is least likely to be directed against the prevailing attitude trend under conditions converse to those named above: (1) if the individual possesses such limited social capacities, and (2) is so absorbed in her own personal conflicts as to be unable to respond to the college community as a community; and (3) if she has attained or surpassed her social aspirations. In view of the first two conditions it is not surprising that, according to our data, these social aspirations were always objectively low.

Students regarded as non-negativistic are least likely to be negativistic toward the prevailing attitude trend under the following conditions, two of which are converse to those named above: (1) if they are sufficiently lacking in energy and (2) in confidence in their own social abilities that they are unable to respond to the college community as a total community and at the same time maintain their home and family relationships more or less intact; and (3) if they feel considerable pull from dominating or demanding parents.

THE NONCONSERVATIVE GROUPS

NON-CO-OPERATIVE AND UNAWARE

teacher relationships: None of the five, except E22 at one particular period, is described as stubborn or resistant. Every one is considered hardworking, eager and enthusiastic but (especially during the first year or two) unsure of herself and too dependent upon instructors. Two characteristics predominate: all are eager to please instructors; and all but Q6 made marked improvement in the direction of self-dependence.

group relationships: All but Q6 were hesitant or inarticulate in groups during the first year or two. E22 is described as highly competitive and anxious to lead. Q6 and Q62 are said to suffer from rather strong inferiority feelings.

Listing them in alphabetical order, numbers of choices received as representative in 1938 and 1939, respectively, were 7, 0, 2, 4, 0 and 17, 0, 2, 8, 1. Choices received as "friend" were 11, 2, 5, 7, 6, of which 4, 2, 3, 2, 3 were reciprocated. As a group they are somewhat low in prestige, somewhat high in friendship status, and about average as to reciprocated choices.

personal stability: One of the five was considered a definite psychiatric problem, and another, very immature emotionally. Two were considered particularly well adjusted personally.

parental relationships: None of the five is considered overdependent upon parents, though one of them experienced considerable conflict over this relationship, and another indulged in overt rebellion against parental standards for a brief period. The other three appear to have developed a reasonably mature relationship.

self-interpretations: Three of the four who were interviewed state emphatically that in a conservative college they would tend to follow the majority trend. "I'm a pretty average person," and "I can't imagine myself in a small minority" are typical answers. Q6's answer is, "I wouldn't go to a conservative college. It would mean too much conflict for me. I would want to follow the majority, but I wouldn't be able to because of my friends at home."

The three individuals who were asked the question as to the major hopes, fears, ambitions, etc. with which they came to college gave astonishingly similar answers, which may be paraphrased as follows: One had felt somewhat defeated in high school, while the other two had had rather happy though inconspicuous high school careers. All three, however, indicated that they had had many misgivings as to whether they could succeed, particularly in the area of social relationships.

These three all express, with light in their eyes, their greatly increased sense of security in social relationships. (Two of them actually used the preceding phrase.) Subjectively viewed, all have been extraordinarily successful. The writer is confident that if the other two individuals in this group had been asked the same questions, one would have expressed the same kind of satisfaction and one would not.

Their summary statements are as follows (in random order): "Social security is the focus of it all with me. I became steadily less conservative as long as I was needing to gain in personal security, both with students and with faculty. I developed some resentment against a few extreme radicals who don't really represent the college viewpoint, and that's why I changed my attitudes so far and no further." "Of course there's social pressure here to give up your conservatism. I'm glad of it, because for me this became the vehicle for achieving independence from my family. I've learned to think for myself, to understand instead of only accepting. So changing my attitudes has gone hand in hand with two very important things: establishing my own independence and at the same time becoming a part of the college organism." "I was ripe for developing liberal or even radical opinions because so many of my friends at home were doing the same thing. So it was really wonderful that I could agree with all the people that I respected here and at the same time move in the direction that my home friends were going." "I think my change in opinions has meant giving me intellectual and social self-respect at the same time. I used to be too timid for words, and I never had an idea of my own. As I gradually became more successful in my work and made more friends, I came to feel that it didn't matter so much whether I agreed with my parents. It's all part of the feeling that I really belong here."

CO-OPERATIVE AND UNAWARE:

Teacher relationships: None of the six is considered stubborn or resistant though Q72 and Q57 are occasionally argumentative. The word "enthusiastic" appears constantly in the records of every one of them. Such adjectives as "plugging," "industrious," "hard working," and "conscientious" also appear frequently in every case. Four are described as impetuous in discussion. Statements like the following are to be found in the records of all but Q57: "so eager and ambitious in her undertakings that she is confused by the tremendous mass of material." Because of impetuosity and overambition they are thought to need pretty constant guidance from instructors. All are eager for criticism, respectful of authority (with some exceptions on the part of Q72 and Q57), and anxious to please instructors.

group relationships: Only E12 is considered hesitant or inarticulate in group discussions. Q72 is considered aggressive and anxious to lead. All the others (including E12 who is described as constantly comparing herself unfavorably to others) are described as gracious, charming, poised, capable and willing to take responsibility.

In alphabetical order, numbers of choices received as representative in 1938 and 1939, respectively, were 4, 2, 18, 13, 60, 14 and 6, 3, 49, 46, 90, 26. Choices received as "friends" were 3, 11, 5, 11, 11, 8, of which 1, 3, 2, 5, 4, 3 were reciprocated. Four of the six are thus very high in prestige and four are high in friendship status.

All but Q57 and Q75 are mentioned by five or more Guess Who raters as being "most anxious to hold positions of community responsibility.

parental relationships: None of the six is considered particularly overdependent upon parents. Two of them are known to have had considerable conflict in attempting to achieve their independence. The other four appear to have achieved a "normal" degree of independence without unusual difficulties.

personal stability: None of the six is considered a psychiatric problem in any serious sense, though two are described in the medical records as pretty tense, and insecure about their social relationships. Two are considered particularly stable and well adjusted.

self-interpretations: Four of the six state without hesitation that in a conservative college they would have "drifted along" with the majority. One of them adds, "In that case I'd have found other ways in which to rebel against my family." A fifth asserts that she would not have become more conservative under these conditions: "I have a definite susceptibility for liberalism, because of my under-dog complex." This question was not asked of the sixth member of this group.

Every one of the six had definite ambitions for leadership on first coming to college. Only Q75, who described herself as "left out," failed to achieve considerable recognition through holding prominent positions, etc., in preparatory schools. All of the others, however, except Q57, refer to some experience of being unpopular at some period of earlier school life. Sample quotations are: "At one time I felt so discriminated against that I refused to go to school for two weeks"; "I wanted terribly to be prominent and while most others thought I succeeded, I considered that I had fallen short. I determined to be really successful in college"; "In Junior High I was the most unpopular girl in the class. I tried desperately to redeem this reputation, and later succeeded. I came to college with the same ambitions, but soon found that I had to go at it differently here"; and "I was a lemon when I first went to —— school. Becoming a leader later brought me great security, but naturally I've never forgotten the former experience, and above all I didn't intend to repeat it here."

All but E12 and Q57 were highly successful, both objectively and subjectively. These two also express a high degree of satisfaction, though they have transmuted their aims into those of intellectual rather than social prestige. All six are almost unrestrained in expressions of happiness during the past four years, although two of them are beginning to dread the prospect of returning home.

Their summary statements are as follows (in random order): "Every influence I felt tended to push me in the liberal direction: my under-dog complex, my need to be independent of my parents, and my anxiousness to be a leader here." "I came to college to get away from my family, who never had any respect for my mind. Becoming radical meant thinking for myself and, figuratively, thumbing my nose at my family. It also meant intellectual identification with the faculty and students that I most wanted to be like." "I met a whole body of new information here; I took a deep breath and plunged. When I talked about it at home my family began to treat me as if I had an adult mind. Then, too, my new opinions gave me the reputation here of being open-minded and capable of change. I think I could have got really radical but I found it wasn't the way to get prestige here." "I take everything hard, and so of course

I reacted hard to all the attitudes I found here to be absorbed. I'm 100 per cent enthusiastic about Bennington, and that includes liberalism, but not radicalism, though I used to think so. Now I know that you can't be an extremist if you're really devoted to an institution, whether it's a labor union or a college." "It's very simple. I was so anxious to be accepted that I acquired the political complexion of the community here. I just couldn't stand out against the crowd unless I had made many friends and had strong support." "Due, I suppose, to my previous experience I naturally affiliated myself with the leaders when I got here, and I gradually came to share their political attitudes. But after a while you get tired of this committee-woman sort of existence, and I've taken more satisfaction lately in intellectual pursuits. Now I think the student leaders tend to be superficial in their opinions, and I've tried to go more to the bottom of things, and so my opinions have changed more than theirs."

It should be noted, finally, that the anxiety on the part of these students to be in positions of prestige and leadership served, more or less consciously, to prevent their acquiring of very extreme nonconservative attitudes. Some of them are very explicit on this point, e.g., the third student quoted above. Only the student last quoted above feels that she has sufficiently renounced ambitions for leadership to be free to continue still further her attitude change in the same direction. In this respect she belongs, as will be seen, with the co-operative and aware group.

NON-CO-OPERATIVE AND AWARE

Teacher relationships: Only Q9, and she only during her first year or two, is described as stubborn or resistant. Every one of the six is described as highly independent, though comments to this effect do not appear for K42 till her last year or two. None, except K42 during her earlier years, is considered overdependent upon instructors or particularly anxious to please them. Every one, by the time she had reached her second or third year in college, had formulated her own goals which were more important to her than praise from instructors. Every one is occasionally described as the best in her class, and four of them are consistently so described. Two of the six were considered so competent that they were graduated after three years. Not one of them is considered too respectful of authority, and all are praised for their habits of critical-mindedness.

group relationships: Four of the six are described as taciturn or reserved in class discussions, but instructors are emphatic that this is not due to lack of ideas or lack of self-confidence. For these four, such phrases as the following appear repeatedly: "bored with discussion which she considers superficial"; "appears arrogant, but is kind to the less intelligent"; "a lone wolf — considers herself exceptional, and she is"; "reserved, almost too perfect"; "shut up in her own world"; "on the fringe of the groups of which she is a member." Of the other two, Q7 is repeatedly referred to as critical of other students, "defensively hyper-critical," as one instruc-

tor puts it, while K42 went through a cycle of being gushy and superficial at first, then silent and discouraged, and finally willing to participate
in discussions on a high level of critical ability.

In alphabetical order, the numbers of choices received as representative
were, in 1938 and 1939, respectively 27, 4, 1, 4, 11, 0 and 13, 6, 0, 3,
11, 0. Choices received as "friends" were 6, 7, 4, 9, 8, 5, of which 3, 5,
3, 5, 3, 1 were reciprocated. Two of the group are thus high in prestige,
two average, and two low; none is low and most are rather high in
friendship status.

personal stability: The medical records of four of these students include
reference to personality problems, two of which were considered fairly
serious; both showed conspicuous improvement with increasing security
during their last two years in college.

parental relationships: Three of this group are referred to in the records
as spoiled, only children. Two of these, and one other have gone through
rather severe battles in the process of casting off what they regard as
parental shackles. Two are considered pretty close to one or both parents, but none is considered particularly overdependent.

self-interpretations: Four of the five who were interviewed state (and
three of them emphatically) that in a conservative college they would be
"even more radical then here." Typical supplementary comments are:
"These ideas are more important to me than being with the crowd";
"I can easily imagine myself being in a small minority, being conspicuous, and getting glory out of it"; "my opinions are in no sense to
be thought of as conforming to those of the majority here, which I
regard as superficial; I react violently if I think my ideas are being
pushed around."

All but one of the five express their ambitions, on coming to college,
in terms of achieving status rather than in terms of making friends,
although the latter is included secondarily by two of them. Three of
these four state these ambitions directly in intellectual terms; the following quotation is typical of all three: "I wanted to stand out intellectually
in the eyes of those older and more advanced." The fourth had enjoyed
considerable prestige through success in various high school activities,
and hoped to do as well in college, but was soon disillusioned about success in such areas, and turned to intellectual goals. The fifth, who did
not state her aims in terms of status, explained her original ambitions
as being due to previous racial discrimination: "I just wanted a fair
chance to be liked as a person." Having achieved more than expected
success, she too, turned to intellectual endeavors during her last two
years in college.[4]

[4] The writer does not possess very complete evidence as to why three of these students had already turned to intellectual areas for their chief security before entering
college. The relationship between their intellectual success and their haughty and
hyper-critical tendencies is, of course, a circular one. Two of them were highly gifted
intellectually. Judging from conversations with life-long friends of these two, their
traits of independence emerged in childhood.

Every one of them was conspicuously successful in the eyes of faculty and fellow students. Only two of them, Q71 and K42, who seem least compulsively driven to succeed, speak of their college years as being genuinely happy ones. As a group, they tend far less than most students to think of college life as an end in itself: they have plans made for years ahead, and so the question concerning the degree to which they have succeeded is met with this sort of answer: "I've got what I needed at this stage of my career, but I'm through with it, and much more interested in the next stage." They view the college as instrument to be used for their purposes, rather than as something to be enjoyed. This was conspicuously true of four of them.

Summary statements are as follows (in random order): "All my life I've resented the protection of governesses and parents. At college I got away from that, or rather, I guess I should say, I changed it to wanting the intellectual approval of teachers and more advanced students. Then I found that you can't be reactionary and be intellectually respectable." "I got my liberal bent from home, but it was vague and sentimental and here I've had the chance to pack it with specific content. Of course, I'm glad that being liberal doesn't make you unpopular here, but I wouldn't give up my ideas even if it did. They are really my own, now, and not merely my family's which I copy." "I simply got filled with new ideas here, and the only possible formulation of all of them was to adopt a radical approach. I can't see my own position in the world in any other terms. The easy superficiality with which so many prestige-hounds here get 'liberal' only forced me to think it out more intensely." "I'm easily influenced by people whom I respect, and the people who rescued me when I was down and out, intellectually, gave me a radical intellectual approach. I'm not rebelling against anything, I'm just doing what I had to do to stand on my own feet." "I started rebelling against my pretty stuffy family before I came to college. I just had to rebel in some way. I felt apart from other freshmen because I was older. Then I caught on to faculty attempts to undermine prejudice. I took sides with the faculty immediately, against the immature freshmen. I crusaded about it. It provided just what I needed by way of family rebellion, and bolstered up my self-confidence too."

CO-OPERATIVE AND AWARE

teacher relationships: None is considered stubborn or resistant, though H32 is described as silently resenting criticism. Every one is considered highly independent, particularly in intellectual areas; this is an extreme trait with Q43. Such phrases as the following appear often: "never accepts a conclusion till she has carefully considered it from every angle"; "persistent in pursuing problems"; "insists on getting at the root of things"; "persistent in probing"; "too good to be easily satisfied." All but one are considered thoroughly open to criticism, and only E72 is described as overanxious for criticism. Five of the seven are referred to as having an insatiable curiosity which has led them not only to study in almost every field, but to interrelate what they have learned in so doing. All but M42 are referred to by such phrases as "meticulous," "something of a perfectionist," "overconscientious."

group relationships: Only Q83 and H32 are ever referred to as quiet or reticent in class, and they only during their first year or two. Every one is described as an excellent group member, such phrases as the following being characteristic: "the mainstay of the group"; "vitalized the whole class"; and "others in the group depend on her." Four of them have been asked by instructors to assist in the teaching of younger students. Only Q43 is described as impatient of shortcomings in other students.

In alphabetical order, choices received as representative, in 1938 and 1939, respectively, were 69, 45, 21, 25, 4, 4, 10 and 77, 35, 32, 25, 9, 5, 9. Choices received as "friend" were 9, 9, 7, 7, 2, 4, 8, of which 4, 4, 3, 3, 1, 3, 2 were reciprocated. Four of the group are thus very high in prestige, and none below average, while five are considerably above average in friendship status.

personal stability: Four of this group are regarded as exceedingly stable, well-adjusted individuals. Among the others, personality difficulties on the part of one were noted only during the first year; one, whose problems were considered rather serious, is described as tense, insecure, and overconscientious, but to have improved considerably; the third is described as having an "independence complex," but to have arrived at a fairly stable adjustment on that level.

parental relationships: None is considered overdependent upon parents. Q43 had done considerable rebelling before entering college. Q83 was definitely overdependent on entering college, but is considered to have achieved a considerable degree of emancipation without much overt conflict. Only E72 has experienced anything resembling violent conflict with parents during college years. H32, B72, and M42 are believed to have worked out their independence from parents in particularly satisfactory manner. (It is doubtless significant that two of these three describe their parents as "very liberal in their political views.")

self-interpretations: All but Q43 and B72 think they would have been more or less "liberal" in a conservative college. "I could easily have gone conservative," Q43 states, "because I needed desperately to identify myself with an institution." B72's statement is: "I bend in the direction of community expectation — almost more than I want to. I constantly have to check myself to be sure it is real self-conviction and not just social respect." Typical supplementary statements of the others are: "I wouldn't rebel outwardly, just go my own inner way"; I don't feel any compulsion to conform, but I'm much happier when I can conform honestly"; "it's not hard for me to imagine myself in a small minority group on such issues, perhaps because I'd be conscious of home influence to back me up"; "I've been in the minority before on matters of conscience"; "I could never believe the typical conservative position; it's too awful — and I know I couldn't marry an obstinate conservative."

Members of this group, more than any other, believe that the basic ambitions with which they came to college have since changed. All of them, in one way or another, state these first ambitions in terms of achieving status and prestige. Q83 and E72 had previously felt left out, and wanted more than anything else the feeling of group inclusion and recognition. Q22 and B72 had pretty much experienced the full measure of "success" in secondary school; they hoped to continue this, but felt some insecurity about it. M42 and H32 had been praised particularly for intellectual accomplishments, and wanted to demonstrate prowess in the new community. Q43 had achieved little but intellectual success, and wanted to "broaden out."

Every member of this group not only achieved a considerable degree of success, both intellectual and social, but she achieved it relatively early. Q22 and Q43, the only two whose prestige scores are not considerably above average, held important college positions during their sophomore years, as did also three of the others. The characteristics which led them to be considered responsible group leaders were noted, in many cases, during their freshman year, and in every case but one, before their senior year. Their testimony during interviews bears out this objective evidence; they felt reasonably secure and successful relatively early in their college careers. The resulting change in the direction of their ambitions may be described in the words of one of them: "It didn't take me long to see that liberal attitudes had prestige value. But all the time I felt inwardly superior to persons who want public acclaim. Once I had arrived at a feeling of personal security, I could see that it wasn't important — it wasn't enough. So many people have no security at all. I became liberal at first because of its prestige value; I remain so because the problems around which my liberalism centers are important. What I want now is to be effective in solving the problems." Another states her present orientation in terms of the college community: "If you feel responsible toward the community you don't care about your personal status. You just want to help make this the kind of college where every student becomes aware and concerned about the important issues she is going to have to face outside of college."

Summary statements are as follows (in random order): "I've always had a strong under-dog complex; I needed the security of personal recognition. Then I found that intellectual self-respect meant more to me; I guess I got my notions of what intellectual self-respect meant from two or three faculty members. By that time my new attitudes were really a part of me, and so I wanted to work for the causes I believed in." "I wanted to accept the liberal ideas which are my parents' and which are dominant here. But I had to make sure they were my own, and so I spent several periods working with left-wing organizations.

Now I'm more critical, and what I believe is my own. In fact, I've gone beyond my family and most of the students here, too." "Prestige and recognition have always meant everything to me, though I cloak it in terms of community responsibility. But I've sweat blood in trying to be honest with myself, and the result is that I really know what I want my attitudes to be, and I see what their consequences will be in my own life. What most distinguishes me is conscientiousness in going thoroughly into what I meet, and applying it to myself." "I was on top of my high school class, intellectually, and hated by all the boys. As a female I was terribly insecure. I had been allowed so much independence by my parents that I needed desperately to identify myself with an institution of such a kind that I could conscientiously conform. Bennington was perfect. I learned how to be a female. I drank up everything the college had to offer, including social attitudes, though not uncritically. Now intellectual pursuits are becoming more important again, and I've become active in radical groups and constructively critical of them." "I've had deep satisfactions in social successes here, but I've had to work harder for intellectual success. Getting less conservative means intellectual respectability to me. I vaguely felt that way before coming to college, partly because my parents are conservative and I never respected them intellectually. There's nothing vague about my opinions now; they really mean a lot to me." "Before I came here I was in a small, withdrawn, nonconforming group, though social attitudes were not involved at all. I accepted liberal attitudes here because I had always secretly felt that my family was narrow and intolerant, and because such attitudes had prestige value. It was all a part of my generally expanding personality — I had never really been a part of anything before. I don't accept things without examining them, however, and I was sure I meant it before I changed." "My family has always been liberal, and they've always given me almost complete independence. So I took such things for granted here. But the influences here made me go further, and for a while I was pretty far left. Now I'm pretty much in agreement with my family again, but it's my own, and it means a lot — it wouldn't be easy for me to have friends who are very conservative."

The various groups may now be compared. Beginning with the two non-co-operative groups it should be remembered, first, that they are in no sense community resistant or negativistic. They are, rather, passively co-operative or conforming. They are also alike in that they are inclined to be reticent in class discussions (though the unawares became less so), and in that they are not above average in prestige but are above average in friendship status.

The two groups differ in several respects. The unawares are considered dependent upon instructors and anxious to please, while the awares are highly independent. The unawares are described as eager and enthusiastic, while the awares are not. The awares are more outstanding academically, and it is clear that they have set higher standards for themselves. The unawares believe that they would follow the majority attitudinal trend in a conservative college, while the awares would not. The unawares describe their major ambitions, on entering college, rather in terms of friendship than of prestige, while the reverse is true of the awares, for whom intellectual prestige is particularly important. The unawares, by and large, had a happier time in college, perhaps because their aspirations were more modest and hence more fully achieved. And finally self-interpretations show that the unawares tend to think of their own attitude change as just one aspect of being assimilated into the community, while the awares tend to think of it as an intellectual achievement in respect to which they have outdistanced most students.

Both of the co-operative groups are composed largely of "substantial citizens." Both are considered hard-working and conscientious, although the characteristic supplementary adjective for the unawares is "enthusiastic," while for the awares it is "persistent." Both show the kind of curiosity that leads them to explore all possible intellectual areas, but the unawares (who are, in general, a less competent group) are more apt to be confused by it all. Both are co-operative and responsible group members. Both groups are very high both in prestige and in friendship status. Both groups had, in general, achieved considerable recognition in secondary school, though memories of precollege "failures" were more acute on the part of the unawares.

The two co-operative groups differ in that the unawares are more anxious to please and more in need of guidance from instructors than the awares. Most of the latter and none of the former are described as "meticulous" or "perfectionist." The awares are much more apt to be intellectual leaders. The unawares feel more definitely successful than the awares in regard to the ambitions with which they entered college, largely because the latter have reformulated these ambitions to a far greater degree than the former; the later ambitions of the awares deal less with personal successes and more with the success of "causes." They differ, finally, in that the awares are far more convinced than the unawares that their present attitudes represent a hard-won victory, and not merely protective coloration. The unawares scarcely raise this question.

The unaware groups are both considered enthusiastic, eager to please, and dependent upon instructors. Most of both groups state that they would probably follow the majority attitudinal trend in a conservative college. Both groups came to college with a good deal of insecurity regarding social relationships, and most of both groups now feel far more secure in this respect; they express, in fact, an extreme degree of happiness and satisfaction about their college years. They feel that they are really a part of the community.

The co-operative unawares possess more of the social graces and skills than the non-co-operative unawares; the latter are described as more hesitant and inarticulate, particularly during early years. In prestige the co-operatives are much higher and in friendship status somewhat higher than the non-co-operatives. The former are thus more "successful" objectively, if not subjectively. The former had achieved more precollege "success," and aspired higher.

Both of the aware groups are considered conspicuous in regard to personal independence, particularly in intellectual areas. Most of the individuals in both groups are outstanding academically. Most of those in both groups believe that they would have become less conservative in attitudes, even in a conservative college. Most of both groups state their ambitions, on entering college, in terms of being accepted. Both groups now phrase their goals in wider than college terms, i.e., in terms of life-long pursuits or of world-wide issues. Hence they regard their "success" as only beginning. Both groups, however, achieved a considerable degree of intra-college success relatively early in their college careers.

The two groups of awares differ primarily with regard to community relationships. Most of the co-operatives came to college with histories of success in social relationship, and their high aspirations in this area were achieved relatively early; thence they turned to more inclusive goals. The non-co-operatives turned early to intellectual ambitions. The former went through the mill of full community participation before turning to more inclusive goals; the latter never went through the mill. Both groups felt somewhat superior, but for different reasons. The non-co-operatives felt (more or less rightly) intellectually superior, and tended to hold aloof. The co-operatives were co-operative rather than aloof, although they

were equally competent academically. But the co-operatives came
to feel superior because they had fought, bled, and died for their
intellectual and attitudinal independence. Their final adaptation
may be said to be still a co-operative one or rather, perhaps, a
participating one, but in terms of a world-wide rather than merely
a college community.

SUMMARY AND INTERPRETATION

The foregoing is what might be termed a two-dimensional analysis. The awareness-unawareness dimension has to do with such
personality factors as determine the degree to which the individual
includes the prevailing attitude trend in her perception of the college community. The personality dimension to which it corresponds
is that of engrossment with personal problems, at the one extreme,
and at the other, freedom to view the community in all its aspects.
The antagonistic-non-antagonistic dimension has to do with such
personality factors as determine the degree to which the individual
tends to resist whatever she does perceive in the community. The
personality dimension to which it corresponds is that of tenacious
resistance in situations in which inadequacy is felt, at the one extreme, and at the other, passive acceptance of such conditions, accompanied by deflection to previously discovered means of satisfaction.

The four personality patterns found to be associated with conservatism may thus be termed the self-absorbed and passive, the
self-absorbed and resistant, the not-self-absorbed and passive, and the
not-self-absorbed and resistant. To some extent, of course, these patterns may be considered artifacts resulting from the kinds of information that the investigator had at hand. He had them at hand,
however, because they seemed to be the most significant kinds of
information to be obtained.

Neither dimension alone seems to account for the observed phe-
nomena. In particular, this two-dimensional analysis permits us to
answer the previously baffling questions: Why do some negativistic
individuals fail to direct their negativism against the prevailing
attitude trend? And why do some non-negativistic individuals show
negativism in this particular respect? An analysis of the personality
correlates of the two dimensions provides this answer to the former
question: because these negativistic individuals are too self-absorbed

to be aware of the prevailing attitude trend; and to the latter question: because these non-negativistic individuals, though not too self-absorbed to be aware of the trend, were too passive in their acceptance of the existence of the trend to face the conflicts necessarily involved in fitting themselves into it.

The two-dimensional analysis may also be applied to the entire group of nonconservatives. The awareness dimension has to do with such personality factors as determine the degree to which the individual perceives the prevailing attitude trend as something to be transcended rather than merely accepted. The personality dimension to which it corresponds is that of seeking acceptance by the group, at the one extreme, and at the other, seeking independence of the group by surpassing it. (This does not mean that the attitude scores of the awares are necessarily less conservative than those of the unawares; it refers only to their manner of viewing their own attitudes in relation to those of the majority.) The co-operation dimension has to do with such personality factors as determine the degree to which the individual seeks to achieve her goals (whether to be accepted or to transcend) through community-wide rather than merely through individual endeavors. The personality dimension to which it corresponds is, at the one extreme, that of fear of or indifference toward participation in community-wide activities, and on the other, the eager embracing of them.

The four personality patterns found to be associated with nonconservatism may thus, for purposes of brevity, be styled the conforming individualists, the transcending individualists, the conforming co-operators, and the transcending co-operators. The reader should remind himself, again, that these are not inevitable patterns, but those resulting from the use of the particular instruments which the investigator found it profitable to apply.

Now let us see whether this two-dimensional approach produces results, which, when applied to conservatives and to nonconservatives, are in any way comparable. The more aware conservatives were found to be less engrossed with personal problems, and freer to view the community in all its aspects than the less aware. The more aware nonconservatives were not only sufficiently free from personal engrossments to include social attitudes in their view of the community, but they had the intellectual capacity as well as the personal freedom to set their social attitudes in a framework far more inclusive than that of the college community. The awareness dimension may thus be thought of as a single one, applying both to conservatives and nonconservatives, and having to do with the degree of inclusiveness of the framework in which the individual's social attitudes are set.

The more co-operative conservatives, while far less resistant to whatever they viewed as majority trends of the community than the negativistic conservatives, were described as passively accepting them providing that such acceptance did not entail too much re-adjustment on their part. The more co-operative nonconservatives accepted whatever they viewed as majority trends of the community not passively, but eagerly, and no matter at what cost of personal readjustment. The dimension is thus from complete resistance to partial resistance (i.e. resistance of the attitude trend only) to acceptance for individual purposes to acceptance for community purposes. This dimension too may therefore be seen as a single one applying both to conservatives and to nonconservatives.

In the last analysis, of course, the only reason for applying these dimensions to the study of individuals is that they serve to illuminate the processes by which social attitudes are acquired. Neither reputation for community-co-operativeness nor belief that one is not more conservative than the majority is necessarily associated with nonconservatism. Each of these, however, is associated with personality characteristics which, in this community, are commonly highly significant for attitude determination. While neither dimension alone is a very safe indicator of what such personality characteristics are, for a given individual, a plotting of the two dimensions against each other does provide a reasonably good indicator of them.

The use of the term "dimension" raises the question of the justification for treating individuals in groups in this chapter. Almost any group of individuals, one might argue, would be bound to have certain characteristics in common. Does not this procedure guarantee in advance that certain "patterns" will emerge? If the dimensions are really dimensional should they not be treated as continua, rather than picking out a few clusters of individuals at different points between extremes?

It must be conceded that the term "dimension" has here been used in a very loose sense. It has been used in a truly dimensional sense only in that *more* as contrasted to *less* is implied. We have not dealt with all degrees of community negativism, but only with more and less of it, and only with more and less of community-co-operativeness. This is also true of the awareness dimension. We have not maintained that every slight difference of degree in respect to this dimension is significant for attitudes, but only that the difference between more and less awareness of positive conservative divergence, and of negative conservative divergence, is significant for attitudes.

This, of course, is the justification for the study of groups of individuals. If only two degrees of only two dimensions are plotted against each other, there are but four possible combinations. Hence four groups of conservatives and four groups of nonconservatives were studied.

But this is a justification only of the procedure as hypothesis. The justification for the retention of the procedure is twofold: it produces results which are congruent with those obtained by other means (e.g. college records and interviews); and it helps to answer the basic questions with which the study began. The patterns which emerge are not merely fortuitous similarities in personality, but they show exactly the kind of consistent interrelationship which should be expected.

The writer has little doubt that other significant "dimensions" could be employed, with the consequent emergence of different patterns. He does not maintain, moreover, that the procedure is foolproof. The discerning reader will have noted that individual exceptions have been noted to almost every generalization and that, in a few instances, individuals assigned to one group belong, in significant respects, in another.[5] He does maintain that individuals classified together have so much in common that is related to attitude formation as to justify the use of the "more-versus-less" dimensional approach, with its consequent emergence of patterns.

[5] This is particularly true of the awareness dimension. After all, the differences between the aware and the unaware groups in respect to estimated majority divergence were rather slight. A few instances could be cited in which an extreme estimate of class response to a single item made all the difference between classification as aware and classification as unaware. The reliability of this measure is less than could be desired.

PART FOUR:

Summary and Interpretation

★ 14 ★

Résumé of Quantitative Findings

THE WRITER KNOWS of few researchers who are able to summarize and interpret their own data to the complete satisfaction of other researchers. Readers who are equally skeptical are bidden to turn directly to the data presented in Part II. The statistically sophisticated reader is asked to refrain from making technical judgments on the basis of statements included in this chapter, inasmuch as some of the more technical problems, such as item validity and scale reliability, are entirely omitted. The attempt has been made, however, to state the findings in a manner satisfactory to both technical and nontechnical readers. The attempt has not been made to include a complete summary of the findings in Part II, but rather to select those findings which have the most direct bearing on the major thesis of the study.

It was found that Bennington students show a significant change in social attitudes, particularly those measured by the scale labeled Political and Economic Progressivism (P.E.P.), between freshman and senior years in college. In terms of the particular content of the scales used, the change may be described as being from more to less conservatism. The change is significant by the usual statistical tests, and is considerably greater than that found in other colleges comparable to Bennington in certain respects. Senior attitudes tend to persist after leaving college, no change at all being observable on the part of those who spent as much as three or four years in college and who had been out of college only one or two years when answering the questionnaire. Changes to more conservative attitudes were relatively slight even on the part of those who had spent less than three years in college, and of those who had been out of college more than two years when answering the questionnaire.

By certain criteria the freshman-senior change seems a large one. Thus in 1936 there were roughly twice as many freshman votes for the Republican as for the Democratic presidential candidate, while among juniors and seniors there were more than three times as many votes for the Democratic as for the Republican candidate. In terms of P.E.P. scores, however, the average change was only about one-fourth of all possible nonconservative change, i.e., to the most "radical" possible position. Neither is it true that the college tends to put out a uniform product, attitudinally speaking. Seniors are scarcely at all more homogeneous in attitude than freshmen. By and large, those who are relatively conservative on entrance are relatively conservative on leaving, and those who enter relatively nonconservative also leave relatively nonconservative. With individual exceptions, of course, all students, regardless of initial attitude, tend to become moderately less conservative.

Relatively few of the attitudes of either freshmen or seniors can be described as extreme. But in spite of the common belief of seniors to the contrary, they do not tend to become less extreme in attitude response than they were as freshmen. Seniors are very definitely characterized, however, by greater certainty as to their disagreement with conservative statements than as to their agreement with nonconservative statements. To a considerable extent college experience has had the effect of "debunking" rather than of building up positive beliefs.

The degree but not the direction of change varied among the various attitudes measured. As the term was applied at this time to the various issues included in the attitude scales, change was consistently from more to less conservative positions. Attitude change must, in fact, be described as a general one rather than as a series of specific ones. This is best illustrated by responses to the scale of attitude toward Loyalist Spain. Although this issue burst upon all students at once, with little or no advance warning to any of them, those who were least conservative regarding other issues immediately took the least conservative (i.e., most favorable to Loyalist Spain) position toward this issue. It seems necessary to explain this in terms of loyalties built up to institutions, persons, or ideologies, which gave direction almost immediately to new issues not previously subsumed under the particular loyalty involved.

Attitude change was only slightly related to courses of study pursued in college. There was a slight tendency for those initially least conservative to choose their major work in Social Studies, and for those initially most conservative to major in Science or Music. These initial differences increased slightly during three or four years of college experience. But the important influences making for attitude change were clearly of a community-wide rather than of an academic-major sort, and for a given individual could be predicted far better from information concerning community relationships than from area of major work.

This conclusion is further reinforced by certain findings concerning values and interests of Bennington students. If, for example, information concerning the Spanish Civil War may be taken as one index of interest in this issue, it is significant that at another college, degree of information was sharply differentiated according as students were or were not enrolled in courses in which the issue had been discussed. At Bennington, on the other hand, there were no differences between Social Studies majors (who presumably had more occasion to discuss the issue in class) and other students. All Bennington seniors, in fact, were somewhat better informed even than students from the other college who were enrolled in classes where the issue was treated.

Certain relationships between social attitudes and values, as measured by the Allport-Vernon test, are illuminating. Bennington seniors, as a group, are very high in theoretical and in aesthetic values, and very low in religious and in political values. (The latter is defined in terms of interest not in politics but in power.) Those whose attitudes are least conservative are particularly conspicuous in precisely these values; they are "like their class, only more so." It is in terms of social value (defined in terms of prizing persons as ends rather than as means to any other end) that the most conservative and the least conservative Bennington seniors differ most. This offers additional support for the evidence offered in the following paragraphs to the effect that nonconservative attitudes are developed at Bennington primarily by those who are both capable and desirous of cordial relations with their fellow community members.

The most substantial evidence for this conclusion is the close relationship between attitude scores and prestige, whether the latter is measured in terms of desirability as a friend or of worthiness to be considered a college representative. In two successive years, and in each of four college classes, the group chosen most frequently had least conservative attitudes; those not chosen at all had most conservative attitudes; and the conservatism of those classified as intermediate increased directly with decrease in prestige. It is also of considerable interest that this same relationship is found, though in lesser degree, between prestige as juniors or seniors and attitudes as freshmen. Thus we see that those who are later to achieve considerable prestige have less conservative attitudes, as just-entered freshmen, than those who are later to achieve little or no prestige. This is significant primarily by way of showing that the histories and personal characteristics of entering freshmen are such that they are impelled to varying degrees of leadership and prestige, and that within a few weeks of entering college they have already "sized up" the dominant community trends, toward which they adapt themselves in proportion to their habits of seeking leadership and prestige.

A study of friendship groupings reveals that those chosen as friends tend to be less conservative than those who choose them; the hierarchy of friendship-desirability is directly related to nonconservatism. The nonconservatives are a more cohesive group than the conservatives; the former tend to choose each other, and to be chosen by the latter. It is also of considerable interest that the only freshmen who have much prestige are extremely nonconservative. Altogether, the evidence clearly suggests that social attitudes are an important component of whatever bonds there are that make for friendships in this community.

Reputation for active community participation is also closely related to less conservative attitudes, while reputation for critical or negativistic attitudes toward the community is commonly associated with greater conservatism. The latter finding is of particular significance in view of the common assumption, in many colleges, that it is the "liberals" or "radicals" who are most community-negativistic. Lesser conservatism is also associated with reputation for energy and enthusiasm, while greater conservatism is associated with reputation for absorption in extra-college social life. Most significant of all, perhaps, is the fact that nearly all of those reputedly much interested in public affairs turn out to be those whose attitude scores are highly nonconservative. Such an interest, in this community, is apparently assumed to be identified with the holding of nonconservative attitudes.

To conclude, however, that community identification inevitably leads to nonconservatism, while community negativism leads similarly to conservatism would be unwarranted unless it is known that all students perceive the community as one in which nonconservative attitudes are dominant and considered "proper." The majority of students in all classes do look at the community thus. Freshman estimates of junior-senior conservatism are slightly lower than their estimates of freshman conservatism, and they estimate faculty conservatism a little lower still. Seniors believe juniors and seniors to be much less conservative than freshmen, and believe faculty to be markedly less so than juniors and seniors. The great majority of all senior attitude responses are believed to be in agreement with the majority position of the class, and nearly all of the senior disagreements with the estimated class majority represent the senior's belief that she is more conservative than her class. Disagreements with the estimated class majority by freshmen are more frequent, although less so than their agreements. Disagreements on the part of freshmen, however, represent individuals' beliefs that they are less conservative than their class about twice as often as they represent the contrary belief. The nonconservative community pull is also attested by the fact that freshman attitude responses actually agree more closely with their estimates of senior responses than with their estimates of their own class attitudes. All but the most conservative freshmen consider themselves more like seniors than like freshmen in attitude, while all but the most conservative seniors believe they are less conservative than freshmen.

Not all students, however, even among seniors, are aware of this community pull, and considerable difference is shown in the degree to which it is believed to exist. Habits of community participation or negativism do not in themselves, therefore, provide an adequate explanation of attitude change. It is for this reason that the several personality patterns described in the preceding chapter are defined in terms of community frame of reference as well as in terms of community participation. Most important of all, the reader should note that both of these concepts which have emerged as most significant for personality in relation to attitude change are community-centered concepts.

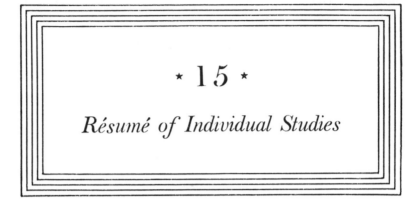

* 15 *

Résumé of Individual Studies

MOST OF THE SUBJECTS selected for individual study in Part III were non-extreme in their attitudes as freshmen, but more or less extreme as juniors or seniors. As the term has been used in these pages, they were relatively conservative as freshmen, and three or four years later either still conservative or definitely nonconservative. The summary statements in this chapter thus deal, in the main, with differences between those whose attitudes did and did not change significantly. They will be referred to as nonconservatives and conservatives, respectively.

The conservatives are chiefly characterized as negativistic or resistant, according to judgments both by faculty and by other students. The latter source also describes many of them as indifferent to community concerns. Several of them are also described by faculty members as being timid and docile. According to both faculty and medical reports, more of them than of the nonconservatives are overdependent upon parents, and fewer of them give evidence of smooth, stable personality adjustment. Few of the nonconservatives are considered negativistic, either by faculty or by other students. Their relationship to faculty members is easier and more secure, in general, than that of the conservatives, and the majority of them are considered self-sustained and independent.

Not all of those characterized by negativism, however, direct their negativism at the dominant community attitudes, and some of those not considered generally negativistic fail to accept the dominant attitudes. These apparent inconsistencies are in large part resolved by the discovery that not all of either group is aware of the dominant, nonconservative community attitudes. The most conservative and least conservative quarters (roughly) of two college classes were therefore classified both according to degree of community negativisim or community co-operativeness and according to awareness of the dominant attitude trend. Some significant variations emerge in the paths by which differing personality characteristics lead to different attitudes. These differing sets of personality processes leading to attitudes are here referred to as patterns.

For purposes of summary and ready reference these nine[1] patterns are paraphrased below. (The emphasis here is upon *process* by which the attitude was arrived at; for the personality correlatives the reader is referred to Chapter 14, and to later portions of the present chapter.) The paraphrasings do not represent the statements of single students, but are composite profiles, as it were. Each of them represents, in substance, what was said to the interviewer by many subjects, both extreme and non-extreme in attitude. In most instances these self-views are entirely congruent with the kinds of community roles which would be assigned upon the basis of the external evidence available. They were obtained, however, exclusively from interviews.

Following each of these statements of roles, the writer has added, in italics, a statement designed to show how role has had its effect upon attitude. The latter statements, while retained in the language of students, are also the writer's paraphrasings. Some of them were uttered almost exactly as they appear; all of them are believed by the writer to represent a fair, though oversimplified, version of how most students in each grouping were led from role to attitude. As in Chapter 14, the classifications of negativistic, co-operative, etc., are based upon Guess Who ratings, and the classifications of aware and unaware are based upon both Per Cent Estimates and interview statements. The first four are characteristic roles of conservatives, and the last four of nonconservatives; the fifth has been added as a role characteristic of many, but not all, of those intermediate in attitude who were not intensively studied.

---

[1] The classification as outlined above yielded eight groups. The fifth, below, has been added to accommodate a considerable number of those non-extreme in attitude who were simply non-extreme in almost every other respect. It is not maintained that all of those non-extreme in attitude belong in this group. See Chapter 17 for further discussion of the point.

reputedly negativistic

1. (aware) I've abandoned my original hopes of success on a community-wide basis, and now I silently resent or overtly resist pressures toward conformity. The important areas of my life are elsewhere. *The community would not accept me, and so I reject it, and what it stands for.*

2. (unaware) I've had more success than I anticipated in being recognized by those who mean most to me as an independent person in my own right, and this is all that is important to me. I rather resent these over-eager references to THE COMMUNITY that you're constantly hearing. *My conservatism would only have been reinforced if I'd ever got into college life enough to realize that my attitudes are disapproved by the majority.*

reputedly non-negativistic

3. (aware) I'm loyal to the community, and positions of responsibility are important to me as a mark of recognition, but I've kept more closely in touch with the outside world than most students have. *I'd only have to revert to conservatism on leaving here for home, anyhow. So why bother?*

4. (unaware) I'm a rather passive member of the community. I tend to go my own way and enjoy my own little circle of friends and put my best into my work. *It wouldn't occur to me to think of public affairs in relation to the college community. I think of them, rather, in connection with home, especially my father and his circle.*

reputedly neither negativistic nor co-operative

5. (relatively aware) I'm neither a rah-rah enthusiast nor a nonconformist. I accept the community as I find it, and enjoy it as such. I'd probably appreciate being given positions of responsibility, but I neither expect nor greatly desire them. *Of course the community has had some influence on my political opinions, just as it has on my opinions about art and music, but I don't take it too seriously.*

reputedly non-co-operative

6. (aware) I've profited enormously from certain aspects of college life, especially the opportunity to develop intellectual independence, but I'm not particularly excited about community life as such. *Being intelligent necessarily involves giving up conservative attitudes, though most students become less conservative on a very superficial basis.*

7. (unaware) I'm no go-getter in a community sense, but I've so appreciated the opportunities offered by the community for general, all-around development that I have come to accept eagerly almost everything it had to offer. *It didn't take me long to see that acquiring tolerant, liberal attitudes goes along with the other characteristics of being a good citizen.*

reputedly co-operative

8. (aware) I'm an enthusiastic community member who has pretty much taken over its standards as my own, so that I am now relatively independent of its approvals and disapprovals. *As one who is regarded as a leader I feel responsible; I've struggled hard to make sure that my attitudes are genuine.*

9. (unaware) I'm an enthusiastic community member, to whom positions of responsibility are an important mark of recognition. I'm eager to conform and to influence others to conform to community standards. *I'm loyal to everything for which the community stands, including the prevailing liberal attitudes.*

Assuming that these are the most common processes by which differing degrees of conservatism are arrived at, we may now present a somewhat more detailed picture of personality characteristics associated with various degrees of susceptibility to community influences upon attitudes.

Those most susceptible were characterized by habits of conformity, with varying degrees of passivity or personal initiative. The more passive among them had fewer social skills and lower social ambitions. Attitude change meant to them either intellectual respectability (the change was greater for this group) or an aspect of good citizenship. The more aggressive among them had greater social skills and ambitions. Attitude change was to them an aspect of the responsibility that goes with leadership. Those among them for whom the change was greater made conscientious attempts to assure themselves that the new attitudes represented genuine beliefs and not merely an avenue to success; they were intensely loyal and conscientious persons. Those individuals changed most, in short, who reconciled the need to conform with the need for independence, by making a greater than average change in attitude. Those whose change was less conspicuous did not face this conflict; they were above all anxious to please, and hence less change was necessary.

Those who were little or not at all susceptible to community influences upon attitudes were characterized by negativism, by indifference, or by divided allegiance toward the community. Habits of negativism were in some cases of precollege standing, and in others represented a reaction to frustrated hopes of social success in college, following some measure of precollege success. (It is the latter group whose attitude scores were most extreme.)

Habits of indifference were in nearly every case traceable to feelings of inferiority accompanied either by strong dependence upon parents, by engrossment with a very limited circle of friends, or by absorption in academic work. Divided allegiance is characteristic of those whose home ties were so strong as to render intolerable overt conflict between home and college standards, but who are otherwise capable of full community assimilation. These individuals were relatively immune to community attitude influences, then, either because they were too absorbed with home ties or personal conflicts to recognize the community influences, because home-versus-college conflict was intolerable, or because they were incapable of reacting to the frustration of what was to them failure in social relationships by any other means than that of rejection of community attitudes.

What seems most clearly to distinguish those who were and those who were not susceptible to the community influences thus appears to be the kinds of adjustments, already pretty well set on coming to college, in two vital areas, viz., toward parents and toward peers. Those who are capable of considerable independence from parents find no great obstacle in the fact that dominant attitudes at college differ from those of parents. Those who are particularly ripe for parental emancipation find in social attitudes a ready symbol. Overdependence upon parents prevents attitude change in two sorts of ways. For some, conflict between home and college standards is simply intolerable; to embrace the latter would be an act of excessive disloyalty. For others the tie is so all-absorbing that the college influences are scarcely felt; hence there is no conflict.

As to adjustment toward contemporaries, two sorts of differences may be seen between those who are most and least susceptible to community influences. The first is that of orienting oneself toward a total community rather than toward a limited group within it. Those who choose the latter orientation are almost invariably those whose sense of personal inadequacy in competing with their peers has prevented them from entering the larger arena. Hence they are not influenced by the dominant community attitudes. The second difference is not unrelated to the first. It is the difference between setting goals, phrased in community-wide terms, within or beyond one's limits of achievement. Those who set them too high and fail to reach them are apt to reject the community attitudes, whereas those whose initial goals are not beyond reach tend to raise their standards of achievement, embracing community attitudes more closely with each added success.

An important personality distinction parallels this last difference. The basis for the discrepancy between goals and capacities seems to lie in a certain unyieldingness on the part of those who have fallen short of their own goals. There is no evidence to suggest that they have any lesser social capacities of any other kind than those whose goals are achieved. Nor is it necessarily true that their goals are any higher, objectively. The difference, rather, is that they expect to achieve them in their own way, i.e., in ways with which they are already familiar and skilled, whereas the others are capable of adopting community-approved ways of achievement. The difference may somewhat oversimply but not unfairly be described as that between achievement by dominating and by pleasing.

Independence from parents, sense of personal adequacy, and sufficient suppleness of personality to permit modification in the means of achieving social ends — such are the major characteristics of those most susceptible to attitude change in this community.

One significant question remains. How much do these attitude changes mean to these students? Precisely what do they mean? The writer assumes that evidence brought to bear throughout both Parts II and III is sufficiently convincing that, in general, the students' attitudes here considered represent more than obliging responses to attitude scales. To most of the nonconservatives, at least, the attitudes really matter. But the personality processes by which nonconservative attitudes were arrived at have been described largely in terms of achieving successful community adaptations. The conclusion might easily be drawn, though quite erroneously in the writer's opinion, that such attitude change as has been reported is in most cases simply a convenient vehicle for transportation to social success.

The different sorts of personality processes described in Chapter 14 indicate, in the first place, that attitude change means different things to different individuals. The question thus becomes not whether attitude change always or ever has such a meaning, but for what kinds of students it has such a meaning; and whether, among such students, its meaning remains such or whether this meaning changes.

It is a common belief among certain groups of students, particularly among the two groups of aware conservatives (cf. Chapter 14), that nonconservatism invariably means just that, i.e., a cheap means of transportation to social success. They are probably not far from wrong as far as the two groups of unaware nonconservatives are concerned. There is little doubt, at any rate, that the nonconservatism of these groups began in just such a way. There is little doubt in the writer's mind that it remained such for some of them, and also that nonconservatism became a value in itself for others.[2] Neither does he doubt that many of the group, average in attitude change (whose personality characteristics have not been studied intensively), were rather passive in their attitude adaptations.

As to initial attitude change, the same thing is also true, probably, of the aware and co-operative nonconservatives. The writer is convinced, however, that their nonconservatism later developed a very considerable degree of autonomy. The autonomy is unquestionable for the aware and non-co-operative nonconservatives. In addition to these two groups, the personal significance of whose attitudes is described in Chapter 14, there are the questionnaire returns from former students and graduates (cf. Chapter 10). Very few of those who had developed any marked degree of nonconservatism in college made significantly more conservative responses one, two, or three years later, and many had become (usually by slight margins) still less conservative. It is hard to see how these ex-students had anything to gain by making such responses. Hence a considerable degree of autonomy is also indicated for most of them.

It is not to be denied that changing attitudes sprang from personal motives, nor that these motives originally had large components of social success in many cases. The question, however, is whether the original significance of the change remained the only or the chief significance. The above evidence suggests that for a large number — probably a majority — of those whose attitudes changed

---

[2] Two sorts of data regarding this point are unfortunately lacking. Adequate personality for former students and graduates who responded after one, two, or three years out of college are not at hand. Hence conclusions as to the personal significance of nonconservatism to those whose later responses were or were not more conservative than their responses before leaving college can not be drawn. Secondly, the Per Cent Estimates questionnaire was given only once; hence changing subjective roles cannot be studied.

significantly, other and more important meanings were acquired. Chief among these, as previously indicated, are intellectual self-respect, independent status as an adult person in one's own right, sense of responsibility to a college, one of whose chief functions it is to create awareness of a changing world (cf. Chapter 18), and sense of responsibility as a citizen in such a world.

Personality Pattern and Community Role

THE ATTEMPT HAS BEEN MADE to observe variations in the ways, in one community, in which social attitudes viewed as adaptive behavior are geared into other forms of personality adaptation. The reader should note carefully that not all possible modes of personality adaptation are considered, nor are all possible conceptual frameworks employed in describing personality factors. The kinds of personality factors noted are, in fact, severely limited. They have to do primarily with perceiving the majority attitude trend, and with participation in community life. In a word, they have to do with degree of assimilation into the college community.

This community, however, has been shown to be one in which the mores call for the development of relatively nonconservative social attitudes. Is the net result of the study the mere banality that those individuals who become most fully assimilated into a community most completely adopt the behaviors approved by it?

From the point of view of *general* theory — i.e., principles applying to all individuals involved — the preceding statement is hardly an unfair summary. The only contribution of the study to the general theory of attitude formation is that, in communities like this one, the acquiring of social attitudes is only one aspect of a total personality adjustment to the total community situation, and that acceptance or internalization of that sector of the mores labeled social attitudes tends to accompany internalization of other sectors.

The study had its origin, however, in queries concerning *individ-*

ual variations in the acquiring of social attitudes, under common influences of community environment. From this point of view the significant questions become such as the following: What sorts of personality variables are associated with various degrees of conforming with the mores-in-general? and with conformity with other sectors of the mores but not with those having to do with social attitudes? and, conversely, with conformity with the attitudinal but not with other mores?

Certain tentative answers have been given, in Part II of the study, to such questions. These answers, too, may be simplified almost to the point of tautology. Those individuals become most fully assimilated-in-general who are most capable of it — or, somewhat less briefly, those who are not too absorbed by private concerns to have developed the necessary social skills and capacities. Those who conform with all but the attitudinal mores are, in general, those who possess the necessary social capacities, but are particularly subject to home and family pulls. Those who conform with attitudinal but not with other mores are, in general, those who do not possess the necessary social capacities, but who view nonconservative attitudes as a mark of community acceptance or intellectual superiority.

The preceding statements are oversimplifications, as a perusal of Chapter 13 will show. But even as there stated in more cautious form, such generalizations regarding selected groups of individuals serve to force the theoretical issue. This issue may be stated indirectly, through the vehicle of answers which have been given to the psychological problem involved. One of these answers is that certain types of personality characteristics tend always to be associated with certain social attitudes, just as height and weight measurements show positive correlations in all unselected groups — e.g., "radicals are maladjusted" or "neurotic"; or "extreme radicals and extreme conservatives tend to be maladjusted," which latter statement carries the implication that non-extreme social attitudes tend to be associated with "normal" personality adjustment. Another answer is that the relationship between social attitudes and other personality variables is always unique for each individual,[1] leaving the implication that more is lost than gained by any conceivable sort of classifying of individuals.

The writer suggests a third sort of answer, as follows: In any

[1] Cf. Allport, G. W., *Personality*, 1937.

community the major characteristics of which, as related to the social attitude in question, are known, certain more or less definite types of relationship between attitudes and other personality variables may be distinguished. Not only is it possible to distinguish them, but it is inevitable that they should occur, and they are discoverable by means no more occult than the ordinary methods of psychological inquiry projected against a community background. Further, it is only by noting the modes of attitude adaptation which appear with a certain frequency that the most fully satisfactory theory of attitude development can be constructed.

This sort of answer constitutes a flat rejection of the first answer cited, because the latter assumes a degree of uniformity among various communities which seems to the writer contrary to fact. It is not a flat rejection of the second answer cited, at least as to its affirmative implications. It concedes the uniqueness of each individual's manner of adaptation, in all its details, but challenges the implicit assumption that significant classifications cannot be made except at great sacrifice. It suggests, as the reason for this negative implication, that inadequate attention has been paid to certain intra-community uniformities.

The above position can scarcely be argued for all communities at once. It might be exceedingly difficult to defend as regards certain types of communities. But for the particular community involved in this study, the outlines of the argument would be somewhat as follows:

Most of the young women who were subjects in this study were between the ages of 17 and 22. Most of them came from upper-middle and upper-class families who lived in urban centers, mainly in the eastern United States. Each had adopted certain unique personality devices for meeting the partly uniform and partly varying social pressures which she had met. But the college community introduced a new set of more or less uniform social pressures to which all of them had to adapt. And with all due allowance for individual uniqueness, the modes of community adaptation which the community recognizes are strictly limited. I.e., reputation for mode of adaptation is forced into a comparatively few molds. The particular mode to which an individual is assigned by reputation may or may not be "fair" or "correct," but it is at least based upon certain manifestations of personality. This phenomenon, which is not limited to this community, may be referred to as the *objective limitation of roles.*[2]

But there is also a *subjective limitation of roles.* For the community which assigns the roles is composed of individuals who must also relate themselves to the community. Thus subjective roles tend to reflect objective roles, in the sense that the latter (already described as limited) tend to set limits within which the former are cast. A given individual's subjective role, however, by no means necessarily coincides with her objective role. Indeed, it is precisely because they often do not coincide that the personality patterns mentioned in Chapter 13 could be discovered by the means there described. For the self-assigned role, like the objective role, is not fortuitously assumed but is the consequence of certain personality adaptations.

We are now in a position to see why there should be sufficient similarity within each of the eight groups of students described in Chapter 13 to justify the term "personality patterns." The groupings were made first on the basis of Guess Who ratings as to community participation, i.e., objective role. There is nothing surprising in the discovery that individuals alike in this respect have, according to other and independent sources of information, certain personality characteristics in common. Further groupings were then made, among those similar in these respects, on the basis of self-estimated majority divergence in attitude, i.e., subjective role. There is nothing surprising, again, in the discovery that individuals alike in the latter as well as in the former respects should have still further personality characteristics in common, since the assuming of a subjective role is a personality function.

The latter point needs to be made more explicit, and for the sake of concreteness the data in Chapter 13 may be briefly reviewed,

[2] The term "role" is not to be interpreted as meaning that each individual is limited to a single mode of community adaptation in all her various relationships, or at all times. Obviously an individual can vary considerably at different times and in different situations. The term has reference only to the data included in this study. *Objective role* may be operationally defined in terms of Guess Who ratings, and *subjective role* in terms of Per Cent Estimates and interview statements.

The term "community role," used later in this chapter, is obviously not used in the all-inclusive sense which the words may imply. It also has reference only to the data included in this study. It is intended to include the aspects of community relationships which those who are similar both in objective role and in subjective role have in common.

from the point of view of personality processes involved in various degrees of awareness. Among the two groups of negativistic conservatives, lack of awareness of their own conservatism appears to be simply another facet of the inability of the one group to cope with the total community as a total community, whereas the awareness of the other group is an aspect of their greater social skills and higher ambitions which were, initially at least, directed at the total community. The pseudo-negativism of the unawares is a protective shell of indifference toward what they cannot cope with; hence their unawareness. The negativism of the awares is an aggressive reaction to the frustration of ambitions which were directed at the total community; hence their awareness.

Among the two groups of non-negativistic conservatives, lack of awareness of their own relative conservatism is the result of the inability of the one group to respond to the total community as a total community and at the same time maintain intact their close home and family relationships, whereas the awareness of the other group is one element in the total-community perception made possible by their greater skills and self-confidence. The indifference of both groups is a mark of their inability to cope with two worlds. One group avoids the threatening conflict by participating only superficially in college life, while the other group is aware of the conflict but prefers minority status (in this respect) at college to discord at home; hence both groups are regarded as indifferent.

Among the two groups of non-co-operative nonconservatives, lack of awareness on the part of the one group is a direct consequence of their arriving at their nonconservatism as an act of conforming, whereas the awareness of the other group is a function of their arriving at their nonconservatism as an act of excelling. Almost the same distinction can be made between the two groups of co-operative nonconservatives. Lack of awareness on the part of the one group represents loyal co-operation in respect to approved social attitudes; as "leaders" they must, of course, be slightly "ahead" of the majority, but not too far. The awares, on the other hand, are not only sufficiently secure so that they can afford to go beyond the majority, but their awareness is a mark of the hard-won struggle by which they reached their nonconservative positions.

In short, it may be said for each of the eight groups that the personality processes which appear to be essentially responsible for whatever adaptation is made are also responsible for whatever degree of awareness is shown. Those who are conservative because they have avoided the community could scarcely have an opportunity to discover that they are conservative. Those who are conservative because they aimed at leadership, failed, and repudiated whatever the community stood for could scarcely fail to be aware of their own conservatism. Those who have acquired more than the average degree of nonconservatism because they are anxious to conform cannot be aware of their own relative extremeness, else they would withdraw to a more moderate position. Those who are extremely nonconservative because they need to excel must be aware that they are somewhat extreme, etc., etc.

Such is the rationale of the personality patterns. Objective roles are assigned, with more or less correctness, on the basis of observable personality characteristics. Among those assigned to similar objective roles, different subjective roles are self-assigned on the basis of other personality characteristics. Those for whom both objective and subjective roles are similar, according to "objective" data, thus have many personality characteristics in common. These common characteristics, moreover, are directly related to the processes of personality adaptation by which the attitudes are acquired.

An important question remains. What evidence is there, in view of the fact that these personality patterns emerged from studies of those rather extreme in attitude, that they also apply to those intermediate in attitude? Only an impressionistic answer can be given, since space limitations have made impossible the inclusion of further individual studies. The great majority of those non-extreme in attitude are neither very negativistic nor very co-operative, according to Guess Who ratings. The majority show little self-estimated conservative divergence, either positive or negative, from the majority position, though there are several whose self-estimated divergences are as extreme as any of those reported in Chapter 13. A comparison of self-estimates with attitude scores shows that a considerable majority of those non-extreme in attitude would be classified as "aware," but that there are representatives of all the eight groups described in Chapter 13. Most of them, according to the interview data, consider themselves more or less "typical" in attitude, and in most instances the interview statements are in agreement with the Per Cent Estimates in this respect.

The writer has not attempted to make intensive studies of individuals not referred to in Part III, but he knew most of them pretty well, and he jotted down a tentative "diagnosis" at the end of every interview. His interpretations are such that, in the main, he feels reasonably confident in saying that (with the exception of one suggested additional group; see Chapter 15) those non-extreme in attitude fit into the same personality groupings as do those extreme in attitude, though perhaps less convincingly so in many instances. To what extent the preceding statement is to be attributed to an increasingly rigid frame of reference on the part of the writer, he is in no position to say.

Even the amateur social psychologist knows, of course, that no two individuals, even within the same family, ever have the same social environment. Adaptations to varying social environments, moreover, are made by organisms possessing different biological capacities. How, then, in an environment far more complex than that provided by a single family can individuals whose personalities have been determined by diverse sets of circumstances be distributed with any semblance of significance into a few personality pigeon-holes?

For purposes of exhaustive personality study, of course nothing of the sort could be attempted. For the present, however, we are interested only in so much of personality as is most directly related to the acquiring of social attitudes. If it turns out that such relevant aspects of personality can be significantly classified, the writer is inclined not to lament that important aspects of personality have been omitted, but rather to inquire what it is about the community that tends to force its members into the classifications.

The anthropologically minded reader will recall that every culture has its characteristic ways of pressing thought and action into a comparatively few molds. Behaviors which seem functionally similar to the outside observer are differently phrased in diverse societies, play different roles in the totality of the cultures. Membership roles in any culture, such as being a father or chief, come to be cast in a more or less rigid framework rather than viewed objectively in terms of their functional significance alone. The possible number of roles which an individual can play is limited, and also the degree of variability within each role. Members come to accept these limitations as "natural," and to view themselves in those terms.

There is nothing astonishing, then, in the finding that a limited number of community roles appears to emerge in such a community as this. It must not be forgotten, of course, that the investigator so planned the study that they could emerge, and this in turn was the result of what he had sifted out as the most significant lines of inquiry. To an unknown extent he probably worded his interview questions in such manner that they inevitably emerged. This would occur not only because of his preconceptions, but also because he was himself a member of the community. Perhaps it is this latter fact which makes it seem so "natural" to him, at the end of the study, to accept the existence of such roles. It is, however, an interesting commentary on the unconscious manner in which one comes to accept them in his own community, that he did not begin to think in terms of specific roles until the study was far advanced.

Beyond all this, however, are certain considerations which suggest that a considerable degree of patterning of roles is inevitable in any such community as this. Few would deny that the culture which is shared by contemporary upper-class urban families includes a rather fixed hierarchy of approved behaviors for young women of this age. Few would deny that this culture admonishes "success" in a comparatively few areas of social relationship. The homogeneity of the college community culture served to limit still further the modes by which "success" could be attained. To the extent that this is true, each community member tends to map out for herself a particular mode by which she will seek, what is for her, success. This mode, in a community like Bennington, necessarily bears some relationship to the community — a relationship of passivity or activity, of inclusion or exclusion, of acceptance or rejection. This study does not seek to ferret out every detail of these modes, but only such as bear most directly upon attitude development — i.e., their community aspects.

This use of the term "success" suggests a conceptual formulation of which the writer might have made more use if it had occurred to him earlier in the course of the study, viz., that of levels of aspiration. If it had, the study would have been planned somewhat differently, but it is doubtful if the final results would have been very different. The results may, in fact, be stated in terms of aspiration-level concepts. Each individual, within the limits of her own selected mode, aspires to a certain level of what she defines as social success. Those who phrase their goals in community terms tend to adopt the normative community attitudes to the degree that they are successful, then to raise their levels of aspiration, and to change their attitudes still further in the direction of those considered most approved, etc.; and to the degree that they are not successful to reject them in favor of goals phrased in terms of other groups or communities. Those who do not so define their goals tend not to adopt the normative community attitudes, except as their more limited goals — e.g., intellectual superiority — happen to lead in the same direction, in which case nonconservative attitudes are developed to the degree that success is attained, aspirations are set higher, further attitude change occurs, etc.

The writer believes that further community attitude research might well be conducted along these lines. But it does not seem necessary to restate at greater length the present findings in such terms, since the study was not so planned.

The writer believes he has made it clear that the community roles and the personality patterns here described are not the only conceivable ones, even in this particular community. Probably no system of patterning is the only conceivable one, in any community. He maintains only that they are significant variables in this community — significant in the sense that more light is thrown on the nature of community forces which serve to mold social attitudes than if no attempt had been made to arrive at a system of patterning. If the main purpose of the study had been to show variations in attitudinal adaptation in all the wealth of their individual details, nothing would have been gained by such a system. But the writer believes he has made a reasonably good case for his position that community factors have been neglected above all others in individual attitude research. He has therefore put the emphasis upon the manner in which individuals participate in community life. The evidence obtained in this endeavor has pointed in the direction of community patterning — whether or not the best possible systematization has been made of this patterning.

To recapitulate, precollege and college community influences conspire to phrase approved behaviors in terms of success in a very few areas. Individuals thus come to view themselves as community participants in terms of a very few roles. The possible degrees of success, particularly as self-viewed, are limited. Individuals distribute themselves among these limited roles not randomly, but in accordance with already existing and currently developing personality characteristics. These characteristics which determine which of the possible roles shall be played by the individual have here been referred to as personality patterns. *It is the community role which mediates between social attitudes and other personality characteristics.* It is the community's limitation of the number of possible roles that results in a limited number of personality patterns — limited, that is, in respect to their significance in determining social attitudes.

★ 17 ★

Personality and Social Change

THE QUERY WITH WHICH these pages opened had to do with personality and acceptance of social change among student groups. The evidence adduced in the intervening chapters was drawn almost entirely from a single small college community, one in which the dominant attitudes favored the kinds of social change being introduced in the 1930's in America. Certain sets of personality conditions were shown to be related to acceptance and to nonacceptance of the dominant attitudes in that community. The question now arises as to the degree to which the relationship between personality conditions and attitude change is a function of the particular community conditions.

Ideally, of course, the problem would have been subjected to experimental control. College communities known to differ in specified ways would have been compared as to the personality characteristics of those of their members whose attitudes changed most and least. Only a limited attempt at such a comparison has been made, the results appearing in Chapters 5, 7, and 8. But even from these data certain modest conclusions may be drawn, and other evidence is available to support them.

First, both at Williams and at Skidmore upperclassmen are less conservative than freshmen. Similar findings have been reported with almost complete unanimity [1] in attitude research among American college students during the past fifteen years. The writer

[1] See Murphy, Murphy, and Newcomb, *Experimental Social Psychology*, 1937, Chap. 13.

does not maintain that the term "conservative," so invariably used in describing these freshman-senior trends, has the same meaning for the widely differing groups to whom the widely differing attitude scales have been given. Indeed, he would stress the great variability in the content of the term.

For the significant finding concerning student attitude changes in almost every kind of American college during these years is not that they are all going through the same changes. It is rather that in each college center certain attitudes considered worthy of measuring by some one in that center are found to be changing. The fact that the term "conservative" is invariably applied indicates, of course, that the varying attitudes have something in common, in terms of contemporary social change. But many kinds of evidence [2] conspire to suggest that each campus has its own brand of conservatism, of which freshmen have more and seniors less. Hence the fact that freshman-senior differences were found to be less at Skidmore and Williams than at Bennington does not necessarily indicate that trends away from conservatism were greater at Bennington. It may indicate principally that the scales used were more suitable for Bennington.

Another kind of finding has been reported with almost equal unanimity by American attitude researchers. Whatever the content of the term "conservatism," those who show it least on any given campus tend to make higher scores on intelligence tests, or to make better scholastic records, or both, than those who show it most.[3] Again we stress the variability of the term "conservatism." Whatever the content of the attitudes to which the term is applied on a given campus, it is found to be associated on that campus with lesser degrees of measured intellectual capacity or achievement.

There are doubtless varying reasons for this widespread fresh-

[2] For a full documentation of this statement the reader is referred to the considerable literature of attitude measurement. By way of summary, the following may be noted: 1) Intercorrelations among scores of conservatism regarding various issues differ greatly in different student groups; 2) Reliability coefficients in a given college center tend to be high for some attitude scales and low for others, with great variation for different groups, indicating that what is regarded as an attitude entity by some groups is not so regarded by others; 3) freshman-senior differences are enormous for one attitude, but slight for another, in highly variable fashion for different student groups.

[3] See the writer's "Determinants of Opinion," *Public Opinion Quarterly*, 1937, Vol. 1, No. 4, pp. 71–78.

man-senior trend away from conservatism, and for the commonly found association between lesser conservatism and greater intellectual performance. But high among them we would place such considerations as the following. For most students in most colleges, faculty members tend to rank high in status and in influence. This is particularly true for those students for whom intellectual concerns are important. In most colleges most faculty members, as "intellectuals," tend to be at once more aware of current social changes and less bound by business and financial ties to the *status quo* than the parents of most of their students. (It is assumed that most entering students have acquired their social attitudes largely through their parents.) In short, faculty members of college communities tend to have most prestige and to be least conservative; whereas freshmen tend both to have least prestige and to be most conservative.

All this is tantamount to saying that the Bennington community is not, after all, so very different from other college communities except, perhaps, in degree. There is, however, one sort of difference of great importance. If, in most other colleges as in Bennington, the order both of nonconservatism and of status and influence is from faculty to upperclass students to freshmen, there is less awareness of the differences in degree of conservatism in the other colleges. The average Bennington student estimates these differences to be greater than they actually are. The average student at Skidmore (the only other college in which such estimates were obtained) underestimates them. There is more community self-consciousness at Bennington regarding the issues to which the term "conservative" is there applied. The issues matter more, and nonconservatism is more clearly recognized as being associated with prestige.

The thesis is thus that in most contemporary American colleges there is under-awareness of the degree to which nonconservatism regarding one or another set of issues actually is characteristic of those having most prestige. There is presumably a circular relationship between degree of freshman-senior difference in conservatism and awareness of it. The greater the difference the greater the likelihood of its being commonly recognized, and the greater its common recognition the greater the difference is apt to become.

It must be remembered that differences in degree of awareness were closely associated, among Bennington students, with differing personality processes by which attitudes were formed. Since it is this matter of awareness in respect to which Bennington is here alleged to differ most from other colleges, does it follow that the personality processes would be essentially different in other colleges? In view of the probable fact (judging from the Skidmore data as well as from the inherent probabilities) that there is in most colleges some degree of awareness of the association between nonconservatism and prestige, it seems likely that essentially similar personality processes would be found elsewhere, though with different frequencies.

For example, at Bennington a majority of students overestimated the actual freshman-senior attitude trend, while at Skidmore a considerable minority overestimated it. If, as here assumed, most colleges resemble Skidmore more closely than they resemble Bennington in this respect, we should expect to find a minority of overestimators in most colleges. It seems reasonable to suppose that among this minority,[4] attitudes would be formed by processes similar to those found in the majority of overestimators at Bennington. A large number, presumably, of those whose attitude changes are great would come from this group.

Again, a minority at Bennington and a majority at Skidmore underestimated the actual freshman-senior difference. Assuming again that Skidmore is the more typical college, the majority of underestimators in most colleges would, we may assume, be found to arrive at their attitudes by personality processes similar to those of the underestimating minority at Bennington. This does not necessarily mean that the lack of awareness of all individuals in the underestimating majorities in most colleges is caused by absorption with personal concerns, lack of social skills, etc., as at Bennington. But it is the writer's best guess that precisely such characteristics would be found among a considerable member of the underestimating majority, and that such individuals would be found there in greater proportion than among the overestimating minority, in most colleges.

The argument, in short, is that Bennington is sufficiently like most other college communities to justify the conclusion that the

[4] It is important to note that members of such a minority would probably not regard themselves as being in a minority; the presumption is that they, being aware that seniors are less conservative than freshmen, would assume most others to be also aware of it. If not, the personality processes might be quite different.

personality processes by which attitudes are formed there may also be expected elsewhere. The principal difference, that of awareness of the lesser conservatism of those having most prestige, is a difference of average tendency, not an all-or-none difference. Bennington majorities may correspond only to minorities elsewhere, but the basic patterns are much the same.

The simple theory of cultural lag may be suggested to explain the assumed common lack of awareness of the greater conservatism of freshmen than of upperclassmen in most colleges. American society, up to a decade or more ago, was a relatively stable one. In such a society the attitude differences between college teachers and those more closely tied to the existing economic system would almost certainly be less than in the more unsettled times of the recent past. If this be the case, college influences in the direction of "liberalizing" student attitudes are greater in the recent past than before. But the change has been too gradual and too recent to be generally recognized. Tradition has bequeathed certain earmarks of sophistication to distinguish the upperclassman from the freshman, but nonconservatism is not one of them in most colleges. Seniors do, in fact, tend to become less conservative, but they are not necessarily supposed to. Perhaps, incidentally, one reason why nonconservatism is included among the marks of senior sophistication at Bennington is that the college, which first opened its doors during the depths of the economic depression of the 1930's, is too young to share in the contrary tradition.

Perhaps, as another aside, this contrary-to-fact assumption may help to explain the common belief that "liberal" or "radical" college students are apt to be a little "queer." Insofar as there is any basis in their own behavior for such a charge, it may simply be attributed to the fact that they conceive of themselves as playing a minority or an isolated role.[5] Ironic though it seems, it is quite probable that such students differ far less than they imagine from "typical" upperclassmen; their minority role is, in part at least, falsely assumed.

One other aspect of the Bennington community is relevant to the

[5] This is a type of community role which would probably have to be added to those listed in Chapter 13, in studying many college communities. Such persons would probably be classified as unaware and negativistic nonconservatives. Only one student (not included in the two classes intensively studied in Chapter 13), out of 140 rather intensively studied at Bennington, fitted this role.

question of its typicality. The writer has more than once suggested that the somewhat unusual degree of "liberalization" which occurs there is to be traced, originally at least, to faculty attitudes. This is true not so much in the sense that there was deliberate intent to "liberalize" student attitudes as in the sense that faculty were concerned to make students aware of their contemporary world. This was a result, not only of the educational policies to which the college was committed,[6] but also of the conviction on the part of most faculty members that many of the students had been "sheltered" to a greater than average degree. The writer would put great emphasis upon this point. The stress upon the contemporary world was, during the years of this study, marked in the areas of literature and the arts as well as in Social Studies. It was particularly noticeable in the repeated series of lectures and discussions which were held with great frequency and attended and participated in by a very large proportion of the entire community.

It was precisely this stress upon the contemporary world which was in large part responsible for students' awareness of freshman-senior differences in conservatism. Upperclassmen had learned more than freshmen about their world, and the forces and conditions making for social change. More than that, those of the upperclassmen who participated most actively in discussions and in activities, in classes and outside of them, tended to be those who had most status and influence. In any community, presumably, those who participate most actively in approved activities are those who have most prestige.

There are probably few who would deny that this emphasis upon the contemporary world represents a trend in recent higher education. It is so conspicuously true, in fact, as to have given rise to a counter-movement toward the classics. To the extent that it is true it seems probable that most other colleges are less unlike Bennington than they used to be, and that the personality conditions associated with attitude change at Bennington should be increasingly approximated in other colleges.

[6] In keeping with these policies, some of which are commonly known as "progressive," attempts were constantly made to begin with problems within the student's range of familiarity and concern. Thus, for example, historical problems were frequently traced backwards. One of the criticisms most frequently raised concerning the curriculum was that it placed too much emphasis upon the contemporary, and too little upon the past.

The argument of this chapter may be briefly recapitulated. Certain aspects of the kinds of social change occurring in the America of the late 1930's tended to be accepted by Bennington students characterized by independence from their parents, sense of personal adequacy in social relations, and modifiability of habits of achieving their goals. In most other contemporary American colleges it may be presumed that comparable adaptations will most readily be made by essentially the same kinds of individuals to the degree that there is common awareness that prestige-endowed individuals within their communities tend to be characterized by acceptance of the social changes in question. This in turn depends largely upon the degree to which there is common awareness within their communities of the significance of contemporary social trends.

The personal characteristics noted above are commonly considered desirable ones. The moral to those interested in smooth social transitions is clear. If those possessing such desirable characteristics are to be enlisted for acceptance of the kinds of social change here dealt with, rather than for rejection of them, there must be relatively greater emphasis in our colleges upon problems of contemporary social change. This must be done not only through academic emphasis, but particularly in such ways as to bring community consciousness of their significance.

APPENDIX A

Concerning the Questionnaires Used in the Study

'I. THE ATTITUDE SCALES

The explanatory material preceding the directions for response was almost unvarying for all questionnaires during the four years of the study. Directions were unvarying for all Likert-type scales. Both the explanatory material and the directions appeared at the beginning of all questionnaires. The following is a facsimile:

Code number ——

This is the (first) of the questionnaires involved in the experiment in which you agreed to participate. Again it is promised that no one will connect your name with your replies as long as you maintain any connection with Bennington College. Only your code number will be recorded.

There are three conditions with which you are asked to comply in replying to this questionnaire:

1. Please do not discuss it with any one else, unless all persons concerned have already completed their replies. It is important that your replies should represent your own opinions and not the influence of some one else with whom you talk.

2. This is in no sense whatever a test of consistency. Some of the statements may resemble each other fairly closely, but you may nevertheless differ in your replies to them and still be reasonable and intelligent in making them. Do not strive for consistency, but *only to state your own opinions.*

3. *Please make some reply to every single statement.* This does not mean that you are expected to have a mature opinion about every statement. It is very likely that you will be uncertain about some of them, but in that case please mark the statement in that manner rather than leaving it out.

When completed, please put in the ballot box in the Store.

On the following pages appear statements about certain contemporary public issues. You will agree with some of the statements, disagree with some, and be uncertain of others. There are no "right" or "wrong" answers. Whatever you happen to think about it is the right answer for you.

Please indicate your replies as follows: [1]

Encircle A if you *agree* with the statement, thus:	SA (A) ? D SD	
Encircle SA if you *strongly agree* with it, thus:	(SA) A ? D SD	
Encircle D if you *disagree* with the statement, thus:	SA A ? (D) SD	
Encircle SD if you *strongly disagree* with it, thus:	SA A ? D (SD)	
Encircle ? if you are *uncertain,* thus:	SA A (?) D SD	

Among the Likert-type scales only the P.E.P. scale is reproduced herewith.

Statements, agreement with which is considered conservative (i.e., scored high), are starred. Agreement with all other attitude statements is scored low, and disagreement with all others is scored high.

THE P.E.P. SCALE

1. The only true prosperity of the nation as a whole must be based upon the prosperity of the working class.
* 2. Recovery has been delayed by the large number of strikes.
3. Some form of collective society, in which profits are replaced by reimbursements for useful mental or manual work, is preferable to our present system.
4. The depression occurred chiefly because the working classes did not receive enough in wages to purchase goods and services produced at a profit.
5. A "planned economy" is not enough unless it is planned for the welfare of workers rather than of business men.
* 6. Most labor trouble happens only because of radical agitators.
* 7. The people who complain most about the depression wouldn't take a job if you gave it to them.
8. The standard of living of the working class can be kept above the poverty line only as workers force it up by the use of strikes.
9. Labor organizations have as much right to bring in outside agitators as do business men to import outside technical experts.
* 10. Any able-bodied man could get a job right now if he tried hard enough.

[1] These directions apply to the Likert-type attitude scales only.

* 11. Most people on relief are living in reasonable comfort.
* 12. The budget should be balanced before the government spends any money on "social security."
  13. Our government has always been run primarily in the interests of big business, and so it is those interests which were chiefly responsible for the depression.
* 14. Labor unions are justifiable only if they refrain from the use of strikes.
  15. Since it is impossible for working people to make any substantial savings, they have fully earned their right to old-age pensions.
* 16. It is all right to try to raise the standard of living of the lower classes, provided that existing property rights are continually safeguarded.
  17. Most employers think only of profits and care little about their employees' welfare.
* 18. Unemployment insurance would saddle us with a nation of idlers.
* 19. Organizations of the unemployed are just a group of chronic complainers.
  20. We have no true democracy in this country, because only business and industrial concerns have economic opportunity.
* 21. If the government didn't meddle so much in business everything would be all right.
* 22. You can't expect democracy to work very well as long as so many uneducated and unintelligent people have the vote.
* 23. The vast majority of those in the lower economic classes are there because they are stupid or shiftless, or both.
* 24. Those who have the ability and the foresight to accumulate wealth ought to be permitted to enjoy it themselves.
  25. The middle classes will never enjoy security or prosperity until they understand that their welfare is identified with that of the working class, and not with that of business and industrial groups.
  26. The real threat to prosperity in this country is the repressive activities of those who wish to keep wealth and economic power in the hands of those who now possess them.

II. THE PER CENT ESTIMATES QUESTIONNAIRE

The purpose of this little test is to see how well you can estimate how Bennington College students and faculty feel about a few contemporary problems. You are therefore asked both to indicate your own reaction, and your estimate of how other students and faculty would respond. "Own responses" will be tabulated and compared with estimates. Results will be posted on the bulletin board. *It is particularly important that you do not consult with any one before replies are made.*

In previous questionnaires you have been asked, not for outright agreement or disagreement to statements, but for degree of agreement or disagreement. For present purposes, however, the latter device is too complicated; comparisons of actual responses with estimates can't very well be made for several degrees of agreement at the same time. You are therefore asked to indicate simply "agree" or "disagree." I am aware that for some of the statements neither of these two simple responses will seem to be accurate. Your responses will not be interpreted, however, as meaning absolute agreement or disagreement, but simply a tendency in one direction or the other. *Please encircle either A (for agreement) or D (for disagreement)* even though you have only a very slight leaning in that direction. Please don't omit any.

Put your own response on the left, by encircling either A or D.

Indicate your estimate of responses of other groups on the right. Please fill out four per cent estimates for each statement, as in the first item which is filled out as a sample.

Your Response			*Your Estimate of Per Cent of Various Groups Who Agree with the Statement*			
			Fresh-men	Sopho-mores	Juniors and Seniors	Faculty
(A) D		SAMPLE: I regret the disappearance of the custom of hazing college freshmen.	10	85	60	20
*A D	1.	Government expenditures for relief and "social security" should be reduced until the budget is balanced.	___	___	___	___
A D	2.	On the whole, the advantages of trade unionism greatly outweigh its disadvantages.	___	___	___	___
A D	3.	Pres. Roosevelt's relief policy, though far from perfect, is preferable to anything practiced or preached by the Republicans.	___	___	___	___
A D	4.	I believe the CIO is more democratic and more concerned about workers' needs than is the A. F. of L.	___	___	___	___

Your Response

Your Estimate of Per Cent of Various Groups Who Agree with the Statement

	Fresh-men	Sopho-mores	Juniors and Seniors	Faculty
A D 5. The National Labor Relations Act has been, on the whole, so fairly and competently administered that it should be continued without amendment.	___	___	___	___
*A D 6. If our government arrangements are such that business can prosper, the rest of the population is bound to share in the prosperity.	___	___	___	___
*A D 7. Trade unions are so greatly influenced by radical agitators that they must be considered, on the whole, a menace.	___	___	___	___
*A D 8. I don't see how any fair-minded person can approve of legislation so obviously one-sided as the Labor Relations Act.	___	___	___	___
*A D 9. Most of those in the lower economic classes deserve to be there, either through stupidity or laziness.	___	___	___	___
*A D 10. Those who are wealthy should be permitted to enjoy the results of their own or their ancestors' ability and foresight without interference.	___	___	___	___
A D 11. There can be no true prosperity of the nation as a whole until adequate incomes for the working class are made secure.	___	___	___	___
*A D 12. I prefer the A. F. of L., which is interested in improving workers' conditions rather than in revolution, to the CIO.	___	___	___	___

| | *Your Estimate of Per Cent of Various Groups Who Agree with the Statement* | | | |
| *Your Response* | Fresh-men | Sopho-mores | Juniors and Seniors | Faculty |

A D 13. Most of those in the lower economic classes are suffering from lack of opportunity rather than as a result of inborn stupidity or laziness.   _____ _____ _____

A D 14. The standard of living of the lower classes should be raised, even if at the expense of those having large property rights. _____ _____ _____

AGREE–DISAGREE ITEMS SUBMITTED TO FORMER STUDENTS [2]

Please encircle A (for agreement) or D (for disagreement) before each of the following statements. You may feel that in some instances neither of these two simple responses accurately reflects your attitudes. Your responses will not be interpreted, however, as meaning absolute agreement or disagreement, but simply as revealing a tendency in one direction or the other. Please encircle either A or D before each statement, even though you have only a slight leaning in that direction.

A D 1. The National Labor Relations Act has been, on the whole, so fairly and competently administered that it should be continued without amendment.

A D 2. I prefer the A. F. of L., which is interested in improving workers' conditions rather than in revolution, to the CIO.

A D 3. Pres. Roosevelt's relief policy, though far from perfect, is preferable to anything practiced or preached by the Republicans.

A D 4. I hope the New Deal will be definitely repudiated in the 1940 elections.

A D 5. I regret that the Spanish Loyalists did not succeed in putting down the rebellion.

A D 6. The Munich agreement was preferable to a general war, which would almost certainly have occurred otherwise.

A D 7. At the present time Americans have more to fear from fascism than from communism.

[2] All these items are taken from the Per Cent Estimates questionnaire. Many of these items, however, are not included in the analysis presented in Chapter 7. These items were presented in this manner in order to afford a direct comparison with the most recent responses of students still in college.

A D 8. The fascist powers succeed by bluff, but fear war; hence their aggressive demands should be resisted, even though a slight risk of war is involved.

A D 9. I don't trust the Russian dictatorship, even though it claims to have no foreign ambitions, any more than I trust the German or Italian dictatorships.

III. THE GUESS WHO RATING SCALE

The conditions under which these ratings were made are described in Chapter 9. Raters were first handed the following mimeographed sheet of directions:

DO NOT SIGN YOUR NAME TO THIS PAPER

The questions asked on the following pages have to do with some personality characteristics of Bennington College students. The form of the questions is that which has been found to be the most satisfactory of all "rating" techniques. It is commonly referred to as the "Guess Who" technique.

I am concerned with only three Bennington College classes, those graduating in 1938, 1939, and 1940, respectively. You will be given lists of the members of these three classes, as this will make it easier for you to answer the questions.

Each question begins with the word "most" or "least," followed by some adjective. Each question is followed by three blank spaces for each of the three classes. You are asked to write in the names of the three individuals in each class who seem to you best to illustrate the characteristic mentioned. It is not compulsory to include three names for each class, in response to each question. Two names of which you feel fairly sure are better than three of which you do not feel sure.

No one actually *knows* the answers to these questions. There are no "true" answers. You are asked for your *opinions*. It is therefore hoped that you will fill in every blank. If you feel that to reply with a certain name would be sheer guess-work, leave it blank, but if that name represents something between guess-work and certainty, please include it.

Suggested procedure. Previous experience indicates that the following procedure works best, though you may find a better one. Start with the list of names in one class. Answer all the questions for this one class. During this procedure names from other classes will occasionally occur to you as particularly fitting; fill in those names as they occur to you. Then repeat the procedure for a second class, adding those names which have not previously occurred to you. Then go through the list of questions once more for the third class.

Your identity will never be known. I am interested only in group replies, not in individual replies.

Accompanying the sheets of directions was a mimeographed list of the names of all students in the three classes referred to. The raters were then given the list of characteristics for which students from each of the three classes were to be nominated. It was in the following form (Item #1 is here reproduced for sample purposes; the other items followed in exactly the same form):

Class Graduating '38   Class Graduating '39   Class Graduating '40

1. *most absorbed* in social life, week-ends, etc.

————————————   ————————————   ————————————

————————————   ————————————   —————————————

————————————   ————————————   ————————————

The 28 Guess Who items were as follows:
1. *most absorbed* in social life, week-ends, etc.
2. *most absorbed* in home and family affairs
3. *most absorbed* in college studies, academic work
4. *most absorbed* in college community affairs
5. *most absorbed* in national and international public affairs
6. *most critical* of college educational policies
7. *most critical* of individual members of faculty or administrative staff
8. *most critical* of student committees (E.P.C., Community Council, etc.)
9. *least concerned* about basic educational policies of the college
10. *least concerned* about activities of student committees (E.P.C., etc.)
11. *most anxious* to be left alone to follow individual pursuits
12. *most anxious* to hold positions of community responsibility
13. *most resistant* to community expectations regarding codes, standards, etc.
14. *most influenced* by community expectations regarding codes, standards, etc.
15. *most resistant* to enthusiasms of the crowd
16. *most influenced* by enthusiasms of the crowd
17. *most resistant* to appeals regarded as moving or emotional
18. *most influenced* by appeals regarded as moving or emotional
19. *most resistant* to faculty authority
20. *most influenced* by faculty authority

The following items have to do with attitudes during the first four or five years after leaving college.
21. *most likely* to be enthusiastic supporters of the college
22. *least likely* to be enthusiastic supporters of the college

23. *most likely* to engage actively in pursuits related to college interests
24. *least likely* to engage actively in pursuits related to college interests
25. *most likely* to lead life of sheltered leisure
26. *least likely* to lead life of sheltered leisure
27. *most likely* to be deterred from some interesting pursuit because of family disapproval
28. *least likely* to be deterred from some interesting pursuit because of family disapproval

APPENDIX B

The Validation of the Scales

The most common procedures in validating questionnaire items are the various methods of testing the "internal consistency" of the entire list of items. The simplest method is that of assigning arbitrary values to each response: i.e., arbitrary in an empirical sense although *a priori* very probable, and then comparing the responses to each item of all individuals whose total scores are extremely high with those whose total scores are extremely low. If the very high and the very low groups (in total score) tend to respond alike to a given item, then that item obviously is not helping to distinguish low from high scores. Responses to that item, in other words, are not determined by the same factors which determine responses to most of the other items, and it is discarded as not belonging.

For determining the interrelationship of the several item-responses this simple method is very satisfactory, although to be fool-proof the responses of a middle group (in total score) should also be analyzed, and those items discarded which the middle group tends to answer extremely. By discarding items which do not meet such tests it is easy to demonstrate that the remaining items are interconsistent. But it is not so easy to demonstrate that the total scale measures what its builder hopes it measures. What the total scale measures is determined by the nature of all the items initially included. In other words, unless the term "validity" is held to be synonymous with "internal consistency," some outside criterion is needed.

No single method was used in validating the several attitude scales used in this study. Since the P.E.P. scale is the *pièce de résistance* of the study, its validation will be discussed at greater length than that of the others. The writer felt that the demand for an outside criterion was adequately met by Stagner's work on the scale in its initial form — work of both *a priori* and empirical nature, which indicated that his scale was actually measuring an attitude toward a single, closely knit group of contemporary issues. The writer's problem, therefore, was to discover whether or not this group of issues was also a closely knit one for the Bennington community.

The test of internal consistency described above is not an easy one to apply to the Likert type of scale, with its five degrees of response to each item, if one wishes to study the interrelationship among *degrees* of response, as well as of *direction* of response to each item. (It would be simple enough, of course, to compare the *mean* response to each item of the high and low groups in total score.) The method has the disadvantage, moreover, that only the responses of the extreme groups, in total score, are used. In a careful item analysis responses of *all* subjects of a sample selected at random should be studied.

A method was therefore used which is almost precisely the reverse of the common procedure. Instead of comparing mean item responses of groups selected on the basis of total score, mean total scores of those making each response to each item were compared. Thus, if responses to a given item are closely related to those to other items, the mean total score of all those who score 1 on that item will be lower than that of all those who score 2 on it; the latter mean will be lower than that of all those who score 3 on it, and so on. If, on the other hand, responses to a given item are not positively related to those given to other items, there will be no increase, or there will be both increases and decreases in mean total score of the respective groups whose responses to that item are 1, 2, 3, 4, and 5. The method used will be made clear from an examination of Tables XXXIV and XXXV.

In Table XXXIV are shown the mean scores *per item,* for all items other than that listed at the left, for four items found unsatisfactory. The responses are those of 100 nonfreshman subjects [1] chosen at random in the fall of 1935. There were 30 items in the initial form of the scale, as used at Bennington, so that each mean score in this table is calculated for 29 items. It will readily be seen that, for these four items, a larger score on a given item is not necessarily associated with a larger mean score for all other items. These

[1] Freshmen were not included in this sample because it was intended to make this scale a valid measurement of an attitude the creation of which was, to some extent at least, a result of experience in this community. To have included in the validating sample subjects who had been members of this community less than two months would have been to flout this basic consideration.

four items were therefore discarded, and all P.E.P. scores (including those of 1935) were calculated on the basis of the remaining 26 items.

TABLE XXXIV. MEAN SCORE PER ITEM, FOR ALL ITEMS OTHER THAN THAT LISTED AT LEFT, ACCORDING TO RESPONSE TO ITEM LISTED AT LEFT

Four Items Found Unsatisfactory (N 100)

Item #	Response 1		Response 2		Response 3		Response 4		Response 5	
	N	Mn	N	Mn	N	Mn	N	Mn	N	Mn
x1	0	—	7	2.55	13	2.06	63	2.68	17	2.48
x2	7	2.38	30	2.60	26	2.76	30	2.79	7	1.48
x3	3	1.65	7	3.16	40	2.71	43	2.45	7	2.74
x4	23	2.21	67	2.77	10	2.75	0	—	0	—

Table XXXV, whose form is like that of Table XXXIV, gives similar data for the 26 items which do seem to be pretty closely related. Mean scores in this table were recalculated, after discarding the four items listed in Table XXXIV, on the basis of 25 instead of 29 items. Examination of this table shows that there is not, for every item, a steady progression in mean score for all other items from those who respond 1 to that item to those who respond 2 to it, to those who respond 3, and so on. The discrepancies, with a single exception (that between response 1 and response 2 for item #12) are between response 3 and response 4, and between response 4 and response 5. The total frequency of response 5 is so small, however, that most of the latter discrepancies are due to a single subject. The response 3-response 4 discrepancies are, with a single exception (item #8), extremely slight. For two items (#4 and 20) there are slight discrepancies both between response 3 and response 4, and between response 4 and response 5.

There is, of course, a relationship between the split-half reliability of such questionnaires as this one and their internal consistency — although it is not safe to draw conclusions about the latter from the former alone. In view of the discrepancies in item relationship noted in the preceding paragraph, scores were recalculated for these 100 subjects, excluding the four most questionable items of the 26, items #4, 8, 12, and 20. The split-half reliability coefficient (stepped up by the Spearman-Brown formula) was .92 for the 22 items and .94 for the 26 items. In other words, while degree of response to these four items was not perfectly related to degree of response to the

TABLE XXXV.   MEAN SCORE PER ITEM, FOR ALL ITEMS OTHER
THAN THAT LISTED AT LEFT, ACCORDING TO RESPONSE TO
ITEM AT LEFT.   P.E.P. SCALE (N 100)

Item #	Response 1		Response 2		Response 3		Response 4		Response 5	
	N	Mn	N	Mn	N	Mn	N	Mn	N	Mn
1	15	2.18	60	2.56	11	2.88	12	2.77	2	3.12
2	5	1.54	43	2.46	39	2.69	13	2.92	0	—
3	13	1.99	35	2.46	29	2.71	20	2.86	3	2.92
4	3	2.00	27	2.36	34	2.69	33	2.62	3	2.35
5	7	1.95	50	2.46	28	2.78	14	2.76	1	3.00
6	21	2.24	54	2.63	12	2.70	12	2.81	1	2.80
7	22	2.28	62	2.62	13	2.89	3	2.93	0	—
8	2	1.44	10	2.16	24	2.54	56	2.20	8	2.66
9	3	1.92	37	2.41	25	2.59	28	2.67	7	2.92
10	31	2.31	43	2.66	23	2.80	3	2.75	0	—
11	24	2.26	42	2.62	25	2.68	7	2.99	2	3.04
12	7	2.44	30	2.39	49	2.60	13	2.77	1	3.40
13	3	1.61	51	2.44	31	2.70	11	2.93	4	2.81
14	9	1.88	63	2.58	22	2.80	5	2.86	1	2.52
15	8	2.09	55	2.55	30	2.69	6	2.64	1	3.28
16	4	1.92	30	2.38	43	2.60	23	2.80	0	—
17	2	2.24	30	2.35	25	2.61	40	2.63	3	3.03
18	14	2.27	41	2.54	35	2.66	10	2.87	0	—
19	19	2.11	60	2.70	17	2.90	4	2.97	0	—
20	4	1.85	46	2.45	30	2.82	19	2.78	1	2.48
21	11	2.29	48	2.45	33	2.72	8	3.10	0	—
22	10	2.28	39	2.47	22	2.48	21	2.77	8	3.03
23	20	2.19	66	2.64	7	2.76	6	2.99	1	3.20
24	6	1.84	29	2.40	38	2.59	25	2.80	2	3.04
25	3	1.44	21	2.23	51	2.62	23	2.78	2	2.98
26	6	1.85	39	2.20	33	2.66	21	2.86	1	3.00

others, it was sufficiently related to improve the reliability slightly —
and the slight improvement seemed to be worth retaining. By and
large, then, these 26 items were closely interrelated. Low, middle,
and high scores on any one of them were associated with low, middle, and high scores, respectively, on the majority of the others.
These 26 items were therefore retained verbatim as the P.E.P. scale
which was repeated once or more during each year of the investigation.

The Internationalism scale was studied for internal consistency in
precisely the same way,[2] the interrelationship of item responses

[2] The table of mean scores per item, comparable to Table XXXV, is not reproduced
herewith. It is highly similar to Table XXXV, with the exceptions noted above.

being in general satisfactory. Likert's original work (the scale as used in this study is almost exactly his) seemed to satisfy the requirements for validity in the sense of being related to some outside criterion. The chief defect of this scale, for this population, is that low-scoring responses were too frequently made; response 5 is rare, and missing entirely to many items. It is, in effect, a four-point rather than a five-point scale. There is no item as unsatisfactory as the four which were discarded from the P.E.P. scale, although for one item (#15) there is almost no difference in mean score of other items for the several degrees of response to this item. One other item (#20) shows a fairly serious discrepancy between response 2 and response 3. The other discrepancies, between response 3 and response 4, and between response 4 and response 5, involve so few cases as to be inconsequential. There seemed, therefore, to be no advantage in discarding any items from this scale. It was not, in the writer's opinion, a very satisfactory scale for this population and few conclusions are drawn from its use.

Most of the remaining attitude questionnaires were designed to measure attitude toward immediately current issues. This meant that they would have to be constructed on short notice, and without benefit of previous try-out by other investigators. In view of the importance of some criterion of validity beyond that of mere interrelationship of item response, their construction bid fair to be difficult. The problem was that of devising new lists of scale items of such nature that those remaining after discarding the unusable items would comprise a valid and reliable scale. The problem of reliability could be solved by the use of a sufficient number of preliminary items to allow for discarding a few. But the problem of validation against some acceptable criterion was not so easy in advance. Yet it was important to insure this in advance, because a revised form might be too late.

An exceedingly simple device was hit upon for three of the scales, those measuring attitude toward the CIO, toward the Loyalist government in Spain (between 1936 and 1938), and toward President Roosevelt's proposals for Supreme Court reform in 1937. The device was that of including, as one of the items, a brief, straightforward statement of avowed preference for one side or the other of the issue involved, in its entirety. These items were: "I hope the Loyalists win the war in Spain"; "I hope the President's Supreme Court plan is adopted"; and both of the following for the CIO scale: "I hope the CIO succeeds in organizing every large industry in the United States"; and "I hope the A. F. of L. succeeds in squeezing the CIO out of existence."

The advantage of the method is simply that these items became criteria for the selection or rejection of other items in their respective scales. The test for internal consistency (i.e., agreement with the key item) became also the test for criterion validity. The method is doubtless too simple; even five degrees of response to a single item do not provide an all-sufficient criterion. But it was a reasonably satisfactory criterion for these specific attitudes, and it seemed to be the best possible method for immediate results.

The method of examining relationship of item responses was as follows: 100 papers, selected at random (representatives of all four classes being included), were divided into five groups, according to scored response to the criterion item. The mean response score to each of the other items was then calculated for each of the five groups. There were thus five mean score values for each item except the criterion item. In Tables XXXVI to XXXVIII, where these mean score values appear, the following groupings have been made: mean score values for response 3, response 4, and response 5 to the criterion item in the scale of attitude toward the Spanish Loyalists have been combined, because there were so few unfavorable responses to this issue. There were two criterion items (#5 and 8) in the scale of attitude toward the CIO, making a possible score range from 2 to 10. Responses unfavorable to the CIO were comparatively few, so that regardless of degree they were all grouped together, making a total of four classifications of response to the two criterion items.

Inspection shows that response to almost every item in all three of these scales is closely related to response to the criterion item or items. In Table XXXVI only item #9 is useless, although three others (#11, 12, 15) have comparatively little differentiating power. In Table XXXVII the mean score for all groups except that giving the most favorable response to the CIO is approximately the same for items #1, 7, 12, and 13, and items #10 and 14 show relatively little differentiating power. In Table XXXVIII, items #4, 6, 7, 8, 10, and 16 show least relationship to the criterion item. For a second use of the two scales of attitude toward Loyalist Spain and toward

TABLE XXXVI. ATTITUDE TOWARD SPANISH LOYALISTS. MEAN RESPONSE TO ALL EXCEPT CRITERION ITEM, CLASSIFIED BY DEGREE OF RESPONSE TO THAT ITEM (N 100)

Score on Criterion Item	N	1	2	3	4	6	7	8	9	10	11	12	13	14	15	16
1	42	1.7	1.9	1.9	2.6	1.4	1.4	2.7	3.1	2.0	2.1	1.7	2.2	1.3	1.9	2.6
2	40	2.4	2.2	2.7	3.5	2.1	2.1	3.3	2.9	2.7	2.4	2.5	2.6	1.8	2.2	3.3
3, 4, 5	18	3.0	2.8	3.2	4.0	2.6	2.3	3.8	3.5	3.4	2.5	2.5	3.4	2.5	2.5	3.8

TABLE XXXVII. ATTITUDE TOWARD THE CIO. MEAN RESPONSE TO ALL EXCEPT CRITERION ITEMS, CLASSIFIED BY DEGREE OF RESPONSE TO THOSE ITEMS (N 100)

Sum of Scores on Criterion Items	N	1	2	3	4	6	7	9	10	11	12	13	14	15	16
2	19	2.2	2.1	2.6	2.5	1.4	2.7	1.4	1.6	1.8	2.1	1.6	1.1	2.2	1.9
3–4	41	2.3	2.4	2.8	2.8	1.9	3.4	2.2	2.0	2.5	2.5	2.2	1.7	2.3	2.5
5–6	22	2.6	2.7	3.1	3.1	2.0	3.7	2.3	2.5	2.9	2.7	2.5	2.3	2.7	2.7
7–10	18	2.5	2.8	3.3	3.3	2.3	3.7	2.6	2.4	3.6	2.6	2.2	2.1	3.0	3.1

TABLE XXXVIII. ATTITUDE TOWARD PRESIDENT ROOSEVELT'S SUPREME COURT PROPOSAL. MEAN RESPONSE TO ALL EXCEPT CRITERION ITEM, CLASSIFIED BY DEGREE OF RESPONSE TO THAT ITEM (N 100)

Score on Criterion Item	N	1	2	3	4	6	7	8	9	10	11	12	13	14	15	16
1	13	1.3	2.2	2.1	2.5	3.5	2.4	2.2	2.8	2.8	2.7	1.9	1.2	1.9	1.3	1.8
2	19	2.0	2.5	2.4	2.9	3.4	2.7	2.6	3.1	2.8	3.0	2.1	2.1	2.5	2.2	2.8
3	20	2.7	3.0	2.9	3.1	3.7	3.1	3.1	3.8	2.9	3.2	2.4	2.4	3.0	2.9	3.3
4	36	3.5	3.5	3.7	3.0	3.8	2.8	3.7	4.2	3.5	3.5	3.2	3.4	3.6	3.7	3.8
5	12	4.1	4.4	3.9	3.4	4.1	3.3	3.4	4.1	3.8	3.6	3.5	4.3	3.8	4.3	3.3

the CIO only the eight best and the six best items, respectively, were retained. This represented an experiment in the use of brief scales, following a preliminary analysis showing that even with so few items, carefully selected, reasonably satisfactory split-half reliability coefficients could be obtained.

Four other attitude scales, used but once, were constructed. They were attempts to measure, respectively, attitudes toward Soviet Russia, toward American isolation, toward the Munich settlement, and toward the New Deal — all given in 1938. In view of the fact that none of these was repeated, and that they were used only in supplementary fashion, rather than as measures from which basic conclusions were drawn (as from the use of the P.E.P. scale), no attempts to validate these scales were made beyond the calculation of their split-half reliabilities.

One further aspect of the problem of the validity of the Likert type of scale arises. Scores on these scales reflect not only direction of attitude, but also intensity of feeling about the items responded to. There is no reason to suppose that the individuals who most consistently favor something toward which attitude is being measured necessarily feel most strongly about it. Tendency to use extreme responses, or to avoid them, is presumably related to certain personality characteristics, and is presumably not perfectly correlated with consistency of attitude direction. Likert scores, in other words, are determined by two sets of factors rather than one. It may be true, in fact, that they reflect tendency toward extremeness of response, or toward the personality trait of caution more directly than they reflect direction of attitude. Thus, in terms of scores on the 26-item P.E.P. scale, an individual might respond favorably but moderately (i.e., "agree" or "disagree") to 16 items while responding unfavorably but extremely (i.e., "strongly agree" or "strongly disagree") to eight items. The resulting score would be the same as if all items had been responded to by "?". Does such a scoring procedure lessen the validity of the scale?

All the P.E.P. questionnaires for three consecutive years were therefore rescored, noting simply the direction of response. Scores were computed in terms of favorable minus unfavorable responses: i.e., frequency of 1's and 2's minus frequency of 4's and 5's. These scores were then correlated with the scale scores. The twelve resulting coefficients (four classes for each of three years) ranged from .884 to .955. Since these coefficients are exactly in the range of the split-half reliabilities of the scale, it may be concluded that *for group purposes* the two methods of scoring are practically identical.[3] (Certain individuals' differences between these two scores are significant; they are discussed elsewhere.)

Since so many conclusions are drawn from the use of the P.E.P. scale, this matter is of some importance. In view of the frequency of the testimony by seniors that they had learned to be less extreme

[3] Even closer agreement between the two methods of scoring was found in the writer's study of attitudes of labor union members toward their unions, previously referred to. See *Industrial Conflict — A Psychological Interpretation*, 1940, edited by G. W. Hartmann and T. M. Newcomb.

in their responses during their college experience, it was necessary to discover whether there was any greater four-year change in *number* of favorable responses (regardless of degree) than in total score. Amount of change on the part of the class which was followed for four years, as computed by the two methods, was then correlated, with a resulting coefficient of .905. Only a very few individuals showed a significant rank order difference between the two scores of four-year change in attitude.

There are two measurable tendencies, conceivably corresponding to personality characteristics of some importance, which contribute to scores on Likert questionnaires. One is the tendency to agree rather than to disagree with statements;[4] the other is the tendency to use extreme rather than moderate or neutral responses. These two tendencies are correlated with 1939 P.E.P. scale scores of the class entered in 1935 to the extent of .62 and .57, respectively. Is there any evidence that these tendencies, as measured by questionnaire responses, are stable ones? The split-half reliability, for the 1939 responses to the P.E.P. scale of the class entered in 1935, of the number of agreements minus number of disagreements, was .68. The corresponding reliability coefficient for number of neutral minus number of extreme responses (i.e., frequency of 3's minus frequency of 1's and 5's) was .87.

At a given moment, then, these do represent fairly consistent tendencies. But these same measures of tendency-to-agree and of tendency-to-be-cautious, computed for different scales, or for the same scale responded to at different times, yielded much lower correlation coefficients. Tendency-to-agree, measured as described above, was scored for two scales (P.E.P. and Internationalism) taken at the same time, 1939, by the class entered in 1935; the correlation was .39 ± .08. The two corresponding measures of tendency-to-be-cautious, computed as described above, yielded a correlation coefficient of .49. Similar scores were computed for three scales responded to in 1937 by the class entered in 1935 (P.E.P., Internationalism, and CIO), with three resulting intercorrelations for each measure. These were, for tendency-to-agree, .59, .18, and .16; and for tendency-to-be-cautious, .39, .20, and .46.

---

[4] Professor E. L. Thorndike, among others, has noted the tendency of most subjects "to answer yes." The writer is not aware that such observations have ever been published.

The degree to which these two tendencies persist over a period of years is also measurable. The *change* in caution score between 1935 and 1936 by the class entered in 1935 was computed for the P.E.P. and the Internationalism scales. The coefficient of correlation between them was .35. Changes by the same class between 1935 and 1939, computed in exactly the same manner, yielded a correlation coefficient of .50. Four-year changes in tendency-to-agree by the same group for the same two scales were correlated to the extent of .06. The 1935 and 1939 caution scores, for the same group, were correlated .29 and .34 for the P.E.P. and Internationalism scales, respectively. The corresponding coefficients of correlation for tendency-to-agree were .33 and .37, respectively. These correlations between 1935 and 1939 scores are to be compared with a correlation between 1935 and 1939 P.E.P. scores of .43.

Most of these coefficients are little more than barely significant. From them it may be concluded that (1) subjects were fairly consistent in tendency-to-be-cautious and in tendency-to-agree for any given scale at a given time, but only slightly consistent for different scales at the same time, or for the same scale at different times; and (2) individual changes in attitude score were affected only very slightly by persistent tendency-to-agree or tendency-to-be-cautious; indeed these tendencies were, if anything, less persistent than the attitude scores. The experience of living in this college community had as much effect upon these tendencies as upon attitude direction. It therefore seems safe to conclude that the validity of the scale scores is not weakened by the fact that they are related to the two tendencies described.

Several of the P.E.P. items, because of their wording, violate some commonly accepted rules for constructing attitude scale statements. The most imperative of these rules is that items shall not be double-barreled. The reason for this is simple: a negative reply to such a statement may indicate rejection of either barrel or of both, and thus identical scores do not reflect identical attitudes. At least four of the items in the P.E.P. scale may be considered double-barreled. They were included in the original form of the scale, but the justification for their retention is an empirical one. Other items were discarded, following the item analysis described later in this chapter. These four not only survived this test, but proved to be among the best of the entire scale. That is, there was a very close relationship between responses to these items and responses to every one of the others in the final form of the scale. The reason for this appears to be as follows: while, theoretically, negative responses *might* be made to such items because either barrel or both barrels were rejected, this particular population — or rather, those of this population who rejected the statements — was highly uniform in its reasons for rejecting each such item. Precisely which part of the item was being rejected is unimportant so long as the grounds for rejection were uniform, so that response to it is closely related to response to other items.

The second heterodoxy in the wording of some items is probably less important. Ideally, every item should be worded in terms of what an attitude scale is designed to measure: i.e., a desired or an undesired state of affairs. The implication of "I want," "ought to be," or "is preferable" should always be present. This does not mean, in the writer's judgment, that precisely such words must always be used. The less sophisticated the subjects the more clear the implication must be, of course. The writer can only record his belief that, for the relatively sophisticated subjects here involved, the implication of "I want" or "should be" is clear if not explicit in every item. Item #18, for example ("Unemployment insurance would saddle us with a nation of idlers."), contains the assumption, which may be assumed to be common to this population, that "a nation of idlers" is undesirable.

APPENDIX C

Reliability of the Attitude Scales

The split-half reliability of all attitude questionnaires was calculated. With few exceptions, the entire sample was used in obtaining each coefficient, and coefficients were recalculated each time
a scale was repeated, for each class separately. Instead of reproducing
herewith all of these hundred-odd coefficients, they are summarized
in Table XXXIX. In general, their magnitude is satisfactory by

TABLE XXXIX. SUMMARY OF RELIABILITY COEFFICIENTS
OF ATTITUDE SCALES [1]

Attitude Toward	No. of Times Given	Freshmen		Juniors-Seniors	
		Range	Median r	Range	Median r
P.E.P.	6	.84 to .91	.89	.91 to .94	.92
Internationalism	4	.48 to .78	.64	.81 to .91	.87
Loyalist Spain [2]	3	.81 to .85	.83	.87 to .92	.90
CIO [2]	1		.84		.91
Supreme Court Reform	1		.86		.90
Soviet Union	1		.89		.89
American Isolation	1		.88		.90
Munich Settlement	1		.87		.88
New Deal	1		.94		.93
Satisfactions	1		.68		.79
Social Distance	1		.90		.94

commonly accepted standards. The chief exception is the low coefficient for freshmen on the Internationalism scale; the Satisfactions scale is also of rather unsatisfactory reliability.

As a general tendency, higher reliability coefficients are characteristic of juniors-seniors than of freshmen. The differences are slight,
but they do indicate that these two scales are measuring attitudes
which are, by and large, more clearly formulated for individuals who
are in the community for their third or fourth year than for those

[1] Stepped up by the use of the Spearman-Brown prophecy formula.
[2] Briefer forms of these scales not included.

who have been there for briefer periods. In the case of the P.E.P. scale this may be partly the result of the initial validation of the scale on the basis of nonfreshmen replies. But the tendency shows more sharply in the Internationalism scale, from which none of the initial items were discarded, and the same tendency appears, in lesser degree, in most of the other scales. In view of the fact that the attitudes selected for measurement were believed to represent vital issues in a community where many issues were taken seriously, it would be queer if junior and senior reliability coefficients were not somewhat higher than those of freshmen and sophomores.

APPENDIX D

Concerning the Selection of Respondents

In Table XL are presented mean P.E.P. scores for the continuing groups within each of four classes: i.e., those members of each class who responded each time the scale was given, from 1935 to the spring of 1938, inclusive. Since the fall, 1938, mean scores of each class are almost identical with the respective scores which precede and which follow them (i.e., spring 1938 and spring 1939), there seems to be no need to examine the fall, 1938, sample. A comparison of this with Table I (Chap. 4) shows that the year-to-year changes appearing in the latter table cannot be attributed to the fact that different subjects are involved in the year-to-year comparisons. The relative amount of year-to-year change is almost identical for

TABLE XL. MEAN P.E.P. SCORES FOR INDIVIDUALS IN FOUR CLASSES WHO RESPONDED ON ALL OCCASIONS [1]

Class Entered	N	Mean Scores				Score Changes [2]				
		1935	1936	1937	1938 (Spring)	1935 1936	1936 1937	1937 1938	1935 1937	1936 1938
1933	26	68.0 (68.6)	60.0 (60.1)			8.0 (8.5)				
1934	21	62.1 (66.5)	59.9 (62.3)	57.4 (58.9)	58.7 (59.9)	2.2 (4.2)	2.5 (3.4)	− 1.3 (− 1.0)	4.7 (7.6)	1.2 (2.4)
1935	35	73.7 (74.5)	68.0 (68.5)	63.3 (64.1)	64.3 (63.7)	5.7 (6.0)	4.7 (4.4)	− 1.0 (0.4)	10.4 (10.4)	3.7 (4.8)
1936	51		73.9 (75.8)	70.8 (72.3)	67.5 (69.1)		3.1 (3.5)	3.3 (3.2)		6.4 (6.7)

the continuing groups and for the total groups: i.e., their rank orders are almost identical. It is of interest to note that, of every pair of these scores, the score of the continuing group is the lower in nearly every case, although the differences are very slight except for the

[1] Corresponding mean scores, taken from Table I, representing all subjects, appear beneath each score in this table for purposes of ready comparison.

[2] Negative change scores indicate that the later score is higher than the earlier one.

1935 scores of the class entered in 1934. (This difference may be attributed to the fact that the continuing group tended to be a cooperating and anxious-to-please group, and in this community it was such individuals whose P.E.P. scores tended to decrease most.) With the exception of this group, mean scores of the continuing and of the total groups in 1935 and in 1938, when response was virtually complete, are almost identical.

One further aspect of the problem of selection remains. Attitude scores change most conspicuously during freshman and sophomore years in college. But each year, during precisely this period, several students drop out of college. Is there a selective factor operating here? Are previous scores of those who remain in college at any given year different from those who drop out? Table XLI is de-

TABLE XLI.   MEAN P.E.P. SCORES IN 1935 OF THOSE RESPOND-
ING AND THOSE NOT RESPONDING IN 1936 AND IN 1937

	1936		*1936*		*1937*		*1937*			
	Responding		Not Responding		Responding		Not Responding			
			In Col-		Not in				In Col-		Not in
Class			lege		College				lege		College
Entered	N	Mn	N	Mn	N	Mn	N	Mn	N	Mn	N	Mn
1933	36	68.6	4	70.0	7	67.7	—	—	—	—	—	—
1934	37	63.6	10	68.2	27	69.8	29	65.3	12	64.7	33	68.2
1935	54	75.6	13	74.3	21	71.8	43	76.8	15	68.0	30	74.5
Total	127	70.1	27	71.4	55	70.3	72	72.2	27	66.6	63	71.2

signed to answer this question. Within any given class, subjects are too few to yield reliable results, but the totals for the three classes indicate that the 1935 mean score of those who later dropped out of college is about the same as that of those who did not drop out but failed to reply. There is, however, some selective influence determining the 1937 replies; the mean score of those in college but not replying is lower, although not significantly so, than that of those who do reply, and lower than that of those no longer in college.

An examination of *previous* scores, however, is not a complete answer to the question of selection. We are as much interested in the process of change as in the matter of initial scores. Table XLII is similar to Table LXI, except that *later* scores of those not replying in 1936 or in 1937 are given. The scores obtained in the spring of 1938 are selected, in this table, because response was 99 per cent complete then, and because these scores are the next ones following

those of 1936 and 1937. (It is not possible to give scores in this
table, of course, for those who have dropped out of college.) Again
it is clear, from this table, that while there are noticeable but not

TABLE XLII. MEAN P.E.P. SCORES IN SPRING, 1938, OF THOSE
RESPONDING AND OF THOSE NOT RESPONDING IN 1936 AND
IN 1937

| | 1936 | | | | 1937 | | |
| Class | Responding | | Not Responding | | Responding | | Not Responding | |
Entered	N	Mn	N	Mn	N	Mn	N	Mn
1934	28	59.6	10	60.8	28	60.0	10	59.7
1935	36	65.2	14	59.8	40	65.1	10	58.0
1936	59	67.5	26	72.7	70	68.7	15	70.9
Total	123	65.0	50	66.7	138	65.9	35	64.0

significant differences, for single classes, between those who do and
those who do not respond, by and large these differences are negligible. It seems fair to conclude that the selection involved, from whatever sources, in the years when fewer subjects responded is not
such as to distort results.

In Chapter 6 certain attitude differences were shown among
juniors and seniors in the several Major Divisions of the college.
Are these differences due to initial selection of students? Mean
freshman scores in each Major Division, which appear in Table
XLIII, show differences somewhat similar to those appearing in
Table XI of Chapter 6. The rank orders of mean scores for the six

TABLE XLIII. MEAN P.E.P. SCORES OF FRESHMEN, CLASSIFIED
BY MAJOR DIVISIONS IN COLLEGE

| Major | Fall '35 | | Fall '36 | | Fall '37 | | Fall '38 | | Total | |
	N	Mn	N	Mn	N	Mn	N	Mn	N	Mn
Science	5	83.8	7	80.7	8	75.4	6	73.2	26	77.9
Social Studies	27	71.4	20	73.5	17	69.3	11	73.7	75	71.9
Literature	12	74.0	12	70.0	9	72.1	9	78.1	42	73.3
Art	20	73.0	6	74.2	19	72.1	9	80.0	54	74.0
Drama-Dance	15	70.3	11	80.7	8	71.5	13	72.6	47	75.7
Music	10	80.9	7	75.3	3	77.3	6	81.5	26	79.1

Divisions are almost identical for freshmen and for juniors-seniors.
The differences between mean scores of freshmen and of juniors-
seniors are approximately the same (about ten points) for all
Divisions except Science, where the difference is only 5.6 points.

The only approximately reliable Divisional differences in freshman mean scores are those between all Science and all Social Studies students, and between all Music and all Social Studies students, the respective critical ratios being 2.5 and 2.8.

But the scores included in these two tables are not those of the same individuals as freshmen and later as juniors or seniors. Several students change majors during or after their freshman year, and many others leave college before becoming juniors or seniors. Mean P.E.P. scores are therefore given in Table XLIV for all freshmen for whom either junior or senior scores are also available. This in-

TABLE XLIV. MEAN P.E.P. SCORES OF SAME INDIVIDUALS AS FRESHMEN AND AS JUNIORS OR SENIORS, CLASSIFIED BY MAJOR DIVISIONS IN COLLEGE

Major	N	Freshmen	Juniors-Seniors	Change
Science	9	79.0	74.0	5.0
Social Studies	27	74.4	63.5	10.9
Literature	10	66.6	58.4	8.2
Art	14	75.9	64.3	11.6
Drama-Dance	11	71.0	60.4	10.6
Music	13	73.5	70.8	2.7

volves only the classes entering in 1935 and in 1936, for whom freshman scores were obtained in the fall, and for whom the latest junior or senior scores were obtained in the spring of 1939. The amount of change in mean score by each Major Division group is about the same as that revealed by a comparison of Tables XI and XLIII, except in the case of Music students, who show very little change in Table XLIV.

APPENDIX E

Reliability of Group Differences
in Mean Attitude Scores

Critical ratios of group differences in mean P.E.P. scores appear in Tables XLV to XLVII. In the first of those tables these are calculated for succeeding scores of each class, and for all members of all classes who responded to either of the two questionnaires involved. All possible comparisons are made except those which are superfluous because of the fact that junior and senior mean scores are so nearly alike. Five of these ten critical ratios approximate statistical significance. None of the three sophomore-junior differences is

TABLE XLV. CRITICAL RATIOS OF P.E.P. SCORE CHANGE
(Single Classes)

Class Entered	Comparison Made	Earlier Score		Later Score		Difference	S.D. Diff.	C.R.
		N	Mn	N	Mn			
1935	Fresh.-Soph.	88	74.5	55	68.5	6.0	2.15	2.79
1936	Fresh.-Soph.	69	75.8	72	72.3	3.5	1.89	1.85
1937	Fresh.-Soph.	64	71.9	62	70.0	1.9	2.24	0.84
1934	Soph.-Junior	74	66.5	37	62.3	4.2	2.41	1.74
1935	Soph.-Junior	55	68.5	50	63.7	4.8	2.38	2.02
1936	Soph.-Junior	72	72.3	58	68.5	3.8	2.29	1.66
1933	Junior-Senior	47	68.6	27	60.1	8.5	3.12	2.72
1934	Soph.-Senior	74	66.5	38	59.9	6.6	2.31	2.87
1936	Fresh.-Junior	69	75.8	58	68.5	7.3	2.25	3.24
1935	Fresh.-Senior	88	74.5	45	62.7	11.8	2.46	5.12

significant, nor are the latest two freshman-sophomore differences. The five which are significant include one freshman-sophomore comparison, one junior-senior, one sophomore-senior, one freshman-junior, and one freshman-senior. Both of the one-year differences which are significant involve the earlier rather than the later classes studied.

In Table XLVI, where comparisons are made between scores of all subjects responding to both questionnaires involved, regardless of

TABLE XLVI. CRITICAL RATIOS OF P.E.P. SCORE CHANGES
(All subjects continuing over period of years)

Class Entered	Date	N	Mean Score	Date	N	Mean Score	Dif- fer- ence	S.D. Diff.	C.R.
1933, 1934, 1935	1935	105	69.2	1936	105	65.0	4.2	1.80	2.37
1934, 1935, 1936	1936	113	69.3	1937	113	65.8	3.5	1.71	2.03
1935, 1936, 1937	1937	98	68.4	1938 [1]	98	67.3	1.1	1.92	0.58
1934, 1935	1935	71	70.4	1937	71	63.5	6.9	2.20	3.14
1935, 1936	1936	58	71.3	1938 [1]	58	66.4	4.9	2.29	2.15
1936, 1937	1937	97	71.0	1939 [1]	97	68.1	2.9	2.08	1.40
1936	1936	55	75.6	1939 [1]	55	68.1	7.5	2.4	3.1
1935	1935	44	74.4	1939 [1]	44	62.7	11.7	2.7	4.3

their class, none of the one-year differences is significant, and only one of the two-year differences. The important observation to be made in this table is that, for both the one-year and the two-year comparisons, the differences become progressively smaller with each succeeding year.

TABLE XLVII. CRITICAL RATIOS OF INTER–CLASS P.E.P. SCORE DIFFERENCES

Date	Group	N	Mn	Group	N	Mn	Diff.	S.D. Diff.	C.R.
1935	Fresh.	88	74.5	Soph.	74	66.5	8.0	1.97	4.06
1935	Soph.	74	66.5	Jrs.-Srs.	92	67.3	− 0.8	—	—
1935	Fresh.	88	74.5	Jrs.-Srs.	92	67.3	7.2	1.86	3.87
1936	Fresh.	69	75.8	Soph.	55	68.5	7.3	2.18	3.35
1936	Soph.	55	68.5	Jrs.-Srs.	60	61.4	7.1	2.44	2.90
1936	Fresh.	69	75.8	Jrs.-Srs.	60	61.4	14,4	2.22	6.49
1937	Fresh.	64	71.9	Soph.	72	72.3	− 0.4	—	—
1937	Soph.	72	72.3	Jrs.-Srs.	72	62.2	10.1	1.96	5.15
1937	Fresh.	64	71.9	Jrs.-Srs.	72	62.2	9.7	2.12	4.58
1938	Fresh.	55	75.9	Soph.	40	69.5	6.4	2.77	2.29
1938	Soph.	40	69.5	Jrs.-Srs.	77	65.6	3.9	2.49	1.58
1938	Fresh.	55	75.9	Jrs.-Srs.	77	65.6	10.3	2.26	4.55

[1] These are spring scores; in 1938, spring responses were more nearly complete than in the fall.

In Table XLVII, mean scores obtained simultaneously for the several class groups are compared, rather than following the same groups from year to year, as in the two preceding tables. Junior and senior scores are here combined, since each class is small. Eight of the twelve differences shown in this table are significant: those which are not are in two cases freshman-sophomore differences, and in two cases, differences between sophomores and juniors-seniors. Again the differences are greater for the earlier than for the later years.

TABLE XLIII. MEAN SCORES AND CRITICAL RATIOS OF DIF-
FERENCES BETWEEN FRESHMEN AND JUNIORS–SENIORS
FOR VARIOUS ATTITUDES

Attitude Toward	Freshmen N	Mn	Juniors-Seniors N	Mn	Differ- ence	S.D. Diff.	C.R.
CIO	47	40.8	41	36.4	4.4	1.4	3.2
Supreme Court	47	51.7	41	42.2	9.5	2.2	4.3
Isolation	49	58.6	68	55.8	2.8	1.4	2.0
Munich	44	45.0	81	42.0	3.0	1.4	2.1
New Deal	37	47.4	76	40.4	7.0	1.6	4.2
Satisfactions	44	39.3	87	42.9	3.6	1.1	3.3
Social Distance	44	60.8	87	54.9	5.9	3.5	1.7

APPENDIX F

Dispersions of Attitude Scores

In Table XLIX are summarized the P.E.P. standard deviations; at the left appear the ranges for each of the four classes for the six times the scale was given, and at the right are standard deviations for all freshmen, all sophomores, etc., grouped together regardless of year of entrance, for the three years when responses were virtually complete (1935, spring 1938, and 1939).

TABLE XLIX. SUMMARY OF STANDARD DEVIATIONS OF P.E.P. SCORES

	Range, for 6 Times Given	Total Group, for 3 Years When Responses Complete	
		N	S.D.
Freshmen	10.8 to 13.8	247	12.9
Sophomores	11.3 to 13.2	221	12.6
Juniors	11.0 to 14.4	155	12.7
Seniors	10.2 to 13.4	128	11.2

Comparison between freshman dispersions of those individuals in two classes (entering in 1935 and in 1936) who also responded at the end of their senior and junior years, respectively, is of some interest. The standard deviation of 44 freshman scores in 1935 was 11.4, and for the same individuals in the spring of 1939, 10.3. The standard deviation of 40 freshman scores in 1936 was 11.5, and for the same individuals in the spring of 1939, 13.8. No other classes could thus be followed through, but these results, together with certain others, suggest that (with regard to P.E.P. scores) there is little or no increase in homogeneity until the senior year, and that during the early years of the college (and of this study) seniors tended to become slightly more uniform in attitude, but that in later years they did not.

In Table L appears a summary of standard deviations for the other attitude scales. Comments concerning this table appear in Chapter 5.

TABLE L. SUMMARY OF STANDARD DEVIATIONS OF OTHER ATTITUDE SCORES

Attitude Toward	No. of Times Given	Freshmen Range	Median S.D.	Juniors-Seniors Range	Median S.D.
Internationalism	4	6.8 to 8.3	7.4	6.5 to 9.1	7.0
Loyalist Spain [1]	3	4.2 to 8.4	6.9	6.6 to 7.5	6.8
CIO [1]	1		5.8		7.8
Supreme Court Reform	1		9.2		12.2
Soviet Russia	1		9.2		9.4
American Isolation	1		9.0		9.3
Munich Settlement	1		10.0		9.1
New Deal	1		11.2		9.5
Satisfactions	1		6.3		7.1
Social Distance	1		3.2		2.1

[1] Briefer forms of these scales not included.

APPENDIX G

Attitude Interrelationships

The intercorrelations of the several attitude scores are presented in Tables LI to LV. Only scores obtained within the same academic year have been correlated. The general conclusions to be drawn from the series of tables are as follows:

1. All correlations are positive, high scores having been assigned, for all scales, to conservative responses, as that term was commonly applied to these issues at this time.

2. By and large, coefficients become smaller with each succeeding calendar year.

3. By and large, coefficients become greater for groups of the same individuals, from year to year.

TABLE LI. CORRELATIONS OF P.E.P. SCALE WITH OTHER ATTITUDE SCALES

Attitude Toward	Date	Freshmen		Juniors-Seniors	
		N	r	N	r
Internationalism	1935–36	88	.27	94	.47
Internationalism	1936–37	69	.40	65	.73
Internationalism	1937–38	64	.34	73	.62
Internationalism	1938–39	71	.42	103	.30
Loyalist Spain	1936–37	45	.52	40	.66
Loyalist Spain	1937–38	63	.69	68	.73
Loyalist Spain	1938–39	55	.60	77	.71
CIO	1936–37	45	.66	40	.60
Supreme Court	1936–37	45	.60	40	.67
Soviet Russia	1937–38	50	.65	68	.50
Isolation	1937–38	49	.71	68	.34
Munich	1938–39	43	.51	71	.53
New Deal	1938–39	37	.69	76	.79
Social Distance	1938–39	43	.36	81	.47
Satisfactions	1938–39	43	.34	82	.41

The P.E.P. scale and the scale of attitude toward Internationalism were given during each of the four years included in the study. Correlations of scores obtained on these two scales with all other

TABLE LII. CORRELATIONS OF INTERNATIONALIST ATTITUDE WITH OTHER ATTITUDES (OTHER THAN P.E.P.)

Attitude Toward	Date	Freshmen		Juniors-Seniors	
		N	r	N	r
Loyalist Spain	1936–37	45	.42	40	.57
Loyalist Spain	1937–38	63	.30	63	.36
Loyalist Spain	1938–39	31	.21	73	.32
CIO	1936–37	45	.58	40	.62
Supreme Court	1936–37	45	.13	40	.64
Soviet Russia	1937–38	49	.22	63	.18
Isolation	1937–38	48	.25	63	.28
Munich	1938–39	37	.20	79	.26
New Deal	1938–39	31	.13	73.	.30
Social Distance	1938–39	42	.18	81	.31
Satisfactions	1938–39	42	.10	81	.30

attitude scores appear in Tables LI and LII. None of the other scales, except that measuring attitude toward Loyalist Spain, was given more than once. All these other intercorrelations appear in Table LIII.

TABLE LIII. INTERCORRELATIONS OF ALL ATTITUDE SCORES OTHER THAN P.E.P. AND INTERNATIONALISM

Attitudes Correlated	Date	Freshmen		Juniors-Seniors	
		N	r	N	r
Loyalist Spain. CIO	1936–37	45	.49	41	.61
Loyalist Spain. Supreme Court	1936–37	47	.27	41	.66
Loyalist Spain. Russia	1937–38	49	.30	68	.62
Loyalist Spain. Isolation	1937–38	48	.55	68	.64
Loyalist Spain. Munich	1938–39	42	.79	70	.51
Loyalist Spain. New Deal	1938–39	36	.57	77	.59
Loyalist Spain. Social Distance	1938–39	31	.67	69	.32
Loyalist Spain. Satisfactions	1938–39	31	.46	69	.51
CIO. Supreme Court	1936–37	47	.36	41	.68
Isolation. Soviet Russia	1937–38	50	.49	68	.36
Munich. New Deal	1938–39	36	.02	69	.40
Munich. Social Distance	1938–39	37	.55	71	.20
Munich. Satisfactions	1938–39	37	.38	71	.43
New Deal. Social Distance	1938–39	29	.56	68	.41
New Deal. Satisfactions	1938–39	29	.05	68	.38
Social Distance. Satisfactions	1938–39	48	.23	47	.25

As to P.E.P. correlations with other attitudes, we find, as might be expected, that they are higher for domestic than for international issues. The freshman coefficients for the three domestic issues toward which attitude was measured (CIO, New Deal, and the Supreme Court) are respectively, .66, .69, and .60; for juniors-seniors the corresponding coefficients are .60, .79, and .67. Several of the P.E.P. items are directly related to each of the first two of these issues. This is not true, however, of the Supreme Court issue, which did not arise till long after the P.E.P. scale had been constructed. The cluster of attitudes represented by these three relatively high intercorrelations was not, of course, peculiar to this college community. Nor can it be said that their interrelationship was significantly increased by college influences, for junior-senior coefficients are scarcely higher than those of freshmen. It is illuminating, however, to compare the freshman correlation of .36 between CIO and Supreme Court attitudes (cf. Table LIII) with that of juniors-seniors, .68. Here are two specific issues, not very obviously related, but they have become so for those who are in this community for their third and fourth years. The generalization seems to be that the P.E.P. scale, as an inclusive measure of contemporary progressivism, is closely related to specific domestic issues for both freshmen and juniors-seniors, but that the specific issues are more closely interrelated for juniors-seniors than for freshmen.

The P.E.P. correlations with attitudes toward the several international issues appear to be contradictory. As for Internationalist attitude, correlations are consistently higher for juniors-seniors than for freshmen until the last year of the study (see p. ? for a discussion of the change in Internationalist attitude during the year 1938–39). P.E.P. correlations with attitude toward Loyalist Spain are also slightly higher for juniors-seniors than for freshmen. The writer is confident that these differences would have been greater had attitude toward Loyalist Spain been measured in the fall, immediately after the arrival of freshmen, rather than in the spring, by which time they had been considerably influenced by the community.

For two international issues, then, freshmen correlations with P.E.P. are lower than those of juniors-seniors. But for three other international issues, Soviet Russia, American Isolation, and the Munich settlement, this is not the case. Junior-senior coefficients are, in fact, lower than those of freshmen for the first two of these issues. The apparent contradiction is explained by the fact that college influences regarding Loyalist Spain, and regarding American nationalism until 1938–39, were almost exclusively in one direction. Regarding Soviet Russia, however, and isolation-vs.-collective security, and the Munich settlement, opposing points of view were both actively defended in the community. Juniors and seniors, as a group, were more influenced by both opposing pulls than were freshmen.

The significant finding from Table LII, in which correlations with internationalist attitude appear, is that only three freshmen coefficients approach or exceed four times their probable errors, these being correlations with attitude toward the CIO and with attitude toward Loyalist Spain in 1936–37 and in 1937–38; the latter two are barely significant. All but one (attitude toward Soviet Russia) of the junior-senior coefficients are, however, approximately or clearly significant. The fact that nearly all the coefficients in this table are relatively low is due, in part, to the somewhat unsatisfactory reliability of the scale of Internationalist attitude, and in part to the fact that this scale represented attitudes which were worn rather lightly in this community. (The latter consideration is perhaps largely responsible for the former.) The fact that junior-senior coefficients are higher, although usually only slightly so, than those of freshmen reflects the general welding-together influence of the college community. As a result of this influence, students come to see that what had previously been seen as relatively discrete issues may be looked at from a focal point of view. Such, at least, is the tendency.

In Table LIII are given the remaining intercorrelations of attitude scores, all those given during the same academic year. These coefficients, in the main, are higher than those in the preceding table. There are, however, two glaring exceptions for freshmen: the correlations of New Deal attitude with attitude toward Munich and with Satisfactions. Of the sixteen freshmen coefficients in this table, eleven are equal to four times their probable errors, or more; all but two of the sixteen junior-senior coefficients are significant, by the same criterion.

The slightness of these differences and the consistency with which they appear may be seen in Table LIV, a summary table. Mean correlations for freshmen and for juniors-seniors are there given for the four groups of intercorrelations listed in Tables LI to LIII. But the problem of selection remains. The attitude intercorrelations of juniors-seniors may conceivably be increased or decreased

TABLE LIV. MEAN ATTITUDE INTERCORRELATIONS *r*

Attitudes Correlated With	Number of Coefficients	Freshman Mean	Junior-Senior Mean
P.E.P.	15	·52	·57
Internationalism [2]	11	·25	·38
Loyalist Spain [2]	8	·51	·56
Miscellaneous [2]	8	·33	·39
Average	42	·41	·48

because of the departure, after their first or second year, of many students. Response was far from complete, moreover, to many questionnaires, particularly to those given but once. In Table LV appear attitude correlations computed for the same individuals as freshmen and one year later as sophomores; and also as sophomores-juniors and again as juniors-seniors. Since only three attitude scales

TABLE LV. ATTITUDE CORRELATIONS FOR IDENTICAL GROUPS IN CONSECUTIVE YEARS

Class Entered	First Date	P.E.P. — Internationalism			P.E.P. — Loyalist Spain		
		N	First Date r	One Year Later r	N	First Date r	One Year Later r
1935	1935	55	·28	·53			
1933, 1934	1935	63	·56	·73			
1936	1936	53	·49	·42	35	·52	·64
1934, 1935	1936	59	·62	·71	39	·73	·85
1937	1937	49	·50	·50 [3]	34	·76	·58
1935, 1936	1937	80	·43	·46 [3]	64	·54	·65

were repeated, only three intercorrelations are possible for follow-up study. Of these three, that between Internationalism and attitude to Loyalist Spain has not been calculated, because of the wholly accidental circumstance that these two scales were never given within six months of each other. The coefficients which appear in

[2] Correlations with all preceding attitudes not included.
[3] Scores obtained 18 months later, but in following academic year.

Table LV seem adequately to confirm previous conclusions. For identical groups, there is a marked increase in degree of inter-relationship among these attitudes for the classes entered in 1933, in 1934, and in 1935, and little or no increase for the classes entered in 1936 and in 1937. We have previously noted the evidence for certain cultural changes within the community during the period covered by this study. Table LV appears to confirm this, and also to suggest that year of entrance is more significant than year of responding. That is, interrelationships in attitude tend to increase for the earlier classes at a time when they are not increasing for younger contemporaries. It is as if the older classes maintained a sub-culture of their own, one aspect of which consisted in viewing various issues from a single focus.

One further finding deserves a comment. The correlations be-tween both Social Distance and Satisfactions and all other at-titudes are low, mostly in the neighborhood of .3 and .4. Murphy and Likert [4] found them to be much higher, particularly with the scale which is almost identical with the present measure of Inter-nationalist attitude. Why are these coefficients so much lower? No single answer will suffice. Most of the *freshman* correlations with Social Distance are, as a matter of fact, not so low; they compare favorably with those of Murphy and Likert. For juniors and seniors, the scale was simply not one of seven points, but more nearly one of three. Thus only one individual in the senior class made a total score equivalent to consistent responses at the third level of the scale — "to my street as neighbors"; all others showed less social distance than that. A forthcoming study by E. L. Horowitz shows that, according to a similar measure, Bennington students were more "tolerant" than those of any of several other colleges studied.

As to the measure of Satisfactions, its mean correlation with five other attitudes, for juniors-seniors, was .41, and considerably less for freshmen. The following considerations are relevant, though not conclusive: judging from interviews and other evidence (see Table III, Chapter 5), freshmen of all degrees of conservatism, with few exceptions, came to college with attitudes which closely re-sembled those of their parents. Whether for the reason that these students represent a fairly sheltered group or for some other reason or reasons, if this is actually the case, then there is little

[4] Murphy, G., and Likert, R., *Public Opinion and the Individual*, 1938.

reason to expect that freshman correlations between conservatism and degree of satisfaction will be high; the more significant relationship is that between their own and their parents' conservatism. Judging again from interview data, a considerable proportion of students broke, to a greater or less degree, with their parents in the area of political and economic attitudes. But it is the major thesis of this study that in this community at this time, they broke because of community influence rather than because of personal dissatisfactions. The fact of correlation yields no automatic answer as to cause and effect, of course. But the writer suspects that the sequence of events was rather "community pressure has led me to be less conservative and hence dissatisfied with things-as-they-are" than "I am dissatisfied and hence forced to be nonconservative." Personal dissatisfactions, of course, play their part, and by some such process as that described by Lasswell,[5] result in lower thresholds for public dissatisfactions. These matters are discussed in Part III, where other evidence seems to show that they play a minor rather than a major part. If the part were major, doubtless the correlations would be higher.

[5] Lasswell, H. D., *Psychopathology and Politics*, 1930.

APPENDIX H

Item Responses to
Per Cent Estimates Questionnaire

TABLE LVI. MEAN PER CENT ESTIMATES OF CONSERVATIVE RESPONSE (BENNINGTON)

Item #	Senior Estimates Attitude Response								Freshmen Estimates Attitude Response							
	Non-conservative				Conservative				Non-conservative				Conservative			
	N	Fr.	J–S.	Fac.	N	Fr.	J–S	Fac.	N	Fr.	J–S.	Fac.	N	Fr.	J–S.	Fac.
1	21	67	36	23	9	70	53	33	17	49	33	28	17	72	74	68
2	28	65	24	13	2	17	17	12	23	38	23	19	11	50	42	40
3	24	73	25	16	6	68	35	18	18	55	42	34	16	61	56	51
4	16	76	23	19	14	68	44	39	16	51	32	28	18	62	55	54
5	15	74	36	30	15	69	58	53	12	40	45	45	22	61	60	57
6	17	68	30	16	13	78	67	65	13	58	44	39	20	77	70	67
7	29	51	23	14	1	50	50	50	25	55	40	38	9	57	49	43
8	27	57	23	13	3	58	58	53	27	44	40	38	5	76	64	52
9	29	39	10	5	1	60	50	50	31	47	34	30	3	32	30	33
10	24	68	27	10	6	80	57	37	22	58	44	34	12	61	51	51
11	28	51	20	13	2	48	68	73	32	33	21	17	2	28	50	45
12	23	66	28	18	7	71	52	41	14	62	48	49	19	65	58	56
13	28	47	17	11	2	50	60	55	27	38	30	26	6	52	38	28
14	28	58	36	23	2	45	63	87	31	43	31	24	2	45	30	15
Mn [1]	—	59	25	15	—	68	53	46	—	47	35	30	—	63	58	54

[1] Mean of the 14 item values, weighted according to number of S's who make either response to each item.

TABLE LVII. COMPARISON OF ACTUAL AND ESTIMATED PER CENT OF CONSERVATIVE RESPONSE TO EACH ITEM

Item #	Freshman Response			Jr.-Sr. Response			Faculty Response		
	Actual	Estimated		Actual	Estimated		Actual	Estimated	
		By Fr.	By Sr.		By Fr.	By Sr.		By Fr.	By Sr.
1	50	60	68	30	53	40	8	48	26
2	32	42	62	7	29	24	12	26	13
3	47	58	72	20	49	27	4	42	16
4	53	57	73	47	44	33	12	42	28
5	65	54	72	50	55	47	28	56	42
6	61	70	72	43	60	46	28	56	37
7	26	56	51	3	43	24	0	40	15
8	16	50	57	10	44	26	8	40	17
9	9	45	40	3	33	11	0	30	6
10	35	59	70	20	47	33	16	40	15
11	6	32	50	7	23	23	4	19	17
12	58	64	67	23	54	34	12	53	24
13	18	41	47	7	31	20	0	26	14
14	6	43	57	7	31	38	4	23	28
Mean	34	52	61	20	43	30	10	39	21

TABLE LVIII. PER CENT ESTIMATES OF CONSERVATIVE RESPONSE BY SENIORS AND BY FRESHMEN AT BENNINGTON AND SKIDMORE COLLEGES

Item #	Skidmore						Bennington					
	Est. by Srs. of			Est. by Fresh. of			Est. by Srs. of			Est. by Fresh. of		
	Fr.	Jr.-Sr.	Fac.	Fr.	Jr.-Sr.	Fac.	Fr.	Jr.-Sr.	Fac.	Fr.	Jr.-Sr.	Fac.
1	41	51	41	45	49	45	68	40	26	60	53	48
2	66	49	41	61	52	53	62	24	13	42	29	26
3	65	58	55	60	59	60	72	27	16	58	49	42
4	68	59	60	68	59	61	73	33	28	57	44	42
5	30	41	45	66	65	59	72	47	42	54	55	56
6	50	48	46	57	60	55	72	46	37	70	60	56
7	46	44	35	46	49	49	51	24	15	56	43	40
8	39	40	36	38	37	41	57	26	17	50	44	40
9	43	39	30	51	49	47	40	11	6	45	33	30
10	61	53	34	60	55	51	70	33	15	59	47	40
11	58	46	40	45	43	38	50	23	17	32	23	19
12	47	51	41	50	52	55	67	34	24	64	54	53
13	47	37	33	48	47	41	47	20	14	41	31	26
14	67	54	48	54	52	43	57	38	28	43	31	23
Mean	52	48	42	54	52	50	61	30	21	52	43	39

TABLE LIX. ACTUAL AND ESTIMATED DIFFERENCES BE-
TWEEN FRESHMEN AND JUNIORS–SENIORS IN PER CENT OF
CONSERVATIVE RESPONSE AT BENNINGTON AND SKID-
MORE COLLEGES [2]

Item #	Skidmore			Bennington		
	Estimates		Actual [3]	Estimates		Actual [3]
	By Fresh.	By Srs.		By Fresh.	By Srs.	
1	− 4	− 10	22 (68–46)	7	28	20
2	10	17	6 (32–26)	13	38	25
3	1	7	9 (63–54)	9	45	27
4	9	9	13 (76–63)	13	40	6
5	1	− 11	− 3 (73–76)	− 1	25	15
6	− 3	2	33 (83–50)	10	26	18
7	− 3	2	9 (37–28)	13	27	23
8	1	− 1	13 (28–15)	6	31	6
9	2	4	4 (15–11)	12	29	6
10	5	12	12 (60–48)	12	37	15
11	2	12	− 3 (10–13)	9	27	0
12	− 2	− 4	25 (71–46)	10	33	35
13	1	10	5 (16–11)	10	27	11
14	2	7	7 (29–22)	12	19	9

[2] Negative differences indicate that senior response (whether actual or estimated) is more conservative than that of freshmen.

[3] The numbers in parentheses represent the percentages of freshmen and of seniors, respectively, responding conservatively. Comparable percentages for Bennington students appear in Table LVII, in the columns headed "Freshman Response" and "Jr.-Sr. Response."

Supplementary Data on Personal Status at Bennington, Williams, and Skidmore

The 1935 sociometric data have been referred to, but not been frequently cited. In Table LX, 1935 data are given which correspond to those of 1938 in Table XXII, Chap. 8. Directions were entirely different in 1935, and probably of considerably less value. They were as follows: "What five nonfreshman students now in college would represent your first choice as living companions in your house suite?" (Student rooms were arranged in suites accommodating, in most instances, four or five or six students.)

TABLE LX. MEAN P.E.P. SCORES OF FRIENDSHIP GROUPINGS OF GROUPS EXTREME IN P.E.P. SCORE (1935)

Class		21 Students Scoring 54 or Less				21 Students Scoring 80 or More			
	N	Those Who Choose Them		Those Chosen by Them		N	Those Who Choose Them		Those Chosen by Them	
		Mn Choices per Person	Mn P.E.P	Mn Choices per Person	Mn P.E.P.		Mn Choices per Person	Mn P.E.P.	Mn Choices per Person	Mn P.E.P.
Soph.	11	4.9	63.9	4.3	61.9	9	3.3	69.8	4.4	66.7
Jr.-Sr.	10	4.8	62.8	4.6	63.7	12	4.7	69.6	4.5	69.5
Total	21	4.9	63.4	4.4	62.8	21	4.1	69.7	4.5	68.3

Frequency of choice in 1935 and in 1938 obviously does not represent the same thing. As a check on the validity of the 1935 responses, the following yes-no question was appended: "Do you prefer to have your closest friends living in the same suite with you?" About 8 per cent answered in the negative. This wording also eliminated several students living off campus from consideration. For such reasons the 1935 responses seem less valuable. This is doubtless one of the reasons why the differences between the two extreme groups are less in 1935 than in 1938, as shown in Tables XXII and LX, respectively. The 1935 differences are in the same direction as those of 1938, but of lesser magnitude. The other reason for the smaller differences is simply that the contrasting groups are less dissimilar in 1935 than in 1938, in terms of raw P.E.P. score — largely because of the fact that freshmen were not included in 1935. But this, of course, only confirms the major point: the further apart two given groups are in score, the further apart are their respective groups of friends.

Mean P.E.P. scores for juniors and seniors at Skidmore College, classified according to college positions held, are as follows:

Positions Held	N	Mean P.E.P.
3 or more	15	72.4
1 or more	33	71.8
None	68	77.6

Similar data, although classified somewhat differently, appear below for juniors and seniors at Williams College. Perhaps the most interesting of these results is the fact that while in general fraternity members do not differ from nonfraternity members, those of the latter group not holding office (probably the most isolated group on the campus) are most conservative. The least conservative group are nonfraternity members holding office, the group which has presumably struggled hardest for its positions of leadership.

Positions Held	N	Mean P.E.P.
One or more major	17	71.4
One or more minor	32	69.4
Fraternity officers only	20	71.9
No offices	41	73.6
Fraternity members holding positions	39	71.0
Nonfrat. members holding positions	10	66.5
Frat. members not holding positions	36	72.2
Nonfrat. members not holding positions	25	74.2
All fraternity members	75	71.6
All nonfraternity members	35	72.0

Index